THE SNIPER ANTHOLOGY

for Bill Lee with best wishes, and thanks for your help.
Tom C. McKenney
15 May 2014
Chapt 3

THE SNIPER ANTHOLOGY

SNIPERS OF THE SECOND WORLD WAR

Adrian Gilbert • Tom C. McKenney • Dan Mills
Roger Moorhouse • Tim Newark • Martin Pegler
Charles W. Sasser • Mark Spicer
Leroy Thompson • John B. Tonkin

Introduction
by

John L. Plaster

Frontline Books
London

Pelican Publishing Company
Gretna 2012

The Sniper Anthology
This edition published in 2012 by Frontline Books,
an imprint of Pen & Sword Books Ltd,
47 Church Street, Barnsley, S. Yorkshire, S70 2AS
For information on our books, please visit
www.frontline-books.com, email info@frontline-books.com
or write to us at the above address.

And

Published and distributed in 2012
in the United States of America and Canada
by Pelican Publishing Company, Inc.,
1000 Burmaster Street, Gretna, Louisiana 70053

Copyright © Pen & Sword Books Ltd., 2011
Chapter 9 © Dan Mills, 2011

Frontline edition: ISBN 978-1-84832-625-5
Pelican edition: ISBN 978-1-4556-1682-4
Pelican e-book edition: ISBN 978-1-4556-1683-1

Cataloging records for this title are available from
the British Library and the Library of Congress.

Printed and bound in Great Britain
by CPI Group (UK) Ltd, Croydon, CR0 4YY

CONTENTS

THE CONTRIBUTORS

Adrian Gilbert

Adrian Gilbert has written extensively on military history in the twentieth century. Among his books are *POW: Allied Prisoners of War, 1939–1945*, *The Imperial War Museum Book of the Desert War*, featuring first-hand accounts from British forces in North Africa, 1940–2, and an oral history of the French Foreign Legion: *Voices of the Legion*. He has a special interest in sniping and sharpshooting and is the author of two best-selling books on the subject: *Sniper: One-on-One* and *Stalk and Kill: The Sniper Experience*.

Tom C. McKenney

Lieutenant Colonel Tom C. McKenney is a graduate of the University of Kentucky and the University of North Carolina (Chapel Hill). He was an infantry officer, parachutist and special operations officer in the U.S. Marine Corps, serving alongside the British Commonwealth Division in the Panmunjam Corridor in Korea, and in Vietnam. He was retired in 1971 for disability incurred in Vietnam. He is an award-winning author of books and periodical articles on military history, most recently of *Battlefield Sniper*, a true story of the American Civil War.

Dan Mills

Dan Mills joined the British Army aged sixteen. He enlisted in his local infantry regiment, The Queen's Regiment, which later became The Princess of Wales's Royal Regiment. During his twenty-four years in the infantry he saw active service in

Northern Ireland, Bosnia, Kosovo, Iraq and Afghanistan as well as travelling extensively around the world. He was awarded Britain's oldest award, a Mention in Dispatches, for gallantry in March 2005 for his actions in Iraq. His first book was the best-seller *Sniper One: The Blistering True Story of a British Battle Group Under Siege* (2007). Dan Mills left the Army in 2010.

Roger Moorhouse

Roger Moorhouse is a historian and author, specializing in Nazi Germany and the Second World War in Europe. A fluent German speaker, he is the author of *Killing Hitler* and the critically-acclaimed *Berlin at War*, and co-author, with Norman Davies, of *Microcosm*. His interest in the story of Simo Häyhä was spurred by his research for his next book – *The Devils' Alliance* – on the subject of the Nazi–Soviet Pact. A regular contributor and reviewer for the national and specialist history press, he has also provided introductions to a number of recent Frontline publications, including the memoirs of Erich Kempka, Heinz Linge, Christa Schroeder and Heinrich Hoffmann. He lives in Buckinghamshire and does all his own ironing.

Tim Newark

Tim Newark is the author of several well-received military history books, including *The Mafia at War* and *Highlander*. Formerly the editor of *Military Illustrated*, he has also worked as scriptwriter and historical consultant on TV documentaries for BBC World-wide and the History Channel, including the 13-part series *Hitler's Bodyguard*. He reviews military history books for the *Financial Times*. Visit www.timnewark.com.

Martin Pegler

Martin Pegler was curator of firearms at the Royal Armouries for twenty years and during his career was able to shoot almost every historic and current sniping rifle. He is the author of a dozen books about firearms, but specializes in the development and technology of sniping. He owns a comprehensive collection of working sniping rifles dating from the nineteenth century and has provided many of them to film and TV companies, for whom he has also acted as historical advisor. He appears regularly as a militaria specialist on the BBC's *Antiques Roadshow*. He lives in France with his wife.

Charles W. Sasser

Author of more than fifty books, including best-sellers like *One Shot – One Kill*, *First SEAL* and *Raider*, Charles W. Sasser has been called 'one of the most respected military writers in the field'. A combat veteran who served with the U.S. Navy (journalist) and with the U.S. Army Special Forces (Green Berets), he is retired from the military after twenty-nine years' active and reserve service. He also served fourteen years as a police officer (in Miami, Florida, and in Tulsa, Oklahoma, where he was a homicide detective). His books have been translated into Chinese, Russian, Serbian, French, Spanish and other languages.

Mark Spicer

Mark Spicer is a twenty-five-year veteran of the British Army, having served with special units, and as a sniper and sniper platoon commander. During his military service he wrote the British Army's field manual for snipers and has since authored three world-renowned books on sniping. Since retiring from the Army he has been involved in training military and law enforcement units from America, Scandinavia and the Middle East and has acted as an expert witness in criminal trials.

Leroy Thompson

Leroy Thompson has trained police and military tactical units, including snipers, for more than thirty years. He also writes articles for numerous magazines on tactical weapons, which includes testing new sniping rifles and optics as they are introduced. He is the author of forty-eight books and over 2,000 magazine articles on military special operations, hostage rescue, tactical operations, and weapons.

John B. Tonkin

An Ohio native and avid student of history, Tonkin enlisted in the U.S. Marine Corps in 1955, joining the 10th Regiment, 2nd Marine Division. He also served in the security unit of a top secret installation during the Cold War. Following military service John began a business career in personnel and labour relations executive management that spanned four decades. Now retired, in addition to his woodworking hobby, he and his wife enjoy their four children and nine grandchildren. John is a Life Member of the Marine Corps League and a current member of the Marine Corps Association.

PLATES

1. Simo Häyhä during his time in action *(Roger Moorhouse)*;
   Häyhä after his severe wound *(Roger Moorhouse)*; a Mosin-
   Nagant 1891/30 rifle with PE scope *(M. Pegler Collection)*.
2. British No. 4 Mk 1(T) rifle, with No. 32 scope *(Courtesy of
   Alamo Military Collectables)*.
3. The No. 32 scope, showing the windage and elevation
   adjustment dials *(Courtesy of Alamo Military Collectables)*; a
   German Kar 98k with Ajak scope on a high turret mount
   (M. Pegler Collection).
4. The preferred British WWII sniper rifle – the P14 *(Private
   Collection, Peter Newark's Military Pictures)*; British sniping
   pioneer of the First World War, H. V. Hesketh-Pritchard;
   sniping trainer and theorist of the Second World war
   Captain C. Shore.
5. The P18 1940 telescopic sight used with the P14 rifle
   (Private Collection, Peter Newark's Military Pictures);
   camouflaged sniper suits designed for the British Home
   Guard *(Private Collection, Peter Newark's Military Pictures)*.
6. Lyudmila Pavlichenko, the most successful Russian female
   sniper of the Second World War with over 300 confirmed
   kills *(Soviet Files)*; Russian sniper Yelizaveta Miranova who
   was reported to have shot 34 Germans *(Major John Plaster
   Collection)*; Pavlichenko, the most dangerous woman on
   earth *(Soviet Files)*.
7. Lyudmila Pavlichenko displays her Hero of The Soviet
   Union award *(Soviet Files)*; Lyudmila Pavlichenko at work
   near Odessa *(Soviet Files)*.

INTRODUCTION

You are about to read an impressive book – the remarkable stories of ten combat snipers of the Second World War. Their ranks include the war's most accomplished sniper, Finland's Simo Häyhä; Germany's finest shooter, Sepp Allerberger; and Russia's famed Vassili Zaitsev and Lyudmila Pavlichenko. Their stories are told to considerable depth, offering interesting details and wartime accounts well beyond their previous exposures in magazine articles and websites.

As well, these pages contain the stories of several hitherto unknown but accomplished snipers, such as Britain's Patrick Devlin and the U.S.A.'s Bert Kemp.

Why so unknown? In retrospect, despite many thousands of books written by WWII veterans of all countries, not a single sniper's memoir appeared in the English language until a decade ago, and even then, the author, Sepp Allerberger, initially concealed his identity. Seventy years ago, snipers often were condemned as cold-hearted killers who took lives without risking their own, an attitude that extends at least back to the Napoleonic era. Second World War sniper veterans often concealed their wartime duties, reluctant to disclose their experiences to a misunderstanding public. And in the case of Japan, few (if any) snipers survived those broiling jungle battlefields, and if they did, their last inclination was to write about their experiences.

Contrast this post-war perception of snipers with the description in the 1940 British Army directive creating sniper teams, requiring that candidates be, 'picked men, and fit men, and proud to be such; the best marksmen, skilled in fieldcraft, confident in their self-reliance, possessed of great courage and unrivalled patience'.

In more recent years, at last, the public has come to respect snipers and their craft very much as that British directive's description. Modern snipers – and those of the past – are properly recognized today as representing the peak of combat skills, a worthy elite offering indispensable capabilities.

It is in this more informed perspective, then, that we can view snipers of the past, and from which these authors tell the snipers' stories.

*

And the authors here are no less impressive than their subjects – a collaboration that includes some of today's greatest sniping authorities – with several personally known by me. Sergeant Major Mark Spicer, for instance, is a retired British sniper instructor and considered one of the world's top sniping experts; Leroy Thompson is a fellow Vietnam veteran and prolific writer on firearms, shooting and special operations; Charles Sasser is a U.S. Army Special Forces veteran and author of a dozen books on such subjects; Adrian Gilbert has authored several major books about snipers and sniping.

Who better, then, to write these accounts? Not only do their pens paint these stories well, but their personal experiences enable them to empathize and understand these snipers as only fellow snipers and combat veterans can. Their insights are not only technically incisive, but disclose the characters and personalities of their subjects, putting a human face to the otherwise one-dimensional snipers portrayed in many motion pictures.

Thus, you will appreciate the bitter cold in which Eastern Front snipers Zaitsev and Allerberger often fought; and the stinking, steaming jungles where Japanese snipers lost their lives atop palm trees. As well, you will better understand the personal revenge that drove Lyudmila Pavlichenko, and how Simo Häyhä applied his skills as a moose hunter and skier to become World War Two's deadliest sniper.

I think you will appreciate this book and its accounts of courage and skill amid great dangers. And come away better respecting these snipers, regardless of the diverse uniforms they wore.

John L. Plaster
Major, Special Forces
U.S. Army (retired)

Chapter 1

SIMO HÄYHÄ

The White Death

It can be rather disconcerting. The face that stares out of the photograph seems to be that of someone who has barely reached adulthood. A smooth, boyish face, almost cherubic in appearance: the eyes closely set, the lips full. Seen full length, the impression of youth and innocence is scarcely reduced. At 1.60 metres (5 ft 3 in), hardly taller than the rifle he holds, Simo Häyhä looks every inch the boy sent to do a man's job. It is hard to believe therefore, that he would become the most prolific sniper of the Second World War, the man with the most confirmed kills in any major war; the man dubbed by his contemporaries as 'The White Death'.

For all his later fame, Simo Häyhä was a simple man. He was born – the seventh of eight children – in 1905 near the town of Rautjärvi in the south of the Grand Duchy of Finland, then part of the Russian Empire. His early life was spent on the family farm, a modest affair with some sugar-beet fields and forestry, as well as a few horses and other livestock, and it was there that he learnt the basic skills of self-reliance and fieldcraft that would later serve him so well.

Like many of his generation, Häyhä would have imbibed the patriotic fervour that accompanied Finnish independence following the Russian collapse of 1917. A few years later, he was called upon to serve the new state himself, when – aged 17 – he joined the Civil Guard. Quiet, reserved and otherwise unremarkable, Häyhä quickly proved himself to be a natural with a rifle, achieving numerous successes in local and regional shooting competitions and being awarded the title of 'Master Marksman'. In 1925, Häyhä was conscripted into the Finnish Army, in which he served for fifteen months, being promoted to the rank of corporal. Then, in 1927, he turned his back on military matters and returned to the family farm. He can have had little inkling of what fate would have in store for him.

In the inter-war years, Finland – like the other states that had emerged from the collapse of the Russian Empire – endured a rather precarious existence. The Soviets viewed the outside world primarily through their own ideological prism – as opponents to be converted and territories to be gained – yet there was also a good deal of old-fashioned Russian nationalism mixed in with the revolutionary thinking; those territories – like Finland – that had once formed part of the Russian Empire were expected to be the first in line once circumstances allowed for a reordering of Soviet borders.

Finnish relations with the Soviet Union were outwardly correct, therefore, even occasionally cordial, but there was a pervasive domestic climate of anti-communism. A non-aggression pact between the two countries was signed in 1932 and renewed two years later, but, by the mid-1930s, the Soviet Union was increasingly making its presence felt and flexing its muscles, for instance by restricting Finnish merchant-ship traffic on the waterways between Lake Ladoga and the Gulf of Finland. By the end of the decade, fear of Soviet expansion was commonplace across the eastern Baltic. Moscow was casting long shadows.

With the German invasion of Poland in September 1939, and the outbreak of the wider European war, naked aggression became the order of the day. Finland, like its Baltic neighbours, soon found itself confronted with a new political reality. Under the terms of the secret protocol to the Nazi–Soviet Pact, which was only made public after 1945, Finland and the Baltic States were consigned to the Soviet 'sphere of influence'. Accordingly, therefore, in late September 1939 the foreign ministers of Latvia, Lithuania and Estonia were invited to Moscow for 'talks', talks which resulted, the following month, in the signing of 'mutual assistance' treaties that would bind those countries ever closer to Moscow, and begin the process of their absorption into the Soviet Union. Finland was next in line.

On 5 October 1939, on the very same day as Hitler was reviewing his victorious troops in the Polish capital, Warsaw, Stalin extended an invitation to the Finns for 'talks' in Moscow. The Finns responded warily, sending the veteran negotiator Juho Paasikivi, to receive the Soviet proposals, which included a northward extension of the border in the Karelian isthmus, close to Leningrad, and a thirty-year lease on the port of Hangö, at the mouth of the Gulf of Finland. Soviet logic was fairly straightforward. Having abetted the Germans in launching the Second World War, even to the point of collaborating in the invasion of Poland that autumn, the Soviets intended to sit back and watch the capitalist Western powers fight each other to another bloody standstill – as in the First World War – thereby hastening the 'inevitable' triumph of communism. In the meantime, all Moscow had to do was to bolster its defences, marshal its forces and make a few adjustments to its frontiers.

The Finns, however, were not minded to accede to Soviet demands, which they viewed as the thin end of a communist wedge, and were unimpressed with what was on offer by way of recompense. Yet, they received little support from either their Scandinavian neighbours, or their German allies – who urged compliance. After over three weeks of inconclusive negotiations, therefore, the Finnish delegation returned home in mid-November, without any agreement having been reached. After the bluster and 'negotiation' had failed, Moscow had to find another way to force its will upon its neighbour. Before the end of the month, the two would be at war.

On paper at least, the Soviet invasion of Finland in the winter of 1939 should have been a straightforward affair. The 26 divisions and 1,000,000 soldiers deployed by the Red Army should have been sufficient to sweep the paltry 10 divisions and 300,000 soldiers of the Finnish Army aside. By every measure available, the Soviets had an overwhelming advantage: three times as many soldiers as their opponents, thirty times as many aircraft and a hundred times as many tanks. On the main front across the Karelian Isthmus, for instance, the Soviets could field 120,000 men, 1,400 tanks and 900 artillery pieces against

Finnish defenders who numbered just 21,000, with 71 artillery pieces and 29 anti-tank guns.[1] In addition, Moscow was confident that the Finnish working class would rise in support of their communist 'liberators' and serve as a fifth column behind enemy lines.

The reality was to be rather different, however. The material and numerical superiority of the Soviet forces counted for little in the extreme conditions of a Finnish winter. Much of the terrain through which those Red Army soldiers trudged was a trackless, snowbound wasteland of thick forests, criss-crossed by frozen lakes, rivers and swamps, which was largely impassable to a modern mechanized army. Moreover, in the south, across the Karelian isthmus, north of Leningrad – through which the main thrust of any Soviet attack was expected – Finnish engineers had constructed an extensive network of bunkers, trenches, obstacles and earthworks, which was known as the Mannerheim Line. In such circumstances, the material advantages held by the Soviets were effectively nullified.

In addition, the quality of the opposing troops also differed enormously from what had been expected in Moscow. Far from welcoming the Soviet Army, the Finns were highly motivated to defend their country. Their morale was high, as demonstrated by a quip that did the rounds that winter: 'They are so many and our country is so small, where will we find room to bury them all?'[2] The Finns were also able to draw on a substantial pool of trained reservists – like Simo Häyhä himself – to bolster their forces. Though many of them lacked modern equipment, and in some cases even rifles, these former Civil Guardsmen nonetheless often brought vital local knowledge with them, as well as fieldcraft and survival skills.

The Soviet Army, in contrast, was ill-prepared. Still reeling from the brutal purges of only a few years before, which had removed over 80 per cent of senior officers and divisional commanders, it was severely weakened, with low morale being exacerbated by defective training regimes and poor leadership. Though well-supplied in comparison to their opponents, Red Army soldiers nonetheless often lacked the winter clothing and camouflage equipment that would be vital for fighting in sub-arctic conditions. Most of the tanks and vehicles that rolled across the Finnish frontier that winter, for instance, bore the same olive-drab livery as the soldiers who manned them. They were certainly not difficult to spot against the blinding white of a Finnish winter.

Tactically, too, the Soviets were guilty of a surprising lack of guile and invention. In most instances, they sought simply to overwhelm their enemy with a massed frontal assault. Coupled with that, they often suffered from a distinct lack of martial dash, adopting an excessively cautious approach in which an advance could be held up for hours by the merest hint of Finnish resistance. Such tactics clearly played into Finnish hands. Given the conditions – with only a few roads and tracks providing a passage through largely impenetrable forest – Soviet assaults quickly turned into enormous traffic jams, with Finnish defenders able to contain the spearhead with relatively small numbers of personnel.

As the Soviet advance stalled, the Finns moved to counter-attack, using small groups of mobile ski troops to outflank the invaders and isolate them from their supply columns. The long nights of the Scandinavian winter were also exploited to maximum effect, with Finnish forces specializing in harrying and ambushing their foes under cover of darkness, often using improvised explosives, such as satchel charges, or the famed 'Molotov cocktail'. There were also rather more unorthodox methods employed. Finnish troops would often target field kitchens, for instance, thereby exposing their remaining enemies more swiftly to the ravages of hunger. In time, Finnish methods evolved into a recognized tactic, by which Soviet forces would be isolated and contained, before being systematically reduced by the combined effects of constant counter-attacks and the harshness of the winter weather, in which temperatures could fall as low as -25 °C. This tactic became known as the *motti*, from the Finnish term for a measurement of cut timber, to be used as firewood. The sinister implication was that Soviet forces thus encircled, were merely waiting to be burned.

In this way, the Finns scored some notable successes: on Christmas Eve 1940 both the Soviet 139th and 75th Divisions were wiped out, whilst the 163rd and 44th Divisions were annihilated in early January.[3] In the latter example, the Soviet 44th Division was ordered to advance in support of the 163rd, which had encountered stiff resistance near Suomussalmi. Soon, the 44th faced a similar fate: strung out for over 30 kilometres along a narrow road, hemmed in by lakes and thick forests, its forward progress was halted by a fortified road-block. Harassed by fast-moving ski-troops, the column was gradually broken up into smaller and smaller sections, whilst the cold and hunger did their work on the encircled soldiers. Each dwindling pocket was then wiped out, one by one.[4] In the aftermath, the Finns gained vital additions of materiel, including 43 tanks, 50 field guns, 270 motor vehicles and over 6,000 rifles. Around 40,000 Soviet soldiers from the two divisions are thought to have perished.[5]

Another tactic in which Finnish forces specialized was the use of snipers. Given the largely static nature of the conflict, as the initial Soviet advance had stagnated, sharpshooters were used to great effect both at the front line and in the reduction of the various *motti* encirclements. Their deployment in reducing the *motti* also had an important tactical and psychological aspect: snipers were well able to maximize the mental anguish suffered by encircled troops, by targeting commanding officers, for instance, or by concentrating their fire on those men who huddled around a camp fire. It would be as a sniper that Simo Häyhä would make his name.

On returning to the Finnish Army, Häyhä was assigned to the 34th Jäger Regiment in the heavily forested area to the north-east of Lake Ladoga, about 280 kilometres north of Leningrad. It was a vitally important area, protecting the Karelian Isthmus from an attack around the northern shore of the lake, which would outflank the Finnish defences on the Mannerheim Line. Though vastly outnumbered, the Finns had managed to stabilize the front, with the line running approximately north to south along the Kollaa River, with the Soviets to the eastern side.

Though a secondary theatre, compared to the Karelian Isthmus, the Kollaa Front would become iconic as a symbol of Finnish resistance.

Initially, Häyhä fought on the Kollaa as a simple infantryman, but it did not take long before his outstanding ability with a rifle was noticed by his superiors. Already an experienced hunter and marksman, he was quickly singled out for more specialist tasks. In one of his first actions, he was called upon to eliminate a Soviet sniper, who had already killed three Finnish platoon leaders and an NCO. Meeting the challenge, Häyhä showed all the qualities of patience and meticulous preparation that would become his hallmarks. After scouting for a favourable firing position, he sat almost motionless wrapped up warm in camouflage fatigues, watching over the sights of his rifle. Several hours later, as the daylight faded and the day drew to a close, he finally had his opportunity. When a glint of sunlight from the telescopic sight momentarily betrayed his target's position, Häyhä saw the Russian rise, rather carelessly, from his hide, doubtless believing that the coming dusk would harbour no threat. A single shot to the head from Häyhä's rifle would prove him wrong.[6]

As time went on, Häyhä's sniping technique developed. In many ways, it was very similar to that of other specialist marksmen, drawing heavily on his skills and experience as an outdoorsman, hunter and trapper. There is a marked similarity, for instance, between Häyhä's background and that of his great Soviet rival, Vassili Zaitsev: both men had been raised in the countryside and were very close to nature, and both were gifted trackers and hunters. With this background, Häyhä found the essentials of observation and concealment to be second nature. He paid particular attention, for instance, to finding good shooting positions – locations overlooking enemy outposts or thoroughfares, from where he could see but not be seen, and where he would not be silhouetted by his surroundings or by a change in the light. His small stature also meant that he had little difficulty in using the natural hiding places that the forest offered.

Camouflage, too, was vital and, as well as his snowsuit, Häyhä used white gauze to wrap around the stock and barrel of his rifle. He preferred to leave his hides as 'natural' as possible, meanwhile, using only the surrounding snow as his camouflage; though he did take care to pat down the snow in front of his hide, so as to prevent a puff of white upon firing, which might betray his position.

Patience was another essential attribute. Häyhä would often spend all of the short winter days in position – moving to and from his hide only under cover of darkness. With just sugar lumps for sustenance, he avoided any unnecessary movement, often sitting motionless for hours on end. He would observe the enemy closely, learning their behaviour, their routines and their habits, biding his time until a suitable target came into view. His opponents never knew of his presence, until the first shot was fired.

Yet, aside from these conventional skills, Häyhä was not short of idiosyncrasies. For one thing, he only occasionally used a spotter – a certain Corporal Malmi – generally preferring to work alone. It is not immediately clear from the few sources available on Häyhä's life why this should be so, but it may be that the necessary arts of movement and concealment were simply easier to achieve by one man rather than two.

The weapon that Häyhä used is also surprising. The M/28-30 was a Finnish variant of the venerable Mosin-Nagant bolt-action rifle, which had made its first appearance in the last decade of the nineteenth century. More remarkably still, it was a rifle without telescopic sights. Though such technology was reasonably well advanced by 1940, the Finnish Army suffered from a lack of higher-specification equipment. Thus, Häyhä was obliged to eschew such technological advantages in favour of the basic iron sights that his stock rifle carried. He made a virtue out of necessity, however, asserting that the iron sights allowed him to present a much less prominent target to an opponent, whilst a marksman using telescopic sights was obliged to hold his head higher and so was much more vulnerable.

By way of compensating for this apparent technological disadvantage, Häyhä was obsessional about maintaining his rifle, spending the remainder of his waking hours, when not in the field, stripping, cleaning and oiling his weapon to keep it in perfect working order. He was also fastidious about zeroing his rifle for differing distances. This was a task that he carried out in the field as a matter of course, and was essential to maintaining his accuracy.

Using these techniques, Häyhä scored numerous successes, often eliminating more than ten enemy soldiers per day. Occasionally, where circumstances and fortune allowed, his totals were greater than that. In one three-day period in December 1939, he accounted for fifty-one Soviet soldiers; and later in that month scored his highest total for a single day – twenty-five confirmed kills. His skills as a hunter and outdoorsman served him well. On one day in early February 1940, for instance, he spotted a newly constructed network of accommodation bunkers close to the front line, but not far from one of his observation posts. Advancing stealthily through the undergrowth with his spotter, he set up a firing point about 150 metres from the bunkers: 'we spent the whole day in our position', he later recalled, 'and killed nineteen Russians. They never learned where we were.'[7]

On some occasions, however, the Soviets were very much aware of Häyhä's position and did everything they could to fight back. Given his prolific nature, Häyhä was soon a marked man and would later suspect that a price had been put on his head. As a result, he found himself engaged in a number of sniper duels during his time on the front line. It was also not uncommon for the Soviets to call in artillery strikes or mortar bombardments in response to Häyhä's sniping, in an effort to eliminate him. In one instance, Häyhä found himself under heavy artillery fire after attempting to knock out a Soviet forward observation post, which was equipped with a periscope. Though peppered with shrapnel and flying debris, he nonetheless survived and was able to withdraw unscathed. Later that day, he returned to the location, approaching from a different angle and finding a new position for himself. On this occasion, he was successful; the periscope was destroyed.[8]

In time, Häyhä's reputation also grew amongst those on his own side. He began to garner plaudits and gifts in equal measure, with many of the latter being donated by ordinary Finnish civilians who had heard of his deeds. Official and unofficial awards followed, and in time Häyhä would be awarded both classes of the Medal of Liberty and two classes of the Order of Liberty. Most famously, perhaps, in mid-February 1940, Häyhä was awarded an honorary M/28 rifle, made by the Finnish manufacturer Sako, and donated by a Swedish benefactor. Despite the award, Häyhä continued using his trusty M/28-30, the weapon with which he would ultimately dispatch an astonishing 542 Soviet soldiers.[9]

Häyhä's attitude to his deadly task was a curiously – if necessarily – detached one. He evidently bore no particular malice towards the Soviet invaders of his country, and took no notice or pleasure in his mounting tally of kills, even refusing to be drawn on the subject in later life. His attitude was much more that he had been given a job to do and he would do it to the very best of his ability. Apparently untroubled by the lethal role that he played in the Winter War, Häyhä claimed never to have lost a night's sleep over it, either during the conflict or subsequently.[10]

Despite his efforts, the wider war would slowly turn against Häyhä and his Finnish comrades, with ever-larger numbers of Soviet reinforcements threatening a decisive breakthrough. On the Kollaa Front, as elsewhere, the Finns were already vastly out-numbered, with barely four battalions facing fully two divisions, as well their attendant armour and artillery.[11] January 1940 would bring further disparity, as additional artillery batteries brought the Soviet total in that sector to around 200 pieces, ten times the number available to the Finns. Despite their superiority in men and materiel, however, Soviet tactics remained stubbornly pedestrian, consisting mainly of headlong, frontal assaults on fortified Finnish positions. Perhaps the most famous example of this approach was the battle of 'Killer Hill', where a single platoon of barely thirty Finns held an entire regiment of 4,000 Soviet soldiers.[12]

Yet, for all their determination and ingenuity, the Finns could not hold out for long against such overwhelming odds. By late February, with Finnish resources running perilously low, and with the once impenetrable forest reduced to a moonscape of shell craters and splintered, broken trees, the numerical advantages of the Soviets finally began to tell. Under such conditions, the static war in which the Finns had specialized began to become more fluid, and though the lines held both on the Kollaa and the Karelian Front, isolated positions were increasingly being overrun, foreshadowing a more general collapse.

Tellingly, perhaps, the end for Simo Häyhä would come as an ordinary infantryman, rather than as a sniper. Commanding a squad of soldiers in early March 1940, he was ordered to resist an advance by the Soviet 128th Division in the forests of Ulismainen on the Kollaa Front. Characteristically, that Finnish defence took the form of a counter-attack. As Häyhä himself recalled:

> We moved to our starting positions in early dawn, about five–six in the morning. There was a swamp, some 300 metres wide which we managed to cross without difficulty as our own machine guns gave us protection. Once over the swamp, we charged against the enemy who were really close to us. My rifle functioned very well; we were so close to the enemy that they were sometimes even only some two metres from me. The enemy were forced to withdraw, but some brave soldiers remained behind to cause havoc amongst us. Suddenly there was a shot, maybe 50–100 metres away and I felt I was hit. I just felt a suppressed bang in my mouth and I lost consciousness.[13]

Häyhä had been shot in the mouth with an explosive bullet, which had entered through his upper lip and exited through his left cheek. The impact had torn away all of his upper left jaw and had shattered his lower left jaw. When he briefly regained consciousness, he later recalled, his mouth was full of bone fragments, broken teeth and blood; he remembered his men frantically calling for a medic, before placing him on a simple sledge and carrying him to the rear. Soon after, he passed out again. He would remain in a coma for a week, only waking up on 13 March, the day that the armistice between Finland and the Soviet Union was signed.

Häyhä's recovery was extremely difficult. At one point, at a field hospital not long after his evacuation from the front, he was left on a pile of corpses when a medical orderly mistakenly thought his injuries to have been fatal. After his condition had been stabilized, he was moved to a military hospital in central Finland, where his treatment could start in earnest. Häyhä would endure as many as twenty-six operations to rebuild his face. His jaw and palate had to be reconstructed – with sections of bone for the purpose being taken from his hip – and for many months he was unable to speak or consume anything but liquid food. Despite his surgeons' best efforts, the severity of his wounds meant that he would be left with severe scarring and disfigurement to the left side of his face for the rest of his life. He was finally discharged from hospital in May 1941, fourteen months after his injury. He returned to the land, taking on a farm in the lakeland of Ruokolahti in south Karelia, where he would breed dogs and work the forest.

Finland's troubles were far from over, however. By the Moscow Treaty of March 1940 Finland had been forced to cede 11 per cent of its territory and 30 per cent of its economic assets to the Soviet Union. Moreover, few Finns believed that the aggressive intentions of the Soviets were sated, and many argued for a reopening of hostilities to regain the lands that had been lost. When Nazi Germany invaded the Soviet Union on 22 June 1941, therefore, the Finns followed suit, advancing to the line of the 1939 border in what became known as the 'Continuation War'. Häyhä volunteered for service in the new conflict, but his wounds were so severe that he was rejected.

In the years that followed, Häyhä lived an ordinary life. The family farm was lost after 1944, when the region was ceded to the Soviet Union, but Häyhä carried on working the 50 hectares of land on his own farm in Utula, 50 kilometres from the Soviet frontier, north of Leningrad. Always active, he enjoyed hunting, skiing and fishing, and otherwise kept himself busy on the farm or in the forests.

Häyhä had no desire to be in the limelight and kept very much to himself; his natural reserve, humility and shyness were compounded by the difficulty in speaking caused by his injury. He never married, preferring the company of his dogs and the proximity of the forest, with which he always felt a special affinity. Nonetheless, he was fêted by the Finnish military and by the Finnish Snipers' Guild, which would organize a sniping competition in his honour in 1978, to be held annually and open to both civilians and military personnel. In later years he was also visited on occasions by sniping enthusiasts from the United States and elsewhere, who were keen to hear of his techniques and experiences. He also collaborated with a Finnish Army officer, Tapio Saarelainen, in telling the story of his life. Simo Häyhä died in April 2002, aged 96.

It is perhaps easy to imagine – especially given his own modesty – that Häyhä's achievements during the Winter War were less than remarkable. One might conclude that Häyhä was an effective proponent of the sniper's art, but little more beyond that. This would be wrong, however. There are a number of factors – aside from the astonishing number of kills that he scored – that serve to make Häyhä's story truly exceptional. For one thing, and in contrast to many of his rival snipers from the Second World War, he scored over 500 kills using a rifle equipped only with standard iron sights. For another, he was operating in the harshest environment imaginable – the depths of a Scandinavian winter – conditions that would test man and machine, friend or foe, to the utmost.

Most remarkable of all, perhaps, is the fact that the Winter War lasted less than four months, from late November 1939 to mid-March 1940, and Häyhä was invalided out of the war after less than 100 days in the front line. On average, therefore, he scored over five kills every day for the entire time that he fought. For all his natural modesty, therefore, that slightly-built man with the boyish face, truly deserves the title of the most prolific sniper of the Second World War.

Notes

1. Philip Jowett & Brent Snodgrass, *Finland at War 1939–1945* (Oxford, 2006), p. 6.
2. William R. Trotter, *A Frozen Hell* (Chapel Hill, 1991), p. 40.
3. See, for instance, Robert Edwards, *White Death* (London, 2006), pp. 162–7, & I. C. B. Dear (ed.), *The Oxford Companion to the Second World War* (Oxford, 1995), p. 374.
4. See Trotter, pp. 162–3.
5. Jowett & Snodgrass, p. 8.
6. Tapio Saarelainen, *Simo Häyhä – The Sniper* (Tampere, 2008), p. 29.
7. Ibid., p. 32.
8. Ibid., p. 30.
9. This figure is disputed, with some sources stating that Häyhä killed as many as 800 Soviet soldiers with his rifle. The figure of 542 is cited in the most authoritative account of his life, Tapio Saarelainen's *Simo Häyhä – The Sniper* (p. 128). In addition to this figure, Häyhä is thought to have scored around 200 kills with his Suomi submachine gun in infantry combat.
10. Ibid., pp. 32 & 64.
11. Edwards, pp. 205–6.
12. Trotter, p. 130.
13. Quoted in Saarelainen, p. 42.

Chapter 2

LYUDMILA PAVLICHENKO

Most Dangerous Woman on Earth

The last train west chugged across the River Bug to the German-occupied side of the Russo-German border at 0200 on 22 June 1941. An hour later, as the short summer night lifted from the central Ukraine, Hitler violated his non-aggression pact with Stalin and launched Operation Barbarossa. German artillery shells screamed across a 3,200-kilometre frontier from the Arctic to the Black Sea. Three million Axis soldiers (182 divisions), 6,000 big guns, 2,000 Luftwaffe warplanes, and thousands of tanks flooded into the Ukraine in what was to be the last German *Blitzkrieg*.

'The sooner Russia is crushed, the better,' Hitler cheered.

Kiev, capital of Ukraine and its largest city, was one of Hitler's first objectives, along with Moscow and Leningrad. Luftwaffe Me-109 fighters and Ju-87 Stuka dive bombers began pounding and strafing the city only weeks after the invasion began. Lyudmila Mikhailovna Pavlichenko, 24, a history student at Kiev University, was walking to college when a swarm of fighters buzzed in low and fast to chew up the block. She dashed for cover. That night, she made up her mind. 'I am going to fight,' she informed her parents. Her father was a veteran of the Russian Revolution, on the side of the winning Reds. 'I'll be at the recruiting office tomorrow.' Within a year, this petite, dark-eyed beauty would become the most dangerous woman of the twentieth century, the deadliest female sniper in any army, in any war.

Pavlichenko arrived at the recruiting office the next morning wearing high heels and a crêpe de Chine dress with her nails manicured and her dark, wavy hair groomed short. She was slim, fit and beautiful, with delicate features and dark brown eyes that seemed to burn into a man's soul. Volunteers were lined up around the block.

The recruiter was an older soldier pulled off the line because of age or ill health. He looked up in surprise when she stood before him and announced her intentions. 'I've come to enlist as a sniper.' This smart-looking woman looked more like a fashion model than a German-killer. He laughed at her.

'Why don't you work in the factories like other women?' he demanded. 'You're needed there what with our men marching off to the front lines.'

Although in the spirit of Soviet equality Russia was arguably less sexist than its Western allies, the Soviet military nonetheless harboured a deep prejudice against recruiting women for combat. The high command maintained women were meant to nurture, not to kill. Females served mainly in administrative, medical and support roles. However, the exceptional circumstances of war on the Eastern Front, with Russia's survival at stake, attenuated objections to women serving on the front lines. By the time the Second World War ended, over 800,000 Russian women had served as pilots, machine gunners, tank crew members, partisans and snipers. Nearly 200,000 would be decorated; ninety-two eventually received the Hero of the Soviet Union accolade, the nation's highest award.

The rapid industrial development of the Soviet Union and the worldwide depression of the late 1920s and 1930s combined to move large numbers of Russians from their farms to the cities. In the spirit of egalitarianism, young women were encouraged to work, go to college and participate in paramilitary training. Women learned to shoot weapons, pilot aircraft, drive trucks and survive in battle. Lyudmila Pavlichenko was one of them.

She was born on 12 July 1916, during the dark years of the First World War in the market city of Bila Tserkva ('White Church'). The family moved to nearby Kiev when she was fourteen, where she completed high school while working as a grinder at the Kiev Arsenal Factory. A gifted but wilful student, a tomboy who would rather hunt small game with a catapult than play with dolls, she was an avid reader of travel and adventure stories.

Like many boys and girls of the times, she was fond of military-related sports and activities. Her taste for adventure included skydiving and flying small planes. She excelled as a remarkable natural rifle shot and won the coveted Voroshilov Sharpshooter Badge while competing in regional rifle matches. As Hitler's spreading war threatened to engulf the U.S.S.R., she prepared by enrolling in a volunteer sniper school arranged by her local Komsomol (Party youth section). She put her diploma in a box and forgot about it until 22 June 1941, when the Nazis swarmed across the River Bug to attack the Ukraine.

By then she was in her fourth year as a history student working on an advanced degree. At the recruiting office, she took out her sniper's diploma, Voroshilov Badge and other shooting and paramilitary honours and dumped them on the table in front of the recruiter who had laughed at her. The expression on his face changed. He looked at the documents and his eyes slowly lifted to regard with grudging respect the impudent young fashion plate across the table from him.

'You're going to get your fingernails dirty,' he said as he stamped her application. Accepted.

With that, Pavlichenko was on her way to becoming one of 2,000 female snipers to serve in the Red Army, only 500 of whom would survive the war.

*

Through bitter experience against Finnish sharpshooters like Simo Häyhä, who picked off more than 500 Russian soldiers during the Winter War of 1939–40, the Soviet Union learned the value of snipers and began to place more emphasis on its sniper training programme. Special sniper units were embedded in nearly all major unit commands. Young Lyudmila Pavlichenko found herself assigned to the Red Army's V. I. Chapayev 25th Rifle Division of the Independent Maritime Army.

She received truncated training in basic military and sniper tactics, such as observation techniques, camouflage and concealment, shot placement and target selection. There was no time for anything else. Although the Red Army's five million soldiers made it the world's largest, it was ill-equipped and inefficient and found itself in chaos as the Germans advanced as much as 450 kilometres within the first week of the attack. By 8 July, the enemy were almost at the gates of Kiev, fighting in the forests less than 150 kilometres away.

Tales of horror and raw courage filtered back to Kiev as Pavlichenko and her fellow replacements prepared to move to the front to join the 25th Rifles – of a Soviet tank ablaze from anti-tank shells charging German positions until its crew burned to death; of a pilot who plunged his damaged warplane into a convoy of German fuel trucks; of rear guards who fought to the death rather than surrender or withdraw . . .

Russian women and children were conscripted to fight. Pretty teenage girls were found dead on the battlefield, still clutching automatic weapons. Soviet soldiers who panicked and fled the fighting were shot by their own officers. Those unfortunates taken prisoner were declared traitors and their families' rations taken away, which often meant starvation.

Before being sent to the front, Pavlichenko was issued the standard infantry weapon, derived from one that had been in Russian and then Soviet service since 1891 – a five-shot, bolt-action 7.62-mm calibre Mosin-Nagant 91/30 rifle that fired a 9.59-gram bullet at 854 m/sec and was effective out to 550 metres. Adopted as the standard sniper's rifle in 1932, it could be fired with authority up to 1,250 metres with the addition of a telescopic sight.

Pavlichenko's 4-power fixed PE scope, a copy of scopes manu-factured by Carl Zeiss, had a 4° field of view, was nearly a foot long and added about half a kilogram to the rifle's weight. Thumbscrews allowed adjustments for windage, drift, lead and angle of elevation.

Armed with her new rifle and a combat load of 120 cartridges, no longer a fashion plate but garbed out in her baggy olive drab male's uniform, with camouflage overalls, sniper's hood and net face mask in her pack, the young history student turned prospective German-killer massed with thousands of other recruits and replacements at the Kiev rail yards for transport to the front. Her unit was already engaged in desperate combat with Romanian and German forces in Moldavia as it attempted to block the southern approach to the Black Sea city of Odessa, the most important port of trade in the Soviet Union and the site of a Soviet naval base.

The rail yards were in turmoil as soldiers with their packs and weapons piled into boxcars, open wagons, and anything else that could be moved by rail. Trains arrived and departed day and night, their steel wheels and shrill whistles signalling an urgency that Russia had not experienced since Napoleon's invasion.

Apprehensive, her nerves drawn tight, Pavlichenko rooted into a boxcar between a grizzled sergeant with bad oral hygiene and a kid of about seventeen who cried a lot. For two days, the train rumbled across Bessarabia towards Moldavia and the Dniester River, where the 25th was making its stand, stopping only long enough to refuel and allow troops to stretch and boil up a few pots of potatoes and cabbage.

Moldavia, formerly part of Romania, was an ancient land known for its castles and wine. Stalin had recently absorbed it as part of his non-aggression pact with Hitler. The Dniester River formed the boundary between Moldavia and the Ukraine. The river entered the Black Sea about 150 kilometres west of Odessa.

Summer dust in clouds obscured the horizons as the troop train neared its destination. Russian forces were on the move by any means available, not only by train but also by trucks, touring cars, horses and wagons, carts, bicycles and on foot. Late in the afternoon of the second day, Pavlichenko and her comrades heard the distant thunder of duelling artillery.

'I knew my task was to shoot human beings,' Pavlichenko later reflected. 'In theory, that was fine, but I knew that the real thing would be completely different.' She was to discover, as others had, that there was a big difference between shooting at a target and shooting at a pair of eyes that jumped out at you through the telescopic sight. She wondered if she possessed that kind of courage, the answer to which she would find within days after her arrival in the wooded, hilly country between the Dniester and Odessa. Her No. 2 Company, 54th Razinsky Regiment, 25th Division, was retreating from the vicinity of the Prut River to dig in on the distant approaches to Odessa.

*

The Romanian General Staff had issued its Directive 31 when Barbarossa began, in it stipulating that its Fourth Army and elements of the German Eleventh Army would defeat the Russians between the Dniester and the Tiligulskiy Banks to occupy Odessa. Odessa was heavily defended by the Soviet 25th, 95th, and 421st Rifle Divisions, supported by the 2nd Cavalry Division, an NKVD (Internal Security) regiment, three squadrons of bombers and fighters and contingents of artillery. Fortunately, the city could not be completely surrounded due to the superiority of the Soviet Black Sea fleet.

Three separate lines formed the Russian defence, the first a thin line of trenches, pillboxes and anti-tank ditches some 50 kilometres outside the city. If it fell, the Russians would withdraw to an alternative defensive line 8 kilometres from Odessa. The final protective line meant house-to-house fighting inside the ancient city originally founded by the Empress Catherine the Great in 1794.

Stalin issued strict orders that cowards would be shot by NKVD troops. It was forbidden in Pavlichenko's company even to think about death, much less talk about it.

No. 2 Company was in the centre of the first defensive line when the German offensive against Odessa began on 8 August 1941, preceded by thunder barrages of enemy artillery that pounded hills and left stands of timber splintered into smoking kindling. Pavlichenko and other soldiers from her company hugged the ground overlooking a narrow open field. Visible through her rifle scope in the pale morning sun were a number of enemy soldiers moving about on the near side of a hill. Easy targets. However, to her dismay, she discovered she could not squeeze the trigger on them. Her finger seemed frozen stiff. Perhaps she hadn't the courage to be a sniper after all.

Nearby lay a young soldier with whom she had become acquainted on the train ride from Kiev. A nice boy with a sunny disposition. The sudden crackle of rifle and machine-gun fire from the opposing tree line signalled a probe. Pavlichenko heard a sound like a hammer striking a melon, followed by a cry of pain and surprise. To her horror, she saw that her friend had taken a round through the head, exploding it in a pink mist of blood and brains. 'After that,' she later recalled, 'nothing could stop me.'

She killed her first Germans a day or so later during the four-day fight for Hill 54.2 near Belyayevka, which her regiment was defending. She and a spotter crawled through thick undergrowth outside the defensive perimeter and set up a hide overlooking the enemy's most likely avenue of approach. Russia's was the first military to employ snipers in two-person teams consisting of a shooter and an observer.

Through his Model 40 trench periscope, Pavlichenko's spotter picked up movement in a wooded area about 300 metres away. Pavlichenko shifted into a better position, the outline of her form broken up by her one-piece overall into which she had woven natural foliage.

Her 4-power scope picked out three Germans stealthily moving in and out of shadow, unaware that they were being watched. She had zeroed in her weapon at 300 metres for point of aim and point of impact. Taking into account variables such as wind speed (light), bullet weight, breath control and trigger squeeze, she cross-haired slightly off centre of mass on the lead enemy soldier. Military snipers usually aimed for the chest area and depended on tissue damage, organ trauma and blood loss to make the kill.

The barrel of her gun danced in front of her eyes from the excitement. She took a deep, calming breath and waited for the right moment. This time she did not hesitate. As soon as her target paused to look around, she squeezed her trigger. The impact of the bullet slapped the German around and dropped him to his knees. Even before he plunged face down in the forest, dead, she acquired and killed a second German. The third soldier panicked and fled before she could finish him. 'There was no change of expression on her pretty face,' her spotter reported, then predicted, 'Russia is going to be talking about Lyudmila Pavlichenko.'

Anger at the Germans for having invaded her homeland turned to hate as Axis soldiers broke through Soviet defences and closed in on the city. The enemy reached the main line of Russian resistance within two weeks after the offensive launched and began shelling Odessa with a reinforcement of ten heavy artillery batteries.

The pretty sharpshooter from Kiev University hardened and quickly adapted to the harsh and dangerous climate of battle. She and other Soviet snipers were granted virtual free rein in carrying out their missions of scouting and slowing down, harassing and demoralizing the advance by long-distance suppressive fire against key targets of opportunity. The roar of artillery, the scream of dive bombers and the clatter of machine-gun fire continued unabated for days, broken only by the occasional lull. Smoke and dust smudged the sky in thick clouds and columns.

A sniper had to possess patience, perseverance, nerves of steel and a steady trigger finger. Pavlichenko proved to be as relentless as she was strikingly attractive. The perfect killing machine. Day after day, she and an observer crept into no-man's land to ply her bloody trade. Fortified by hatred and her sense of mission, she often crawled into a hide and remained for up to eighteen hours at a time, living on dry bread and water, conducting bodily functions in place, all just to get the one shot, one kill of the sniper's trade. Her body count grew almost daily.

Her preferred targets were enemy officers, followed by communications specialists, NCOs, dog handlers that were often used to track snipers, and, of course, enemy snipers, a deadly cat-and-mouse game played out in the wreckage and rubble of war. Losers received no second chance.

Crafty and deceptive, with a strong sense of survival, she employed various ploys and tricks to keep going when the life-span of the average sniper was about three weeks. Captured snipers from either side were summarily executed on the spot.

Thunderstorms or artillery barrages that masked the report of her rifle were her favourite times to hunt since her targets were less alert to her presence and her location more difficult to pinpoint. She rarely fired more than once from the same position and never returned twice to the same hide. She tied strips of cloth to bushes in danger areas to flutter in errant breezes and distract enemy observers. Grenades, mines and smoke booby traps provided further protection against intrusion. Sometimes a clothing store mannequin disguised as a tempting target lured enemy snipers into exposing themselves.

She proved unequalled in the cold-blooded act of sniper psychological warfare. Consistently taking out the second man in a patrol or column struck panic in advancing squads or platoons to the point that no one wanted to be placed in that position. Occasionally, she deliberately shot a man in the legs so that his pleas for help would entice other targets into her sights.

The single crack of Pavlichenko's 7.62-mm Mosin-Nagant in no-man's land was enough to strike terror into the hearts of German and Romanian soldiers. Whenever she went to the rear, infantrymen gawked in disbelief that this slip of a girl could be the ruthless killer whose reputation was beginning to spread throughout the Ukraine. By 29 August, twenty-eight days into the Odessa offensive, her body count stood at 100, or an average kill rate of nearly four per day. Few snipers in any war had been so successful in such a short period of time. In effect, she was already becoming the world's most accomplished bringer of death.

*

A small cemetery held by the Russians near Il'Ichevka State Farm was strategically important because of the Voznesensk– Odessa highway that ran across the farm. Snipers were deployed ahead of the defensive perimeter. Working alone for the day, Pavlichenko climbed a tree inside the graveyard to obtain a better view of the terrain, thinking the foliage would conceal her.

Barely had she settled in than the sharp crack of a rifle sent a bullet scything through the leaves inches above her head. A second shot followed in the echo of the first. Realizing she was in dire straits, with at least two enemy snipers zeroing in on her, she let go and fell twelve feet to the ground, landing on grass between two graves. Pain shot up her spine. She gritted her teeth against it and lay perfectly still, pretending to be dead, knowing that to move even a finger would draw more fire to finish her off.

Hours passed. The midday sun baked her body. Stinging, biting insects crawled on her face.

Finally the sun went down. She crept from the cemetery under cover of darkness and back to her own lines, where she spent two days in bed and more than a week afterwards hobbling around with the aid of a makeshift crutch.

*

The enemy continued to pound Odessa. No quarter asked, none given. Russia suffered an unrecoverable blow when the north-western heights fell and Germans occupied the area south of the Sakhoy Bank, which allowed their artillery to reach any sector of Odessa and the Soviet defences.

Choking summer dust stirred up by boots, horses and tank tracks hung in clouds as high as city buildings, turning to mud when the cold rains of late September began. Downpours lasted for days and turned tracks and roads into impassable bogs. Horses sank up to their collars, men to their knees, and vehicles to their axles.

Scarcely a building in Odessa remained intact. Fighting raged in Mikhailovsky Square, on the Potemkin Stairs and around the imposing dome of the First Orthodox Church. Fires burned almost constantly. It was a target-rich environment for snipers like Pavlichenko, now promoted to senior sergeant. She chalked up another eighty-seven kills.

On 9 October 1941, a shell splinter gashed her scalp during fighting in the Dainitskiy sector. Her company commander, Junior Lieutenant Petrenko fell dead. Sergeant-Major Leonid Kitsenko, a sniper and senior NCO of Pavlichenko's sniper element, was wounded. Pavlichenko assumed command, a valiant figure wearing a dirty bandage around her head, cap pulled low to hold the dressing in place, face masked by blood, struggling to maintain consciousness.

'Cowards!' a political officer railed against her frightened comrades. 'Look at the woman. Pavlichenko has the balls of a man.'

She was eventually moved to a medical battalion, from which she was released only days before Odessa fell on 15 October. In accordance with Stalin's scorched-earth policy, Russian sabotage groups destroyed as much of the city as they could and land-mined the rest while the Black Sea Fleet evacuated more than 350,000 soldiers and civilians under cover of darkness. The Soviets lost 16,578 dead and 24,690 wounded during the siege. German and Romanian casualties numbered 17,729 dead and 63,345 wounded, among whom were 187 killed one shot at a time by Sergeant Lyudmila Pavlichenko.

More savage fighting lay ahead for her at Sevastopol, which by this time was also soon to come under siege.

*

Lyudmila Pavlichenko the sniper cannot be considered apart from the times and circumstances that created her. Without the war, she would likely have lived out her life as an obscure history teacher somewhere in the Ukraine. As it was, however, with 187 confirmed kills, she was becoming celebrated throughout the Crimean region by the time her 25th Rifles escaped Odessa to reinforce Sevastopol. The entire world would soon hear about 'the most dangerous woman of the century'.

Sevastopol, lying at the tip of the Crimean Peninsula jutting into the Black Sea, was one of the most defensible locations on the Eastern Front – ringed by mountainous terrain whose rugged lines of ridges provided the city and harbour with natural protection. German forces would have to push through the narrow and desolate Isthmus of Perekop and then drive across the Crimea, often being compelled by the terrain to attack frontally along narrow strips of land. The battle for the isthmus, and the advance to the city and the Soviet fleet harboured there, began on 24 September 1941, and raged fiercely for the next nine months. It would require six German divisions and two

Romanian brigades with air support and some of the heaviest artillery ever built to defeat the Russian enclave.

Pavlichenko landed by ship with the 25th Division during a lull in the fighting. The battle-worn and under-strength reinforcements from Odessa were immediately hurled into the struggle.

In the fighting around Sevastopol during the Crimean War of the previous century (1853–6), Russians developed the art of sniping from 'rifle pits' in no-man's land. As then, and as at Odessa, Russian snipers at Sevastopol in 1941–2 were cast forward of the main defensive line in a thin screen of modified 'rifle pits'. Sometimes alone, at other times working with a spotter or fellow sniper, Pavlichenko continued the practices that had made her so successful at Odessa. She generally crept into her hide at around 0300 and sometimes waited for as long as two days for a single shot.

Winter was coming. Morning ice appeared on brown grass and the bare limbs of trees. Miserable conditions exacerbated her previous injuries. One day at the front was like a month or even a year in peacetime. She lost weight, grew thin and gaunt and developed the haunted 'thousand-yard stare' that marked a combat veteran. Streaks of white appeared in her raven-black hair.

Nonetheless, she persevered. Clad in trousers and baggy camouflage known as a *mochalniy* suit with its large hood and loops to permit the use of foliage, she knocked off one or two enemy soldiers every few days. She was constantly on the move, transferred from sector to sector so her true eye and steady hand could be used to their best advantage. No one from the old days in Kiev would have recognized in her the young college student in heels and crêpe de Chine.

The new Pavlichenko, sniper, became familiar to the entire country as word of her exploits spread. The Communist Party used her to inspire ordinary people, who were suffering horribly from cruel wartime conditions. 'If this beautiful young woman can endure,' went their spiel, 'then how can we who are not at the front complain about food rationing and other hardships.'

Even the Germans were aware of her and her unerring eye. One afternoon, she killed a radioman in a squad rushing from a shell-gutted farmhouse towards a barn filled with mouldy hay. It was a long shot in cold rain that impaired proper visibility. A shot like that could only have been made by 'the Russian bitch from hell'. A German officer stood up long enough to shout, 'Lyudmila, leave your Bolshevik friends and come and join us.' She killed him.

*

The Soviet outer defences collapsed on 28 October, leaving the entire Crimea with the exception of Sevastopol itself in German hands. Through autumn and into early winter snowfalls, fighting see-sawed as counter-attack followed attack and the Russians clung stubbornly to their spit of land on the Black Sea. German artillery and mortars pounded the city relentlessly until it was little more than a pile of rubble with scarcely a building left standing. Day by day, Soviet forces that originally numbered some 235,000 soldiers dwindled in the attrition of lead and steel.

Snipers were, as usual, an integral part of the city's defence. During the siege of Sevastopol, which eventually lasted until July 1942, a Russian sniper contingent estimated at fewer than 300 shooters wiped out about 10,000 German soldiers, almost an entire division. Pavlichenko, who won a battlefield promotion to junior lieutenant, was the siege's top scorer, followed by Sergeant-Major Leonid Kitsenko, now recovered from his wound at Odessa.

After the Russian withdrawal into the city, Pavlichenko and Kitsenko became a team so effective that commanders described them as worth an entire division of infantry. They often returned from a hunt claiming three or four kills between them for the day. On at least one occasion, they were seen embracing with more than comradely enthusiasm.

Continuing horror stories of German atrocities helped fuel Pavlichenko's rage. Special *Einsatzgruppen* units made a full-time job of killing Russian prisoners of war, as well as civilians and Jews. At Kiev and elsewhere, Jews were shot and thrown into mass graves; hundreds of thousands were murdered in this way. In Minsk, SS pulled 280 Russian civilians from jail, lined them up in front of a ditch and mowed them down. Following the fall of Kiev on 26 September 1941, cattle trucks hauled off 38,000 Russians to slave labour camps; most of them never returned. In an attempt to depopulate the Ukraine to make room for German settlers, occupiers encouraged starvation and the spread of diseases by neglecting sanitation measures and prohibiting food being sent to needy areas. 'This enemy consists not of soldiers but to a large extent only of beasts,' Hitler declared. 'This is a war of extermination.'

German snipers were encouraged in their deadly trade by rewards for kills and by bounties on the heads of successful Russian snipers like Pavlichenko, whose fame had spread as far as to Berlin. Twenty kills earned an expensive wristwatch, forty a hunting rifle, and sixty a personal hunting trip with Hermann Göring. Few German snipers involved in the siege of Odessa and Sevastopol lived long enough to earn a hunting trip. Pavlichenko alone was to slay thirty-six enemy snipers.

Not only was she deadly, but, even more humiliating, she was a woman. As the Wehrmacht closed its steel bands on Sevastopol, German snipers made a pact to put an end to the Russian bitch with the long-reaching rifle.

On 11 November, 60,000 Axis soldiers launched a four-day attack against a sector of the city's defences where mountainous terrain was prohibitively difficult. It was one of Pavlichenko's favourite hunting grounds precisely because it offered good cover and concealment. As was her custom, she crawled into her hide before dawn on a clear, frosty morning with the smell of snow in the air and settled down to wait for a target of opportunity. Her usual partner, Kitsenko, was assigned elsewhere.

In the early morning light something moved in a copse of new-growth trees that rimmed the military crest of a ridge about 400 metres to her front. She glimpsed a helmet through her binoculars. Snipers were often unable to resist the temptation of an easy kill. Pavlichenko held off and waited. The movement of the helmet seemed unnatural. Then she detected the flutter of branches to the left of where the helmet had disappeared, just enough movement to attract her attention. She herself had sometimes used the old trick of tieing a line to a bush and shaking it from a distance in order to draw fire and pinpoint an enemy sniper's location.

She waited, tense and edged for action. The sun climbed higher, its rays sparking jewels from the frost in the lowlands. Several times over the next few hours she detected movement – but never a clean target. She knew these were simply distractions to encourage her to compensate by shifting the barrel of her rifle or the tilt of her camouflaged head, small adjustments only a trained eye would notice. The guy out there knew what he was doing. The prudent sniper under such circumstances might withdraw to fight another day. Pavlichenko, however, held her ground, not only because of pride, although that certainly figured in the equation, but also because her worthy adversary had undoubtedly killed many of her comrades and would kill others unless she stopped him.

Her peripheral vision caught the suspicious shifting of a shadow, just in time to see the blink of a muzzle flash. The crack of the enemy's high-powered rifle reverberated from the distant ridgeline. A rock within touching distance of her head disintegrated into a stinging shower of particles.

A second shot snapped at her head, again only centimetres away. She wriggled backwards out of her hide and, crouching low and using the reverse slope of her knoll for cover, scrambled towards a nearby rocky upcropping where she burrowed into a thicket of briars interwoven with old growth timber. The site provided a view of the lowlands between her and the ridgeline occupied by her deadly foe.

She dared not move. Her eyes snapped from side to side, scanning. Cold, stress, hunger and thirst plagued her as she lay in wait for the German – and he lay in wait for her. A high stakes poker game in which each challenged the other to blink.

The strange stand-off continued all through the afternoon. Clouds rolled in and snow began to fall. Pavlichenko determined she would not miss her shot if the opportunity presented itself. The name of the game was patience coupled with accuracy.

Artillery thundered like a storm on the horizon. Small birds and animals scurried about.

Ultimately, the German proved the less patient of the two. Succumbing to curiosity, he made the mistake of lifting his head to take a better look across the clearing. Pavlichenko's crosshairs locked onto his forehead. He seemed to be looking directly at her when she massaged her trigger. It was her first shot in the duel. No other was required.

Later, a Russian patrol confirmed that the dead man was an expert sniper whose 'kill log' supposedly recorded the deaths of more than 400 Allied soldiers by his hand at Dunkirk.

*

Pavlichenko and partner Kitsenko continued to create mayhem with their rifles all through what the Germans referred to as the 'Winter Crisis'. Although starving, cold, and suffering from injuries both old and recent, the two fought on in the snow. By spring 1942, Lyudmila was an 'old timer' serving as a front-line sniper leader near the embattled Imgarmansky Lighthouse and taking novices under her wing to teach them how to become sharpshooters.

At some point, probably in early May 1942, Sergeant-Major Leonid Kitsenko was killed, either by an enemy sniper or by the ubiquitous shelling. Although little has been recorded about the relationship between Lyudmila and Leonid, it is assumed that they were at some point married. It has been noted, almost in passing and without providing a name, that Pavlichenko's 'husband, also serving with the Red Army, was killed in the [Sevastopol] siege'.

Fellow snipers noticed Lyudmila's increased bitterness following Kitsenko's death. Anger burned deeper into her being. In late May, the Southern Army Council cited her for killing 257 Germans. During a meeting of her sniper unit, she vowed to raise her score to 300 within the next few days – and kept her word.

During 2–6 June 1942, the Luftwaffe dropped 570 tons of bombs on the beleaguered ruins of Sevastopol and its harbour. As preparation for the final assault, heavy artillery that included some of the largest guns ever built, such as the 600-mm *Karl* mortar and the 800-mm *Gustav* railway gun, fired 42,595 rounds, the equivalent of 2,449 tons of munitions. On 7 June, the Germans attacked and breached the outer defensive rings round the city to seize most of the bay's northern shore. While strong pockets of Soviet resistance held firm in the rear and on the flanks, no one harboured any illusion about how much longer the Russians could last. The fight was down to its last days.

Shrapnel riddled Pavlichenko's worn young body during the hell of raining bombs and shells. Unable to continue her vendetta, she was moved to a Severnaya Bay champagne factory converted as both an ammo dump and a field hospital. She was not to see personal combat again. Because of her growing status, she was evacuated by submarine at night before Germans entered the city on 1 July. Her final tally stood officially at 309 kills, including more than 200 officers and 36 enemy snipers. Since she often worked alone, however, and every kill had to be verified independently, the actual number may have been nearer 500. In comparison, Russia's other famous Second World War sniper, Vassili Zaitsev, killed 225 German soldiers during the Battle of Stalingrad.

While the Germans declared victory over Sevastopol on 4 July 1942, it took them twenty-seven more days to mop up. Russia suffered 18,000 killed or wounded and 95,000 captured. Only 25,157 were successfully evacuated. German casualties numbered 24,000 dead or wounded; the Romanians listed another 1,597 killed and 6,571 wounded. Pavlichenko's 25th Rifle Division was declared combat ineffective and disbanded, its banners sunk in the Black Sea and its remaining soldiers reassigned to other units.

*

Due to her fame, Lyudmila Pavlichenko was sent to the United States and Canada at the end of 1942 to drum up war support. She delivered speeches in forty-three American cities and was the first Soviet citizen to be received at the White House, where she had dinner with President Franklin Roosevelt and First Lady

Eleanor. Celebrities all over the continent lined up to be photographed with her. Folk musician Woody Guthrie recorded a song dedicated to her, 'Miss Pavlichenko'. She was featured in a 1943 comic book, *War Heroes*. She played with Laurence Olivier in the documentary film *Chernomortsy*. Actor Charlie Chaplin gallantly kissed her fingers one by one, saying, 'It's quite remarkable that this small, delicate hand killed Nazis by the hundreds.'

Interviewed by *Time* (28 September 1942), she gently derided American women and the American media:

> I am amazed at the kind of questions put to me by the women press correspondents in Washington. Don't they know there is a war? They asked me silly questions such as do I use powder and rouge and nail polish and do I curl my hair. One reporter even criticized the length of the skirt of my uniform, saying that in America women wear shorter skirts and besides my uniform makes me look fat.

'The most dangerous woman in the world' saw out the war as a sniper instructor at the Central Women's Sniper School near Moscow. Her military awards included: Order of Lenin with Gold Star; the Bravery Medal, awarded to snipers with forty or more kills; and the title Hero of the Soviet Union, the highest distinction any Soviet citizen could receive. Of 11,635 HSU recipients, only 92 were women, 50 of whom received the award posthumously.

She was discharged with the rank of major in 1945 and returned to Kiev University to finish her postgraduate degree. Russia issued two postage stamps in her honour and named a Ministry of Fisheries vessel after her. She served out her life as a historian working for the Navy Central Staff and was active in veterans' affairs.

She married a second time, in 1943, and gave birth to a son. Husband and son remained out of the spotlight to the point that almost no records exist about them. Lyudmila rarely spoke publicly of her sniper career. She published several magazine articles and a book about her division's role in the defence of Sevastopol, but, other than one small section in a Russian book published posthumously, wrote little about her own exploits. One of her only recorded comments resulted from a 1968 visit to London where a reporter asked about her feelings at Sevastopol.

She killed without hesitation, she responded, and with not a twinge of regret afterwards. 'If you are going along a road with your child and you see a snake, what do you do?'

She died of natural causes on 27 October 1974, at the age of 58 and was buried in the Novodevicheye Cemetery in Moscow. Sevastopol named a street after her, not far from where Sergeant-Major Leonid Kitsenko died.

References

Due to the guarded nature of Soviet society during the Second World War, I have had to resort to numerous sources to fill in the gaps of detail left by the official histories of Lyudmila Pavlichenko. Relying upon my own knowledge and experience with war and people at war, as well as my extensive research into the Second World War era, I have on a few occasions in this narrative resorted to re-creating scenes and dialogue in an effort to depict Pavlichenko as a well-rounded individual. Where re-creation occurs, I have striven to match personalities with the situation and the action while maintaining factual content. None of the facts has been altered.

Ian Baxter, *Hitler's Defeat on The Eastern Front* (Pen & Sword, 2009)

Kazimiera J. Cottam, *Women in War and Resistance* (Focus Publishing, 1998)

N. Krylov, *Glory Eternal: Defence of Odessa, 1942.* (Moscow, 1972)

L. Ozerov, 'The Girl with the Rifle', in *Soviet Women in the War Against Hitlerism* (Moscow, 1942)

L. M. Pavlichenko, 'I was a Sniper', in I. M. Danishevskiy, *The Road of Battle and Glory* (Moscow, 1977)

The World at War 1939–45 (Reader's Digest Books, 1998)

Russia Besieged, The Soviet Juggernaut (Time/Life Books, *The Second World War* series, 1980)

Time magazine (28 September 1942)

Wapedia. 'Wikki: Snipers of The Soviet Union.' (Wapedia.
 Mobi/en/Soviet_sniper – accessed 13 August 2010)

Wikipedia article, 'Lyudmila Pavlichenko' (www.wikipedia.org. –
 accessed 27 July 2010)

Chapter 3

BERT KEMP

A Reluctant Warrior with a Deadly Gift

Bert Wilson Kemp was a fairly typical product of the time and place into which he was born: a family farm in rural West Tennessee, in the early years of the twentieth century. Yet he was more than that – much more – for he was born with an amazing ability for precision, almost supernatural, marksmanship with weapons. And this gift, this ability applied to weapons of virtually any kind: catapult, bow and arrow, pistol or rifle. The choice of weapons didn't seem to matter; he was equally gifted, and comfortable, with any of them. Whatever that rare combination of genes is that creates such a marksman, Bert Kemp was one of the tiny fraction of 1 per cent of the human population who are born with it. He had electrochemical circuits, almost cybernetic programmes, hard-wired on the surface of his brain, that naturally calculated, at lightning speed, such things as distance, trajectory, motion, wind and time, determining the sight picture and aiming point, sending the perfectly timed impulse along the neurological pathways to activate the flexor muscles in his trigger finger, bringing about the perfectly timed squeeze.

Bert also had exceptional vision and depth perception. This gift gave him an additional 'edge' because, when hunting, he usually saw the game animal before it saw him. And later, in the war, when scouting ahead or when he was stalking a designated German, Bert could consistently see his target before the target saw him. His grand-nephew, Odie Kemp, who became Bert's protégé and hunting companion in his later years, expressed this advantage succinctly and emphatically: 'He could see like a hawk.'

Combine these gifts with the ongoing need for food on his family's table, in the years before and during the Great

Depression in rural Tennessee, and the rare product is a Bert Kemp.

Bert was born in 1919 on a remote farm in Weakley County, Tennessee, the son of Whit Allen Kemp and Ludie Jean Nichols Kemp. The nearest town was the village of Cottage Grove, about four miles away, in adjacent Henry County. Bert was the next-to-youngest of six children; in a pattern typical of that time and place, only three of them would live to adulthood. His mother died of tuberculosis when he was six years old; his father never re-married. He grew up on the farm where he was born, learning early that survival depended on hard work, careful use of available resources, and self-reliance. Like the other children, Bert worked hard on the farm, where there was work to do the year round. But in the autumn and winter there was also time for hunting; this became his passion, and pre-determined much of what his life would become.

Hunting for food (and money)

As was the case with most remote farm families in that hard-scrabble time and place, there was little disposable cash in the family, and the rule when something was needed on the farm, was 'make it, make do, or do without'. Being something he could make for himself, with no cash outlay for materials, the catapult (or slingshot as Kemp and his family knew it) was very naturally his first weapon. He would later take one to war, and it would serve him well. Even after the war, and for the rest of his life, he never lost his fondness for the slingshot, and it was always with him. It became a family proverb that 'if Bert had his trousers on, he had the slingshot with him'.

A major source of meat for the family table was wild game. At the time, deer were scarce, and reliance was heavily upon rabbits and squirrels. Growing up in the forest, Bert quite naturally learned to move through it as if he were a natural part of it, disturbing nothing, making no noise. He learned early to kill a squirrel high in a tree, or a rabbit on the run, with his home-made slingshot. Under those circumstances he would get only one shot, and he had to make the first shot the killing shot, which meant a head shot. Although he could never have imagined it, this also contributed to what he would become in 1942.

At age 9 he was given his first gun, a single-shot, bolt-action, .22-calibre rifle, and it dramatically altered the economy of his life. He killed squirrels and rabbits at an increasing rate, and sold his surplus kills to Mr Miller, owner of the local country store. Other boys in the community did the same thing, but used shotguns or made body shots with rifles. Bert was paid more for his game because they were all taken with head shots, and the meat was not damaged. He then used the money to buy more .22-calibre ammunition, for killing still more squirrels and rabbits. What money was left over, he gave to his father to help support the family. With the expending of each box of fifty rounds of ammunition, Bert's God-given ability to hit small targets in difficult situations developed to still higher levels. 'I hunted just about all the time when I was a boy growing up around Cottage Grove,' he would tell a reporter for the county newspaper after the war, 'It was the Depression, and rough times, and you had to learn to adjust your sight picture carefully to add food to the table.'

Another ability with which Bert was blessed was in baseball; he was a natural. He could play any position, and he could throw a natural curve ball; but the need for his help on the farm ended his school days, and baseball, in the elementary grades. When he could get away from chores, he would walk to the one-room school at recess time, play baseball with the boys there, and walk back home; but even that soon ended.

His love of baseball would never leave him, and in later years he would watch his children and grandchildren play, quietly teaching them things that their coaches probably did not know.

Learning to look for 'What shouldn't be there'

As he grew to manhood during the Great Depression his woodcraft skills and amazing marksmanship continued to improve. His father taught him to spot game standing still in deep cover.

When scanning ahead, he was taught to look for things that should not be there – perhaps an ear, a leg, or a foot of a game animal, not quite concealed. When the forest was quiet he could sometimes hear a deer walking, even though he couldn't see it, and at times he could even smell one.

Bert's 'small game business' prospered as he continued to kill squirrels and rabbits, selling the meat and buying more cartridges at such a rate that by the late 1930s and up until he was drafted into the Army, he was firing 500 rounds a week at small, distant and quickly moving targets.

As basically serious, if not grim, as life was in that time and place, there was always time for fun. On one occasion when his Aunt Bertha was gathering eggs she found an unusually large one, and it was briefly a conversation piece. Bert showed her a nickel (a significant amount of money then) and bet her that if she would throw the egg up in the air a few feet above her head, he could hit it with his .22 rifle before it came back down so she could catch it. He said that if he missed he would give her the nickel. Being a good sport, Aunt Bertha tossed the egg up, higher than her head. Bert easily shot the egg dead centre at the top of its flight, but Aunt Bertha had made a slight mistake in trajectory: the egg was higher than her head, but it was also directly over her head when Bert's little projectile smashed it, and the contents of the large egg drenched Aunt Bertha's hair. She gave Bert a scolding that could have peeled the paint off the henhouse, but he heard little of it for he was rolling on the ground, convulsed with laughing. And he kept his nickel.

Bert could make a game out of his shooting and, being a boy, he often did. His nephew Odie (son and namesake of Bert's oldest brother), who was only eleven years younger than his Uncle Bert, had a baseball of which he was very proud. Bert told him to go around on the other side of the house where he would be safe, and Bert could not see where he was. He told Odie to throw the ball up, from anywhere, in any direction, and he bet that he could hit it with his .22 rifle. Odie went to the other side of the house, threw the ball up above the house and Bert hit it. Then Odie threw the ball up, from a different spot and at an angle, and again Bert hit it. This challenge was repeated, over and over. Bert was totally focused on hitting the ball and, in the excitement of the contest, it did not occur to young Odie, until it was too late to matter, that Bert was shooting his prized ball to pieces. Nephew Odie, not quite sure whether to laugh or cry, joined Bert in his laughter and a family legend was born.

One memorable summer the three Kemp boys decided to make some wine – in clear violation of their father's rules and the law during Prohibition. Clandestine wine-making was pretty simple in that time and place: there was plenty of fruit juice, the very air contained yeast, as did the skin of the fruit, and there were plenty of places to hide most anything in the surrounding fields and forest. So Odie, Chesley and Bert gathered wild grapes in the forest (muscadines were the best), crushed out the juice, left it open for a day or two to allow plenty of yeast to add itself to the brew, and then hid it until fermentation was complete. But the amateur vintners made two mistakes: they decided to hide it under the house; and they corked the bottles too soon. Fermentation was not finished, and the process was accelerated by the heat of the summer night. The carbon dioxide produced in the fermentation process built up until the corks could no longer contain it. Corks began to fail, each with a loud 'pop' as it left the neck of the bottle and thumped against the underside of the floor, eventually waking their father. They lost their wine, got a sound whipping, and another family legend was born.

The outside world comes calling

By 1940, at age 21, the reputation of this obscure farm boy from the Tennessee back country had spread, without benefit of advertising or promotion, from the cracker barrel and checker board culture in Miller's store and the shady, dirt streets of Cottage Grove, until it reached the Remington Arms Company in far-off New York state. A Remington recruiter was sent to find the young phenomenon and offer him a lucrative job as an exhibition shooter. This would not only bring him more money than he had ever dreamed of, but would also make him famous in the world of guns and hunting. But Bert was a quiet, private person. His world consisted of the family farm, the familiar hills, valleys and forests around it, Johnson Chapel, their little Methodist Church, and the village of Cottage Grove. The thought of travelling to strange places and being on display before strange people was not appealing. Also his brother Odie, thirteen years older than Bert, had already married and moved away. His other brother, Chesley, was slowly dying with tuberculosis, and Bert was needed on the farm. Bert declined the offer from Remington, and stayed on the farm.

But not for long.

War comes to Weakley County

On 7 December 1941 the Japanese surprise attacks on Pearl Harbor, the Philippines and other places in the Pacific, plunged the U.S. into the war. A month later, in January 1942, the war had reached all the way into Weakley County. Like Sergeant Alvin York of the First World War, another country boy from the hills of Tennessee who had become a reluctant warrior, Bert Kemp was drafted for Army service. Both Tennesseans were remarkable for their God-given talent for accurate shooting; also, like Sergeant York, Bert's religious training and gentle nature made him reluctant to kill. Unlike Sergeant York, Bert would capture few German soldiers; but in terms of killing them, Sergeant Kemp would far outdo his famous Tennessee predecessor.

But all of that almost didn't happen. When Bert reported for induction he didn't pass the physical examination. One of the examining physicians, however, knew Bert and his family, and knew of Bert's amazing accuracy with weapons. He was re-examined, and this time no fault was found. It was 18 January 1942 and Bert Kemp was Private Bert W. Kemp, Serial Number 34 185 517, Army of the United States.

'Get this man off the firing line!'

The medical problem that was 'overlooked' at his induction physical was apparently a hernia, for shortly after beginning basic training he underwent surgery for hernia repair, and missed the training on the rifle range. After Basic Training he joined the 1st Infantry Division at Camp Blanding, Florida. On the rifle range, as the division prepared for combat, an officer watched Bert as he reduced the target's bull's eye to tatters, with a group so tight that individual hits could not be scored. 'Get this man off the firing line', the officer said, 'and get someone up here who needs to be here.' Army authorities were beginning to take official notice of Bert's amazing skill with the rifle, the skill that would force this gentle, kind man from rural Tennessee into becoming a killing machine of seldom seen efficiency.

One soldier in Bert's unit became aware of his uncanny ability to shoot and, for a while, it made him prosperous. Unknown to Bert, the man was taking bets on Bert's ability to hit small targets – bets he knew he could not lose. Bert found out what he was doing and put a stop to it – he strongly disapproved of gambling, especially when the victims could not win.

The offending peep sight

On the troop ship carrying him to England, Bert decided to improve the sights on his M1 Garand rifle. He was accustomed to open sights; and the small, circular peep sight at the rear of the barrel bothered him. It seemed to limit the sweep and scope of his peripheral vision. He didn't like it, and he knew that he could shoot better without it. It had to go. Unacquainted with the realities of Army ways, he made his way below decks to the ship's machine shop where he borrowed a file. Back on the weather deck, he sat and filed on the peep sight until it was completely gone.

Everything was fine until an officer saw what he had done to his rifle. He stared with disbelief at the vacant spot where the peep sight had been, unable for a moment to comprehend what Bert had done to this piece of government property. Then he exploded, threatening every punishment conceivable, short of the gallows. When he calmed down, he asked Bert why he had done this terrible thing to Mister Garand's masterpiece. Bert replied, simply and honestly, 'It gets in my way.' This answer caused another eruption, and Bert was promised disciplinary action when they landed. Charges were filed against him and, after arriving with his battalion in Dorset in England on 7 August 1942, his case was set in motion. The charges were serious, but before they could be carried out, a senior officer who had heard of Bert's amazing shooting ability, said 'Leave him alone – he has demonstrated that he did the right thing.' The charges were dismissed.

The 1st Division trained in England for three months, went back aboard ship and sailed for North Africa, landing at Oran in Algeria on 8 November 1942. After a brief defence, the Vichy French forces surrendered; but the rest would not be so easy. From there on it would be heavy, sometimes vicious, combat with Erwin Rommel's German and Italian forces at places like Maktar. Tebourba, Medjez el Bab, the bloody disaster at Kasserine Pass, Gafsa, El Guettar, Béja and Mateur. They would fight in North Africa until May 1943. And after that there would be Sicily.

Bert's first kill

At times Bert fought with his rifle company, Company L, 3rd Battalion, 26th Infantry Regiment, as a scout-sniper, sent to advanced positions from where he could see the enemy dispositions, provide timely intelligence, and kill selected targets (usually officers) at long range. It was on such a mission, in the North Africa campaign, that he got his first kill. He spotted a German soldier in an observation post, and had a clear field of fire, but he couldn't bring himself to squeeze the trigger. Finally the German spotted Bert and fired; he missed. He fired again and missed. The German fired eight times, with each round coming closer. When his eighth round spattered dirt in Bert's face, he squeezed the trigger, fired one round, and the German dropped. Bert's deeply ingrained reluctance to kill another human being was not a thing easily overridden.

At times he functioned as a distant point man, scouting far ahead of his advancing unit, seeking always to see without being seen by the enemy. This was the case as his regiment approached a 5-kilometre gauntlet called Kasserine Pass, where the Americans would suffer a major defeat at the hands of Erwin Rommel, and learn some hard lessons at a high cost in lives and careers. This battle was actually a series of battles in which poor American leadership and training led to a major disaster. On one of those hillsides overlooking the pass Bert, with his keen vision and common sense, could see clearly what his unit was walking into, and he radioed his command post to warn them. The commanding officer said he wasn't going to change his battle plan based on the opinion of a low-ranking enlisted man. 'We know what we are doing,' he said. But they didn't. And Bert could only watch and grieve as Rommel's forces chewed them up.

It was cold that winter in the mountains of North Africa, and on one occasion this proved to be Bert's redemption. Taken by surprise by a German column coming from an unexpected direction, Bert had no chance to run and no place to hide. In desperation, he buried himself in a snow bank and lay still, something he had done for fun as a boy. The Germans passed by so close to him that he could hear them talking and coughing. When he was sure they were far away he carefully emerged from the snow, and looked around. They had passed, he was now behind them and they were taking no care for their own security. He could easily have killed several of them, but was glad just to get away and continue his patrol. Remembering that day he said it wasn't so bad under there. 'If you stay under the snow long enough, you get warm.'

A ditch, a tank and a great many Germans

On one occasion Bert was alone, well in advance of his unit, concealed in a ditch. He was watching German units assemble, when he was apparently spotted. The German infantry opened fire and began to attack the ditch. With no place to go, and the Germans closing in on him, he began to take a deadly toll on the advancing infantry. To reload he would shove a new clip in his M1 with one hand, while continuing to fire with his pistol, then resume his deadly rifle fire. Because he favoured head shots, when the Germans went down they stayed down. So many Germans were dying in front of his ditch, they could not believe that they were fighting only one man. They called up a tank. As the huge machine rumbled towards him Bert knew that he couldn't fight a tank and win, so he began to run down the ditch towards some woods. The German infantry were now up to the edge of his ditch, and every time a head appeared above the rampart Bert, still running, fired and the head disappeared. Unintentionally, it became what amounted to an amazing slaughter of a locally significant force, but by only one man.

Reaching the end of the ditch, he still had a space of 50 metres ahead of him before he could reach cover. He burst forth and sprinted for the woods. The tank's machine gunner opened up on him, with the bullet strikes spraying mud on him, and he was still only half way to the woods. He thought he was a goner, when a P-38 fighter suddenly appeared behind him at treetop level, making straight for the tank. Bert had never seen an aircraft fly so low; when it passed over him 'it was so low that it nearly jerked my topcoat off'. The P-38 killed the tank, and then went to work on the exposed German infantry. Bert made it to the woods without being hit and never looked back. His rifle barrel was still so hot that when night fell and dew settled on it, the oxidation process was accelerated and it rusted overnight. His unit moved out the next morning with Bert scouting in front; and when they reached the ditch they found so many dead Germans in front of the ditch that they covered the ground. Bert remembered, 'we could have walked for 40 yards without stepping on the ground'.

But soon Bert would find a sniper team-mate and he wouldn't be operating alone any more.

A sniper partner and lifelong friend

Bert was promoted to private first class, and then to corporal. It was in an assault on an enemy-held hill that he found the man who would be his sniper partner, and lifelong best friend.

The hill was prepared by artillery and mortar fire, and the assault platoons moved in. Casualties were heavy, and the assault platoons were driven back several times. Finally, in a last attempt to take the hill, Corporal Kemp was the senior man standing and he led the assault. Throwing grenades, he made it to the top and hit the deck. Knowing that he must immediately set up a hasty defence against a German counter-attack, he looked around to see how many men he had with him on the hill. There was only one. That man was Wesley Holly of Mississippi; the rest of his men had either gone down as casualties or stopped short of the crest and turned back. He and Wesley hung on to the top of that hill until reinforcements could arrive, and it was the beginning of a friendship that would end only with Wesley's death forty-five years later. In the months of fighting that followed, the two would be inseparable, and each would save the other's life at least once.

The sniper team concept as we know it today, with a designated shooter and a spotter with a spotting scope, had not been fully developed in the North Africa and Sicily campaigns of 1943. The teaming up of Bert and Wesley was more of their own design, more out of necessity than established doctrine. They knew that they could trust one another, and they came to know one another so well as to be able to communicate at times without words.

Like Bert, Wesley had grown up on a remote farm – his in Noxubee County, Mississippi. And, like Bert, he had grown up in the forest, hunting to put meat on the table. Quite naturally Wesley, like Bert, had developed the skills and patience necessary for a sniper to function effectively and stay alive. In this sense, they were a matched pair.

After the Kasserine Pass disaster, many commanders were relieved, and tactics were quickly re-thought to match the terrain, German tactics and circumstances. It is fair to say that when Bert's division landed in North Africa there was no established doctrine for the use of snipers. They were thought of as 'scout-snipers' and were called upon, when it seemed necessary, to do a variety of things, but sniper doctrine and training as we know it today was still far into the future. In the First World War, sniping had been developed to a high degree in the static years of trench warfare, but it was abandoned after the war. In the Second World War the same was true in static situations, such as the battle for Stalingrad, but in the fast-moving combat in North Africa and Sicily, it was more a matter of multi-faceted improvisation. Bert and Wesley were making it up as they went along; and it was only the grace of God and their experiences growing up in the forests of Tennessee and Mississippi that kept them from being killed early in the game. They had no spotter scope and no telescopic sights; they had only their sharp eyes, easy familiarity with the outdoors, and their marksmanship skills.

No surrender for Bert and Wesley

Both Bert and Wesley were acquiring reputations for success in the kills count, and they both felt very strongly that they must never allow themselves to be captured, for they had heard that, if they were captured, the Germans would torture and kill them. This, of course, was not necessarily true, but it was what they heard – it was 'the word'.

They were often well in advance of their attacking units, in established, concealed positions, from which they could observe enemy activity for several days. And from these positions they could fire on selected targets. On one occasion, when they were preparing to move out, they were told that there would be a third man going with them. A new lieutenant had joined the company and he was being sent out with Bert and Wesley to gain some experience. The patrol did not go well. Spotted early by the Germans, they came under small arms fire which steadily increased in volume as the German unit moved into the attack. The lieutenant, who had never before been under fire, panicked and said that they should surrender. Without taking his eyes off the enemy, Bert merely said, 'No sir' as he continued to fire. When he next glanced at the lieutenant he saw him absorbed in tying a white handkerchief to the barrel of his M1 carbine. When the lieutenant looked up, he was looking into the muzzle of Bert's rifle. Turning mutely to Wesley for support, he found himself looking into the muzzle of Wesley's rifle. With that the lieutenant collapsed, curled up in the bottom of the hole and began to weep, as Bert and Wesley turned back to the fight. Soon Bert heard firing to his right; looking around he saw that the lieutenant had regained his composure and re-joined the action. The fighting grew fierce as the Germans brought up a light machine gun, firing so close that the muzzle flash briefly blinded Bert before it was put out of action. Finally, punished by the deadly rifle fire, reinforced by the lieutenant with his carbine, the Germans withdrew to a covered position and Bert's three-man team disappeared to the rear, into the forest.

Back at the unit, Bert told the lieutenant that nothing would be said about his attempt to surrender. But he hoped that he would never again have to go on a patrol with an inexperienced officer, where he might have to risk a mutiny charge to keep from being captured.

BARs and German machine gunners

Sniping came naturally to Bert and he established his own tactics and techniques as he went: a combination of what he had learned in the forest growing up, and the hard lessons of on-the-job training on the battlefield. One thing he quickly learned concerned the Browning Automatic Rifle (BAR) and German machine gunners. The BAR was a product of the genius of John Moses Browning, an 8-kilogram automatic rifle – in effect a lightweight machine gun – which could be fired from the shoulder standing, lying prone with a bipod, or from the hip on a sling. Like all Browning weapons, it was utterly dependable. The Germans learned to fear it, and Bert learned about this fear. As a result of the BAR's effectiveness, the BAR men became a target of choice for German machine gunners. Realizing this, Bert and Wesley learned to move, when they could, into a position well off to both sides of a BAR man, find a place with concealment and a field of fire, and wait for the Germans to bring up their machine gun. As they set up their heavy gun, with their attention focused on the BAR man, Bert and Wesley would pick off the German crew, leaving their gun un-manned and the BAR man, for the moment, a lot safer.

Fighting in hedgerows and thick brush, Bert profited from a lesson that his father had taught him in hunting when he was growing up: to stop, be still, and 'look for something that shouldn't be there'. Back home in the Tennessee forest, hunting game, that 'something' might be a part of a leg, a rabbit's exposed ear, or a squirrel's tail. In combat it might be a boot tip, the edge of a pack or helmet, or a flash of light reflected from a binocular lens or telescopic sight. A German soldier might be still, thinking he was completely concealed, and therefore invisible; but when something 'that shouldn't be there' showed, it usually cost him his life.

'Light up and die'

Wesley was an expert marksman, but not in the sense that Bert was. Wesley was deadly at long-range sniping, when he had time to study the target, estimate windage, elevation and effects of light. He could squeeze off such a shot with deadly accuracy. Bert, of course, could do the same; but Bert was also deadly as a snap-shooter. That rare electrochemical circuit board that was naturally wired into his brain made him able to perform all those calculations in a fraction of a second and hit a small target that was visible only briefly and then lost in darkness. This was the case when, at night, a careless German would light a cigarette or his pipe. During the one or two seconds that the German's face was illuminated by the flame Bert could fire, and the soldier would pay with his life for his moment of carelessness. Telling of this after the war, Wesley would swear that, in the flicker of time that the light existed, the German's head would disappear, leaving just a glimpse of ashes, suspended in the dying light. Did he exaggerate? Maybe – stories have a way of growing with the retelling over the years, even when we don't intend it. But I wasn't there, and Wesley was, and I will give him the benefit of any doubt. At any rate, it is a fact that in combat, in the dark, the rule has been, for a very long time, 'light up and die' – especially if there is a Bert Kemp on the other side, watching.

Stalking key targets

At times Bert was assigned a specific target – usually a certain German officer. The loss of such an officer, especially in his own rear area where he was supposed to be safe, could create command confusion, undermine morale and, at least temporarily, make that unit less effective. These missions could take several days, just to get into position without being seen, where the target was expected to appear. And then, after the kill, it was even more difficult to escape unseen and return to allied lines.

Bert had been told, not necessarily correctly, that the typical German soldier was trained to obey, not to think and act independently; as a result, a unit would often become confused when its immediate commander was killed. One such mission left a particularly vivid picture in Bert's memory: a German lieutenant, leader of a special operations unit. The man was good, and his excellent performance and resulting reputation became his death sentence. When Bert, from an unseen firing point, dropped the officer with a head shot, his men reacted immediately; they scattered. Instead of reorganizing and moving aggressively in the direction from which the shot had come, those around the dead officer remained for critical minutes in confusion, while Bert was escaping. He found this kind of mission the most difficult, in every way. In addition to the patience required and the danger, it was very personal – it seemed like murder. He would find these kills the most difficult to forget, especially one of them.

The kill that Bert would never forget, the one that bothered him most, occurred in the fast-moving, sometimes confused and poorly coordinated fighting in the desert. Bert's battalion found itself isolated, temporarily cut off from the regiment, and completely surrounded by German infantry. The Germans did not have sufficient forces to overrun the Americans, and a stalemate ensued. With neither force able to break through the other, the Germans called up an English-speaking soldier who had been educated in the U.S.. With a megaphone, he launched into an ongoing effort to convince the Americans that their situation was hopeless, and that they should surrender. After a long time, with the propaganda speeches more or less continuous, Bert's commanding officer walked up to his position on the perimeter and said, 'Kemp, I've heard all I want to hear from that guy. Take care of him.'

Bert moved out, crawling up shallow gullies, using desert shrubbery where it appeared, and rock outcroppings for cover and concealment. It took a long time for him to reach a vantage point from where he could see the German speaker without being seen, and with a clear field of fire; when he did, he was looking at him face-on. He really didn't want to kill the man, but orders, as the saying goes, are orders. He lined up his sights for a clean head shot and the German's last surrender speech was cut off suddenly in mid-sentence. Slowly, reversing his path to the firing point, Bert made his way back to his unit and resumed his position on the perimeter.

For the rest of his life this one kill bothered Bert. He would say, 'That man had done me no harm. He was just making speeches. He was a threat to nobody – not to me or to anyone else – he didn't even have a weapon.'

Bert's reputation spread to the allied armies and, at times, they requested his help. He was assigned to temporary duty with both the British and with the French. For his outstanding service to the French he was decorated with the Croix de Guerre. It has been reported that he was recommended for a high British decoration, but if so it was lost in the administrative confusion of the battlefield, for no record of it has been found. It is interesting that, on a large and confused, rapidly changing battlefield, Bert's reputation spread outward, all the way to the high levels of command in both the French and British Armies. Some have even reported that Adolf Hitler, through Rommel, became aware of this deadly sniper with the American 1st Infantry Division. There is no record to substantiate this, but a sniper who could stalk and kill key officers at a great distance without being seen and then escape was a very great threat.

This spreading reputation as a sniper is reminiscent of the way the reputation of an unknown farm boy, in the back country of rural Tennessee, once spread all the way to high levels of executive authority at Remington Arms in New York. It seems that when one is that good, the fact cannot be contained.

A slingshot on the battlefield?

The slingshot, the first weapon Bert mastered as a little boy, remained a favourite for the rest of his life, and he was almost never without one. He carried one with him all through combat in the Second World War, and at times it was a critical part of his armament – not for killing Germans but for killing rabbits. Many times, when he and Wesley were on extended patrols behind German lines, or long stays in an observation post, they needed food. On Sicily they found the Corsican hare, a relative of the rabbit, but much larger than the cottontail rabbits they had hunted as boys. And they seemed to be everywhere. When they were behind enemy lines and in need of food, Bert's slingshot and the large Corsican hares provided it, because the slingshot made no sound that would give away their presence. When they were in a place where they could build a small fire without being seen, they cooked the meat and feasted, or cooked it and carried it along with them. Remembering his boyhood 'meat business' with Miller's store, Bert thought about how much more money he could have made if he had been bringing in these big Corsican hares.

A Silver Star in Sicily

In ferocious fighting on Sicily Bert, by then a sergeant, found himself in a key position in the savage battle for some vital terrain. Bert, as usual in an observation and firing point in advance of his unit, saw a major German attack on his unit developing, and his firing point became the key to saving his comrades. His citation for the Silver Star medal reads:

> Undaunted by an intense enemy tank, artillery and
> machine-gun barrage, Sergeant Kemp fearlessly remained
> in an exposed vantage point, and with accurate and rapid
> fire skillfully covered his comrades' withdrawal to more
> advantageous positions, mortally wounding a number of
> Germans, and destroying a hostile strong point, thereby
> contributing immeasurably to repulsing a determined
> enemy counter-attack.

The expression 'mortally wounding' in the citation is interesting.
Because Bert always preferred head shots, virtually all that he
wounded were indeed 'mortally' wounded – dead before they hit
the ground.

The presentation of this medal made it all the more meaningful
to Bert because it was made by Brigadier General Theodore
Roosevelt, son of the 26th President of the United States. After
pinning the medal on Bert, General Roosevelt told Bert to turn
about, facing the formation, and told the massed soldiers to 'look
at this man'. He said that he had plenty more of those medals,
and challenged all of the other soldiers to perform as Bert had
performed. Bert was mortified. He was always embarrassed by
praise. After the war he consistently objected to being called a
hero; the heroes, he said, were those who died. But that moment
with General Roosevelt was nonetheless a treasured experience
that he never forgot.

Five wounds take their toll

Bert was wounded five times: three times in North Africa and
twice in Sicily. On one occasion he was knocked unconscious
and left for dead. In the confusion of the battle, he had been
separated from Wesley, and those around him had left him
among the corpses. When Wesley discovered what had happened
he returned alone, through a hail of fire at great risk to his life,
to that corpse-strewn hilltop. He found Bert and dragged him
back to a place of relative safety. From there Bert was carried to
the aid station, thence to the field hospital. Had it not been for
Wesley's courage, and his refusal to leave his friend among the

corpses, dead or alive, the wound would have been fatal. Each had saved the other one's life at least once. Neither was decorated for these heroic acts; but they never forgot.

Each time Bert was medically evacuated to a hospital for treatment he felt guilty for leaving his buddies to fight without him, a common emotion for wounded combat infantrymen. Finally, severely wounded, he refused to leave his unit and continued fighting, saying he was needed where he was; but that fifth wound would end his career as a master sniper, and, in time, as a soldier. In savage fighting on Sicily a piece of shrapnel hit him just behind his ear, fracturing his skull, and penetrating five centimetres into his brain. This wound, with suddenness and finality, ended Bert's combat service, for it left him with permanent brain damage, double vision, migraine headaches, and deafness in one ear, and it made the recoil and muzzle blast of firing .30-calibre weapons painful. Hospital treatment was needed, first overseas and later nearer home. He would wear glasses for the rest of his life to correct the double vision; when he didn't wear them the migraines returned.

Bert and Wesley, as a scout-sniper team, were no more, and they would lose track of one another. Their friendship, however, would be renewed unexpectedly years later, when Wesley, again facing death, would call out to Bert for help.

Aftermath

Bert's career as a combat infantryman and master sniper was over. There would follow months of surgery and hospitalization before he was finally returned to the States, where there would be still more hospitalization before he was able to return to duty. He was briefly assigned duty as a military policeman, guarding German prisoners of war in Georgia, but he was too badly broken, and really wasn't up to it. It is the nature of severe head injuries that our mental mechanisms for controlling emotions are greatly reduced. Without such injury we are, as Bert put it, 'able to kill by staying mad 90 per cent of the time', by trivializing the horror, or simply by burying it somewhere deep inside. But in

Bert's severely weakened condition the emotional toll of all the killing, and the death and mutilation of his friends, descended upon him like a cloud of lead.

He wasn't mad any more – just exhausted – and vulnerable. He remembered his dead friends and worried about Wesley; and the cumulative weight of it all, in spite of his inherent toughness, overwhelmed him. The quiet, gentle, sensitive man, whose amazing gift had forced him into the role of master sniper, stalker and killer, began to crumble inside. To paraphrase Mark Antony, master snipers should be made of sterner stuff.

Bert, in spite of his innate gentleness, had risen to the occasion, answered the call of duty, and performed superbly under the most difficult circumstances. Now, privately, he grieved and wept and prayed, and in time found the peace he needed in the God he served. He was finally discharged for disability; his discharge document lists his character as 'Excellent' and his physical condition as 'Poor'. He was spent – no less courageous than before, but used up.

He returned home, thin and weary, still suffering from migraines, dizziness and double vision, and deaf in one ear. The gentle, kind, sensitive man who never wanted to hurt anyone, wore the Silver Star, five Purple Hearts, the Soldier's Medal for heroism, the French Croix de Guerre with Fourragère, the Good Conduct Medal, the European, African and Middle Eastern Campaign Medal with three bronze battle stars, the gold-framed blue ribbon for two Presidential Unit Citations, and the blue and silver Combat Infantryman's Badge.

Bert returned to Weakley County and the farm where he had been born and reared; it was Christmas 1944. His father needed help with the farm work, and Bert moved easily back into his role there. He spent time in the woods, and found it to be a peaceful, friendly, healing environment, but he didn't feel like hunting.

Shortly after his return he attended a basketball game at Cottage Grove High School (the high school he didn't get to attend), and here he met Thera Peale. Their meeting was unexpected, sudden and violent. She came running around a corner of the building at just the wrong time, and crashed into

Bert, literally knocking him down. She was a senior at Cottage Grove, and she had bowled him over in more ways than one; they were married the following November, 1945. She was 18 and Bert was 26.

They bought a farm near Thera's father's, and in December 1947 the first of four daughters, Ludie, was born. Two years later their house burned and all contents were lost. They sold the farm and, like many others in the South, moved north, to Chicago, to find work. The climate was unhealthy for Ludie, and both Bert and Thera were unhappy in the industrial North. They returned to Henry County, bought a house in Paris, the county seat, where Bert worked for Holley Carburetor. Thera had a natural gift for mathematics and book keeping, and they conducted several small businesses from their home. In 1955 twin girls, Vanesia and Theresia were born.

Crisis reunites Wesley and Bert

When the twins were eighteen months old, a telephone call during a Sunday lunch changed their lives. Bert took the call, and when he returned to the table he was weeping. The call was from the local police, who had received a call from a woman in Mississippi. She was trying to reach a man named Bert who had served with her husband in the war. It was Wesley Holly's wife. Wesley had been critically injured in a farm accident, was near death and delirious, and continued to call for someone named 'Bert'. The attending physician said that he believed this Bert must be someone who had been with Wesley when he was in trouble in the past, and it would be important to find him and have him come to the hospital. Mrs Holly had heard her husband speak of a close friend in the war named Bert, but she didn't know his last name. She only knew that he had once lived near Paris, Tennessee. She called the police in Paris and told her story, and thus their call to him.

Bert left immediately. He stayed by Wesley's bed, held his hand, and talked to him for several days before he finally regained consciousness; and he stayed with him until he was convinced that Wesley would recover. The friendship that was born in crisis on a faraway battlefield was re-born in crisis in a Mississippi hospital, and they would be close until Wesley's death, thirty years later. The relationship was so close that Bert's children came naturally to call Wesley and his wife 'Uncle Wesley' and 'Aunt Mattie'; and they refer to them this way today, although both are long dead.

In later years

In October 1962 Tammy, the fourth, and final, child was born to Bert and Thera. In 1966 Bert's father died, and in 1969 his younger sister Gertie died. His brother Odie was all that was left of his family. During these years Bert and Wesley enjoyed frequent hunting and fishing trips together, and various of the children joined in. They were times they never forgot, and times that their children, grandchildren, nieces and nephews continue to talk about today. Those times together with Wesley and the children were Bert's happiest.

Bert killed his first deer at age 39, with a bow and arrow. In spite of his late start he still set records for deer kills in both Mississippi and Tennessee. For gun hunting he used small-bore rifles because they were easier on his injured head. His favourite rifle was a .223 made in Finland. And he killed many deer with his .22-calibre pistol, with a 14-inch barrel and telescopic sight. Most deer hunters try for a heart or a neck shot, but Wesley still preferred a head shot (except for trophy specimens). His grand-nephew Odie says that when he wanted to 'show out' he would make a called eye shot.

There were long-standing problems in the marriage which Bert approached with his characteristic patience, hoping that things would improve; but they didn't. By 1977 the divorce was final. Bert never allowed the girls to say anything critical about Thera; 'Remember,' he would say, 'she is still your mother'.

During those difficult years, Bert had become both mother and father and, without complaint or comment, had moved smoothly into cooking, laundry and all that was necessary to keep the home running. According to Ludie, his oldest, 'He could iron a dress as well as any woman, and he was world-class in braiding pigtails or making a pony tail.' She marvelled that hands as rough and scarred as his could be so gentle in caring for his daughters.

Dealing with his memories

At times, when questioned, Bert would speak of the war to close friends; but otherwise he internalized it. If with a group of family or friends and a war movie came on the television, he would quietly leave the room without a word. When his daughter Ludie learned in school of the Kasserine Pass battle, she came home and asked Bert if he knew anything about it. He stood looking at her, wordless, for what seemed like a long time; and then his eyes filled with tears and he left the room. When he returned he continued with what he had been doing, as if her question had never been asked. He never spoke of the war with his daughters, except to assure them that he was not a hero.

His amazing gift for shooting never left him. The twins have happy memories of times when they were five or six, and Bert would have them throw two pennies up in the air at the same time. He would shoot centre holes in both, and they would excitedly search until they found the pennies. Only recently, twin Theresia's daughter, Mika, told her own story. She told her mother that she too had played that game with her grandfather, only he had her throwing dimes into the air, making for a much smaller target. Neither the twins nor Mika had ever known him to miss.

That ever-present slingshot

Since boyhood, Bert and his slingshots were inseparable. He always had one, made of dogwood, and it was always with him. Not infrequently wild animals ('varmints') would get into the carburettor plant where Bert worked. Killing them with a firearm was too dangerous; but Bert would solve the problem with his ever-present slingshot.

At the wedding of his daughter Ludie he and she were photographed as they knelt at the chancel rail for prayer. Looking at the photo after the wedding, she noticed a bulge under his suit jacket. It was his slingshot, in the hip pocket where he always carried it!

Losing Wesley and brother Odie

In 1988 Bert lost Wesley to cancer. He sat by his bed, as he had after the accident, talked to him and held his hand until he died. His brother Odie died the same year, and Bert was without both his brother and his best friend.

In time, Wesley's son Jimmy, Bert's grand-nephew Odie Kemp, and David Bumpus, a young Paris policeman, became his fishing and hunting buddies. Although David was much younger than Bert (who routinely called him 'Boy'), he became more than a hunting and fishing companion to Bert; he became a friend and confidant. When David was on midnight patrol he always drove past Bert's house; and if the kitchen light was on, he knew that 'the war was bothering him' and that Bert needed a friend. Not infrequently what was bothering him was that unarmed, English-speaking German with the megaphone. Bert would cook something special for them to share, and he would tell David things he didn't tell anyone else, now that Wesley was gone. Bert's daughter Ludie accurately observed that, 'Jimmy, Odie and David were the sons Daddy never had.'

Requiem for a reluctant warrior

Cancer, which Bert had survived earlier, returned in 2000 and there was no stopping it. Knowing his end was near, Bert prepared. He asked David to see to it that the girls were spared as much pain as possible. He made it known to the family that he wanted to die at home, and that he wanted a 'no-resuscitation order'. His daughters watched over him during those last weeks and Theresia, who is a nurse, saw to it that his wishes were carried out. Bert was comatose during the last two weeks and the twins stayed by his side. He was moved from the hospital to his home on a Wednesday afternoon; and on the following Saturday morning, 23 September 2000, with Theresia by his side, Bert Wilson Kemp, the reluctant warrior with the amazing gift, stepped quietly into eternity.

Maybe, somewhere beyond the sunset, Wesley was waiting for him.

References

Books

Martin Blumenson, *Kasserine Pass* (Boston, 1967)

Kenneth Macksey, *Crucible of Power: The Fight for Tunisia 1942–1943* (London, 1969)

U.S. Army Center for Military History, *The Sicilian Campaign* (Fort Lesley J. McNair, Washington, DC, 2009)

James Scott Wheeler, *The Big Red One: America's Legendary 1st Infantry Division from the First World War to Desert Storm* (Lawrence, Kansas, 2007)

Periodicals

[Anon.], 'Henry Infantryman Has Five Wounds', *Paris Post Intelligencer*, Paris, Tennessee, 1 September 1944, p. 1

[Anon.], 'Sgt. Bert Kemp Wins Silver Star Award', *Paris Post Intelligencer*, Paris, Tennessee, 28 March 1945, p. 1

Ken Clayton, 'Living Rifleman Ranks with Tennessee Legends', *Post Intelligencer*, Paris, Tennessee, 6 November 1987, p. 1B

——, 'Bert Kemp a Local Hunting and Shooting Legend', *Post Intelligencer*, Paris, Tennessee, 15 January 1988, p. 1B

Jim Dumas, 'Army Sets Its Sights on Bert Kemp's Uncanny Marksmanship', *Paris Post Intelligencer*, Paris, Tennessee, 11 May 2000, p. 6A

Documents

Honorable Discharge Certificate and Summary of Service, Sergeant Bert W. Kemp, Serial Number 34 185 517, Army of the United States, 22 December 1944

Internet sources

Charles R. Anderson, 'Tunisia', www.history.army.mil/
brochures/Tunisia/Tunisia.htm, 2003

'Battle Analysis, Kasserine Pass', www.usaiac.army.mil/cac2/
csi/docs/MHIC_Link04a.ppt277,13,Basic Battle Analysis.

Andrew J. Birtle, 'Sicily1943', www.history.army.mil/
brochures/72-16/72-16.html, 2009

Wikipedia article, '1st Infantry Division (United States)',
www.wikipedia.org

Witnesses interviewed

Roland Alexander, Paris, Tennessee

David Bumpus, Paris, Tennessee

Theresia Kemp Gregory, Greenbrier, Tennessee

Vanesia Kemp Hill, Cordova, Tennessee

Jimmie Holly, Shuqualak, Mississippi

Ludie Ann Kemp, Memphis, Tennessee

Stanley Kemp, Paris, Tennessee

Crockett Mathis, Paris, Tennessee

Tammy Kemp Wimberly, Paris, Tennessee

Chapter 4

OPERATION FOXLEY

British Sniping and the Hunt for Hitler

Adolf Hitler, Nazi Germany's Führer, was very well aware that he was a marked man – and that it was a sniper that stood the best chance of killing him. As he told his first Gestapo chief, Rudolf Diels, in 1933:

> One day a completely harmless man will establish himself in an attic flat along Wilhelmstrasse [in the centre of Berlin]. He will be taken for a retired schoolmaster. A solid citizen, with horn-rimmed spectacles, poorly shaven, bearded. He will not allow anyone into his modest room. Here he will install a gun, quietly and without undue haste, and with uncanny patience he will aim it at the Reich Chancellery balcony hour after hour, day after day. And then, one day, he will fire![1]

It was a remarkably prescient description of the kind of assassin who would target victims in the later twentieth century. Hitler repeated his fear of death by sniper during one of his appearances at major party events while having lunch at the Berghof on 3 May 1942, with Martin Bormann recording his conversation:

> In the midst of such crowds, it is easy for some fanatic armed with a telescopic-sighted firearm to take a shot at me from some corner or other; any likely hole or corner, therefore, must be kept under careful observation. During the hours of darkness police searchlights must be so sited that their rays light up these danger-spots and are not, as happened to me in Hamburg, concentrated all the time on my own car. Narrow streets should, as far as possible, be

avoided on official occasions; the five-metre-wide lane leading to the Kroll Opera in Berlin is potentially one of the most dangerous bits of road I know.[2]

Hitler was dismissive of the efforts of the thousands of security officers surrounding him whose attentions seemed more likely to attract assassins than dissuade them. He frequently drove them mad by ignoring their carefully planned schedules, changing his mind at the last moment on routes and modes of travel. As far as he was concerned this was the best way to protect himself. 'The only preventive measure one can take is to live irregularly – to walk, to drive and to travel at irregular times and un-expectedly,' he said

Hitler knew there was little he could do against a determined attacker and, until the last months of the war, was not prepared to hide away from his supporters:

> As there can never be absolute security against fanatics and idealists on official occasions, I always make a point of standing upright in my car, and this method has again and again proved the truth of the proverb that the world belongs to the brave. If some fanatic wishes to shoot me or kill me with a bomb, I am no safer sitting down than standing up.

Several assassination attempts were made against Hitler throughout the 1930s, but these mostly came from disaffected Germans. It was only in the months leading up to war that a Briton first thought of killing the Führer and that was by sniping at him. In 1938, Colonel Sir Noel Mason-MacFarlane was the British military attaché in Berlin and had witnessed Hitler's triumphant entry into Austria in March of that year. Watching the German convoy full of heavily armed troops and armoured vehicles had sent a chill down his spine. He was convinced Hitler posed a threat to Britain and was determined to avoid another world war by doing something practical about it.

Mason-MacFarlane lived in Berlin at 1 Sophienstrasse, just a hundred metres from where Hitler regularly stood to review his troops. 'All that was necessary,' he recalled, 'was a good shot and a high velocity rifle with telescopic sight and silencer. It could have been fired though my bathroom window from a spot on the landing some 30 feet [10 metres] back from the window.'[3] Since he was a diplomat, Mason-MacFarlane's house was within the security zone put round Hitler by his SS bodyguards and the noise of marching men and cheering would have disguised any noise from his rifle. He was quite prepared to pull the trigger himself.

'He discussed the plan with me in the summer of 1938,' said the Germany correspondent of the *Times*, Ewen Butler, 'as I sat looking out of the window of his Berlin flat – the window from which his rifleman would have fired the shot which would have ended Hitler's career.' Both men believed the Führer's personal security was a shambles and could be easily penetrated. Just weeks later, the British journalist got to within half a dozen metres of the Nazi leader outside the Anhalter station in Berlin:

> In my case the Gestapo security arrangements had collapsed. I was not searched, although I had no right to be where I was and might have had several Mills bombs in my pocket. In that case I could have disposed not only of the Führer but of most of his accomplices. I told Mason-Mac about this and he reproached me bitterly for having missed such an excellent opportunity.[4]

Mason-MacFarlane reported his golden opportunity to Foreign Office officials in London but was told not to proceed. They said it was un-sportsmanlike to assassinate the dictator. More importantly, the mood of the moment was appeasement. British Prime Minister Neville Chamberlain wanted to avoid a war in Europe at any cost and preferred to do this by giving Hitler exactly what he wanted. Mason-MacFarlane was unrepentant, however, saying in October 1938, just after the Munich agreement: 'I regard that sheet of Munich notepaper with Hitler's and Chamberlain's signatures on it as already a "scrap of paper".'[5]

Further British plans to assassinate Hitler in the early years of the war were discouraged by the Venlo Incident in November

1939. Tempted by the prospect of meeting German officers plotting to kill the Führer, two British Secret Intelligence agents working in then-neutral Holland drove to a rendezvous near the town of Venlo on the German border. Unfortunately, the meeting was a sting organised by the German Security Service, whose operatives kidnapped and interrogated the two British agents, gaining much information from them about the Allied intelligence network in Europe. Most damagingly of all, it made the British very wary of dealing with any Germans claiming to be part of a conspiracy to kill Hitler.

This caution continued until 1944 when discontent within German ranks was so widespread that the British felt confident they could again begin to trust information forwarded to them from German sources. It was at that moment that a series of very thorough plans was made to assassinate Hitler. Called Operation Foxley, this was devised by SOE – Special Operations Executive – under the command of Brigadier Colin Gubbins, Director of Operations. One of the chief weapons deployed by SOE would be the sniper's rifle and it depended on the very high quality of British sniper training.

*

Sniping in the British Army had rapidly developed in the First World War. As their officers were picked off with pinpoint accuracy by Germans using high-velocity sporting rifles equipped with telescopic sights, so the British retaliated by turning to their own hunting experts. Combining the talents of scouting, observation, and stalking, they placed an emphasis not only on accurate shooting but also on a mastery of fieldcraft. This included the development of a variety of camouflage and decoy techniques. Papier-mâché dummy heads were placed on the edges of trenches to distract German snipers, while the highland ghillie suit evolved into the scrim-decorated Symien Sniper Suit with hood.[6] These lessons were resurrected in the Second World War by Lieutenant Colonel Nevill Armstrong.

Chief Reconnaissance Officer and Canadian Army Chief Instructor at the Second Army School of Scouting, Observation and Sniping in Flanders in 1915–16, Armstrong ended the First World War as Commandant of the Canadian Corps School of Scouting, Observation and Sniping in France in 1917–18. Twenty-two years later, he put his talents at the service of the British Army as Senior Instructor, Sniping Wing, at the Small Arms School, at Hythe and Bisley, and then as Commandant of the Royal Marine Snipers' School. When he came to write up his knowledge in a book entitled *Fieldcraft, Sniping and Intelligence*, running to six editions up to 1944, Armstrong paid tribute to 'that intrepid band of hunters, scouts and snipers', members of the battalion intelligence sections of the British Expeditionary Force in 1914–18. The foreword to the book was written by Lord Cottesloe and reiterated the hunting analogy: 'What indeed is the human animal in war but a special variety of soft-skinned dangerous game?'[7]

Armstrong's book gives us a comprehensive record of the state of sniping in the British Army in the Second World War, but much of it was built on combat experience gained in the First World War. He even referred to the use of dummy heads. In Belgium in 1916, he recalled, he was asked to help out a brigadier whose soldiers were suffering heavy casualties from German snipers:

> So we gave special training to two of his officers and sixteen men and sent them off. Some two weeks later we received a letter from this Brigadier, stating that the sniping had been checked and the tables turned, and that one of the most dangerous and persistent snipers had been spotted by using a camouflaged head, two of which we gave the sniping officer and trained him in their use. The head was carefully exposed and the Hun immediately bit, but missed with his first shot; the second shot, however, hit the dummy head in the eye and came out behind. By looking through the holes with a periscope the Boche was spotted in a tree and killed.[8]

Armstrong's preferred sniping rifle was a First World War model – the P14 Lee-Enfield. First appearing in 1914, the gun included modifications from the P13, itself based on the Mauser front-locking lug bolt-action rifle. With greatly improved accuracy, it was set to take over from the Short Magazine Lee-Enfield (SMLE) Mk III to become the standard British Army rifle, but with the beginning of the First World War, it was considered confusing to introduce a brand-new weapon at that moment. This attitude changed in 1915 with the enormous expansion of the British Army and a need for more guns. With British factories already busy, the manufacture of P14s was contracted out to the expert American gun-making firms of Winchester and Remington.[9]

Design glitches halted the wide acceptance of the P14. It was considered too long for everyday infantry use and its U.S. production meant spare parts were harder to find. As a result, the half-kilogram-lighter and 5-cm-shorter Lee-Enfield remained the primary British infantry weapon, but the superior accuracy of the P14 made it the first choice for British snipers using it with telescopic sights. Eighty years later, a former U.S. Army officer and firearms expert tested the P14 to see it how it compared with later rifles. The P14, he concluded, 'is certainly as good as many sniper rifles seen in today's armies. An L42A1, which is still used in the British Army in the 1990s, with similar ammunition will shoot similar groups, and it is just as long and heavy. I do not think the P14 sniper rifle is a great 600-yard-plus rifle, but for 400 yards or less it could be deadly even today.'[10]

With modified 1940 P18 telescopic sights, the P14 remained the best British sniping rifle in the Second World War, although Armstrong also conceded it was 'heavier and less easy to handle' than the SMLE Mk III, and its magazine held only five rounds, but none of this was a major problem for a sniper. Regarding the recruitment of soldiers as snipers, Armstrong had a very definite kind of man in mind. 'Stalkers, keepers, poachers, prospectors, trappers, out-of-door people, hill and moorland farmers', he put at the top of his list. 'It is useless to try to make a sniper out of every man in a battalion.' He wanted men who had first-class observational skills and could read a landscape. They should study the movement of mammals and birds and note how their actions can give away the presence of humans. Animals provided other clues too. 'In position warfare we are very much like animals,' he said. 'We do the same thing more or less in the same way day after day.'[11] Understanding the habits of a target was vital to a successful kill.

Outlines could prove a dangerous give-away and Armstrong spent much time recommending all forms of disguise. Camouflage had been taken up with enthusiasm in the Second World War and many official government manuals appeared covering every aspect of it, from hiding buildings, tanks and vehicles to protecting soldiers. Former surrealist artist Roland Penrose wrote a guide to camouflage for the Home Guard and in it he made the point that camouflage was not about selecting the right colour, but the correct texture. He also explained the technique of disruptive patterning, which meant breaking up the outline of a figure or object.

For the purposes of the Home Guard, Penrose had to choose readily available materials and he recommended that a cheap and quick sniping suit could be made out of hessian sacking in less than ten minutes:

> If the seams are turned outwards, a jagged edge can be obtained. In painting them disruptive patterns will be found to be useful and as in nature the upper surfaces, such as the back of the hood, shoulders and back, may be kept darker in tone than the front. It is sometimes a good plan to make the pattern cut across the back and legs, as this part is likely to be most visible when a man is lying on the ground.[12]

When it came to using the urban environment for sniping, Lieutenant Colonel Armstrong recommended securing a room in an upper storey of a house. This would help protect the sniper from an enemy armed with hand grenades:

> He should take up a position in the room which will give him an oblique line of fire protected by the wall of the room and well clear of the window. If unable to get a good view while standing on the floor of the room, the sniper can pull

out a bed or chair or table, and for protection may possibly use mattresses, pillows, furniture etc.

A position in the rafters of a ruined house or behind rows of chimney pots also provided excellent cover for snipers. Further chapters in Armstrong's book covered care and use of telescopic sights, sniping in attack and defence and at night, scouting, observation and landscape sketching.

It was not the only manual available for teaching sniping in the Second World War. Hesketh Vernon Hesketh-Prichard was an explorer and big-game hunter who founded the First Army School of Scouting, Observation and Sniping at Linghem in the Pas de Calais in 1916. He put all his knowledge into a book called *Sniping in France*, published in 1920. John Buchan, the best-selling thriller writer, then *Times* correspondent, encouraged Hesketh-Prichard and even raised funds for his sniping school.

It was Hesketh-Prichard who originated the use of dummy heads to fool enemy snipers:

> The uses to which the heads were put were varied [he recalled]. They were most useful in getting the enemy to give a target. It was also possible, by showing very skilfully the heads of Sikhs or Gurkhas in different parts of the line, to give the German Intelligence the impression that we were holding our line with Indian troops, and I have no doubt they were considerably worried to account for these movements.[13]

He described in detail how dummies could also be used to track shots by looking through the bullet holes left in the front and back of a fake head.

Early on, Hesketh-Prichard had faced prejudice against setting up his sniping school from superior officers who preferred the blunt impact of massed musketry rather than, what they termed, 'an excess of accuracy'. 'But this war,' argued Hesketh-Prichard, 'was largely a war of specialists [and] changed many things, and among them the accurate shot or sniper was destined to prove his extraordinary value.' At first, the duty of British snipers in the Great War had been to dominate German snipers, destroy their morale, and make life in the trenches secure for their own comrades. Later in the war, as British forces took the offensive, the sniper was put out in front to keep enemy heads down while his companions consolidated their newly won positions. 'Many a sniper killed his fifty Germans in a single day, and whether as a rifleman or scout, he bore a part more perilous than that of the rank and file of his comrades.'[14]

Hesketh-Prichard's anecdotes in *Sniping in France* often turn on a hunting analogy and when it came to spotting the enemy he recommended the use of a telescope rather than field glasses. 'Anyone who has tried to count the points on the antlers of a stag will know this,' he concluded.

Hesketh-Prichard died in 1922, but his advice continued to inspire snipers over the following two decades. One of them was Captain Clifford Shore, a sniping instructor who saw action during Operation Overlord in 1944, and wrote *With British Snipers to the Reich*, first published in 1948. Shore referred to the game-hunting Hesketh-Prichard as the main inspiration behind sniper training in the Second World War. Along with Armstrong, Shore favoured the intuitive hunter-sniper over the trained marksman, saying that sniper instructors could quote many instances of 'brilliant performers on the range at normal targets failing to retain that shooting capacity on "live" targets – game in general, deer – and Man!'

Generally, Shore was unimpressed with the employment of British sniping on the battlefield and felt that more could have been made of snipers on covert missions:

> During the Second World War snipers were not used enough, and the real lone sniper was very seldom, if ever, used. Lone snipers could have been used in a deep penetrative role, well behind the enemy lines. Given guts, absolute fieldcraft ability, stealth, cunning, supreme confidence in his own prowess, and a splendid shot, the death and confusion that such a man could have caused in the enemy's rear is inestimable.[15]

Shore feared that, in the months immediately following the end of the Second World War in Europe, a similar lone German sniper could cause havoc among the Allied occupiers. 'In the forest areas of Germany a man knowing the country like the back of his hand could add many scalps to his totem,' he warned, 'and escape the dragnet which would be sent sweeping against him.' Only a like-minded British sniper would be able to track him down.

It was just this kind of deep-cover sniping operation that SOE had in mind when they came to consider methods of killing Hitler in 1944.

*

To kill Hitler, SOE followed the advice of Lieutenant Colonel Armstrong and concentrated on getting to know his daily habits. That way, a sniper could lie in wait for him, just as a hunter would track an animal. SOE focussed on the Führer's daily routine at his favourite location – the Berghof – his mountaintop lair near the town of Berchtesgaden in the Bavarian Alps. It stood on the Obersalzberg and reminded the Nazi leader of the mountain landscape of his childhood in Austria. He claimed that it stimulated his imagination and gave him space to think. 'All my great decisions were taken at Obersalzberg,' Hitler recalled. 'That's where I conceived the offensive of May 1940 and the attack on Russia.'[16]

Hitler loved the outdoor life and his one main regret about becoming leader of Germany was that he could no longer pull on a pair of leather shorts and go hiking. In his early years at the Berghof, he would set off into the forest with a few friends, frequently bumping into hikers curious to see the man who claimed to be able to save Germany, but as he came close to power in 1933, more and more crowds were drawn to his Bavarian retreat, until it became a security problem. Land was bought, barbed-wire fences raised and the surrounding area divided into security zones patrolled ultimately by 20,000 SS bodyguards and soldiers. During the war, the Berghof was Hitler's alternative power base, his other main residence after the Reich Chancellery.

For Operation Foxley, SOE made a thorough study of the area around the Berghof – its geography and its climate. Most of the land on the Obersalzberg was heavily wooded and hilly, making it a difficult place to guard and offering good cover for covert action by a sniper. The Berghof complex was known to contain members of Hitler's elite bodyguard – the SS Begleit-Kommando. They slept in bedrooms in the same house and on the same floor as he did. Nearby were barracks containing SS Leibstandarte soldiers. An attempt on the Führer's life near any of these buildings would be suicidal.

Instead, there were moments in the day when Hitler walked away from the main buildings in the compound and wanted to be more alone. It was at this point that the sort of lone sniper described by Captain Shore – with 'stealth, cunning, supreme confidence in his own prowess' – could target him.

The information about Hitler's private daily movements came from German prisoners of war interrogated by SOE. One of these was a member of the SS Wachkompanie Obersalzberg – a bodyguard unit recruited from SS mountain troops and part of the Leibstandarte guard. The informers revealed that Hitler was a late riser, rarely getting up before 1000. Given a shave by his barber, he would then either go for a morning walk to the tea-house at Mooslaner Kopf for his breakfast or attend a conference. The stroll to the teahouse would take fifteen to twenty minutes at a normal leisurely pace. Most importantly he would walk alone. There was an SS guard at either end of the walk and one man would patrol the route, but Hitler hated seeing him. If he did, the Führer shouted at him 'If you are frightened, go and guard yourself.'[17]

When Hitler arrived at the teahouse, he was given a breakfast of milk and toast and then driven back to the Berghof. Probably because he felt safe within the Berghof environs, the Führer ignored his own advice of leading an irregular life to avoid assassins. That brief period of time when he didn't wish to be observed in the woods appeared to be the first chink in his armour. In the SOE proposal for Operation Foxley, the planners outlined a possible assassination mission. Two separate snipers would cut their way through the Berghof perimeter wire fence and position themselves 100–200 metres away from Hitler's route near the teahouse. They would arrive no earlier than 1000, so as to miss an earlier security dog patrol of the area.

The equipment to be carried by each of the snipers was listed by SOE and included a 'Mauser sniper's rifle, telescopic sight (carried in pocket), explosive bullets in a magazine, wire-cutters (for making hole in wire fence), HE grenades carried in haversack for close protection and assistance in making get-away'.[18] The Mauser was the Karabiner 98k, a bolt-action rifle that was a shortened version of the First World War Mauser Gewehr 98. The 98k was the most common German infantry rifle in the Second World War and with an added Zeiss scope was a popular sniper weapon.

Interestingly, recent firing tests of the Karabiner 98k with Zeiss 1.5-power scope concluded that it was ill-balanced with poor optics and was probably intended less as an expert sniper's rifle and more one designed to enhance the accuracy of the ordinary infantryman – 'a marksmanship rifle'.[19]

The most important factor, as far as SOE was concerned, was that the rifle was German – not British. SOE had no wish to create a martyr out of Hitler by openly killing him, but if they blamed it on forces within the German Army, then that might work. The failed bomb plot against Hitler in July 1944 confirmed the existence of German resistance at a high level and provided good cover for a British assassination attempt. SOE considered the best operatives for such a mission would be Austrians or Bavarians with a grudge against Hitler, but the large number of foreign workers – especially Czechs and Poles employed on building work within the Berghof security zone – were also seen as potential recruits.

Any of these foreign agents could be given a fake uniform copied from detailed notes made on the outfits worn by Hitler's various security forces at the Berghof. The operatives would be trained in sniping and sabotage techniques in Britain or by British instructors based abroad, then infiltrated into the Obersalzberg via Salzburg. From there, they would make contact with foreign workers who would smuggle them into the Berghof, or, wearing German security uniforms, they would penetrate the forest and fences surrounding Hitler's residence.

If the teahouse snipers failed to kill Hitler, then a back-up unit would be placed in the woods to intercept Hitler in the car taking him up the hill later. For this, a sniper's rifle was thought to be less useful. Instead, men armed with a PIAT rocket launcher or bazooka would blast him in the vehicle. The PIAT was reasonably light to carry and packed an enormous punch, able to penetrate through a dozen centimetres of armour plate of the sort used to protect Hitler's Mercedes cars.

Other more elaborate assassination missions were designed for the Berghof, one of them being a combined arms aerial assault on the mountaintop complex. After an attack by low-flying bombers, aircraft would drop SAS paratroopers to kill Hitler. Such an option, however, would be too high-profile and could be easily traced back to Britain. The foreign operative with a sniper rifle was by far the preferred option.

Away from the Berghof, Operation Foxley considered killing Hitler in his mobile headquarters, an armoured train dubbed the Führer Special. Inside information about this came from a steward who had worked on the train. He revealed that Hitler was protected by at least twenty bodyguards, comprising his Begleit-Kommando SS elite, soldiers from the SS Leibstandarte, and Gestapo agents. Whenever he got off the train these men surrounded him. It was a formidable ring of steel to break through, but one weak point was thought to be the railway sidings at Klessheim, near the Berghof. A regular stopping point used to service Hitler's train, the sidings were surrounded by thick woods and could provide good cover for a sniper armed with a high-velocity rifle. When Hitler stepped down from his carriage for a breath of fresh air, the sniper could shoot him. The main obstacle facing this attempt was that soldiers of the Führer Begleit-Bataillon were housed in the nearby Schloss Klessheim. Patrolling the landscape around the railway sidings, they would make it difficult for any sniper to get close to him. Bearing in mind the lower level of track security in Austria, SOE considered simply bombing the railway – with the subsequent derailment having a bigger chance of success.

In the end, events overtook Operation Foxley. The relentless advance of the Soviet Army on the Eastern Front demanded Hitler's constant attention. Hitler flew out from the Berghof in mid-July 1944 to go to his battlefront headquarters at Rastenburg – the Wolf's Lair – in East Prussia. His staff at the Berghof expected him to return to enjoy a holiday away from the fighting, but he never came back. Having narrowly avoided being blown up by his own generals a few days later, Hitler spent most of the last months of the war at Rastenburg before the proximity of Soviet soldiers forced him to flee to Berlin. With the Berghof remaining unused, the detailed plans by SOE to kill Hitler by sniper fire were redundant.

The SOE author of the Operation Foxley report is usually identified as Major H. B. Court. Recent research, however, suggests this may be a typing error and that the author was really Major H. D. Court – Harold Darlington Court – a military engineer.[20] Major Court gained useful experience during the First World War in Bulgaria setting up observation posts looking out for enemy firing positions. The meticulous observational fieldcraft skills he learned there, similar to those outlined by Lieutenant Colonel Armstrong in his Aldershot sniping manual, may explain why he selected a sniper as one of the best military technicians to kill Hitler.

*

Despite the imagination shown by Operation Foxley and the central role to be played by British sniping, it is hard to disagree with Captain Clifford Shore that British snipers were generally underused as weapons directed against enemy commanders. In the event, no British snipers or foreign agents trained in British sniping were sent undercover to assassinate senior Nazis. It may well be that the terrible retribution suffered by Czech civilians as a result of the killing of Reich Protector Reinhard Heydrich in 1942 by British-trained assassins dissuaded similar such ventures early on in the war. Certainly, by 1944, it was probably believed by the British that Hitler and his generals were doing a good enough job of losing the war that there was little value in hastening their end with a sniper's bullet.

Notes

1. Quoted in P. Hoffmann, *Hitler's Personal Security* (Da Capo Press, 2000), p. 24. See also R. Diels, *Lucifer ante Portas: Zwischen Severing und Heydrich* (Zurich, 1950).
2. Bormann notes, midday, 3 May 1942, *Hitler's Table-Talk* (Oxford University Press, 1988), p. 453.
3. Quoted in Hoffmann, *Hitler's Personal Security*, p. 99. See also Mason-MacFarlane Papers in Imperial War Museum, London.
4. E. Butler, 'I talked of plan to kill Hitler', *The Times*, 6 August 1969.
5. Mason-MacFarlane's Berlin report on Sudeten transfer, 11 October 1939, in British National Archives, WO 106/5421.
6. Plate 5, *The Principles and Practice of Camouflage*, British Army pamphlet March 1918, Imperial War Museum, 182.7 K.37025. See also Tim Newark, *Camouflage* (Thames & Hudson, 2007), pp. 64 & 84–5.
7. Lt-Col N. A. D. Armstrong, *Fieldcraft, Sniping and Intelligence* (Gale & Polden, 6th edition, 1944), p. vii.
8. Ibid., p. 24.
9. T. Gander, *Allied Infantry Weapons of the Second World War* (Crowood Press, 2000), p. 16.
10. T. J. Mullin, *Testing the War Weapons*, (Paladin Press, 1997), p. 157.
11. Armstrong, *Fieldcraft*, pp. 23–4.
12. R. Penrose, *Home Guard Manual of Camouflage* (George Routledge & Sons, 1941), p. 98.
13. H. V. Hesketh-Prichard, *Sniping in France*, (Hutchinson, 1920), p. 7.
14. Ibid., p. 58

15. C. Shore, *With British Snipers to the Reich* (Greenhill Books, 1997), pp. 141–2.

16. *Hitler's Table-Talk*, 2–3 January 1942, p. 165.

17. Operation Foxley, SOE report, British National Archives, HS6/624, p. 60. See also M. Seaman, *Operation Foxley: The British Plan to Kill Hitler* (Public Record Office, 1998).

18. Operation Foxley, SOE report, p. 66.

19. Ibid., pp. 114–15.

20. B. Ross, 'The Foxley Report: Plotters against Hitler', BBC History website.

Chapter 5

A JAPANESE SNIPER

A Long Walk to a Short Life

The malodorous, combined scent of rotting coconuts, fetid jungle vegetation, decaying human remains and his own body odour assault his olfactory system as he rises towards the upper branches of a tall coconut palm tree. Using a rope and pulley, his friend is hoisting him to his hide. With rope now securely tied to the tree trunk, their eyes meet – briefly – both keenly aware of what the future holds. With his back to Taki and forgoing a backward look, his friend shuffles away, bound for the rescue barges waiting on the beach.

Imperial Japanese Army Corporal Taki Nakamura[1] is aware that this palm on Guadalcanal, Solomon Islands, could well be the last tree he ever ascends. But to die for the Emperor is honourable. After all, when he became a soldier in the Japanese Army, he also became the Emperor's property and, in accordance with the *Bushido* code he was taught, dying for the Emperor is praiseworthy. Even though a wave of doubt mixed with fear occasionally sweeps through him, he is committed to his mission. He is but twenty-two years of age and has served the Empire since he was officially conscripted into the Army just after his twentieth birthday at the start of 1940.

Once he is in the perch he erected four days ago, he knows full well he will sit silently in his treetop hideout protected only by ripening coconuts, palm fronds and what his friends laughingly call his 'hair shirt', the camouflage netting that holds bits of coconut husks and palm leaf. His rifle locked and loaded, he will wait for enemy targets of opportunity. And as he waits he will sweat profusely. The dysentery that afflicts him rumbles deep in his gut almost continuously and quickly relieving the resultant urge has become second nature to him. But once in a tree hide, he must use the self-discipline the Imperial Japanese Army has taught him.

The tropical heat of the South Pacific eases only during the torrential rains that inevitably follow when the atmosphere can no longer hold the weight of the moisture evaporated from surrounding seas. It is the relative humidity more than the heat that causes the perspiration from his malnourished body (he has not eaten an adequate meal in almost four months) to trickle down the back of his neck between his shoulder blades to his belt line. There it is stopped by the service belt buckled around his waist. It now hangs loosely on his emaciated frame even though it fitted perfectly the day he arrived on the island. His now-rusting Arisaka rifle with its 2.5-power telescope mounted left of the receiver is hung by its sling across his chest, and hugs his back as his friend pulls him higher towards the spread of palm fronds above.

By any reasonable standard, he should be dead, a casualty of the seemingly endless ranks of U.S. Marines, with their tons of materiel, that have come ashore here over the past six months. He is a survivor, well trained in his craft. As a scout originally assigned to the Seventh Army's 28th Regiment, he was always in the forefront of the action. He endured multiple battles with the enemy and has the wounds to remind him. Now, with his own forces aboard the ships that will free them from this hell-hole of an island, he is no longer in front, but is the last of the last rearguard. It is a rotten assignment, but duty is supreme and he is honoured to have volunteered for the job. As he finds his place among the palm fronds, try as he might, he cannot forget the friends who preceded him in death on this stinking piece of land in the midst of an ocean. It is a terrible place to die.

Finally, high in his palm tree hide, waiting for the enemy, he wonders if his family will ever learn his fate. The question has ricocheted around his mind: how did he come to this time and place in his life?

*

Basic training lasted six months (including indoctrination) even though it seemed much longer to Taki. After initial physical conditioning that included strenuous physical training, running, marching, and martial arts instruction, all recruits were given extensive bayonet drill. *Bushido* required that the true warrior must attack, attack, attack and with his superior spirit and will to win, close with and destroy the enemy face-to-face. There were field exercises with emphasis on unit tactics, forced marches under difficult conditions, close order drill, marksmanship; then more immersion in the *Senjinkun*, the warrior code. He had been taught, beginning in his third school year, that the destiny of the Army was the destiny of the Empire and the Emperor. No matter what the soldier did, it was for the Emperor, a deity. The Imperial Rescript was the motivation:

> If you all do your duty, and being one with Us in spirit do your utmost for the protection of the state Our people will long enjoy the blessings of peace, and the might and dignity of Our Empire will shine in the world.

The state religion of Shintoism that was a fusion of Confucianism, Zen and Buddhism reinforced this mind-set when it stressed a martial spirit, self-sacrifice, loyalty, justice, a sense of shame if dishonoured, polite social behaviour, modesty, frugality and honour. Honour was valued as more important than life.[2] These principles did not apply to the enemy. They were Taki's study subjects during off-duty hours in the barracks.

To Taki, barracks life was not significantly different from his civilian world. Conformance, unthinking obedience and crowded living conditions were part of his prior life. As a new conscript, he found himself at the bottom of the 'pecking order' and anyone who had been inducted earlier than he could punish him at any time. Constantly reminded that he was worth only *issen gorin* (one *sen*, five *rin* – less than a penny) and far less than a good artillery horse, he understood that he was subservient – immediately, early and often. This sort of seniority system went well beyond rank.

Taki quickly came to understand that within his barracks, soldiers divided themselves into divisions: those with less than three months' service were the lowest category; those with over six months further sub-divided themselves into those who had been promoted and those who had not. Older soldiers assumed the status of NCOs when regular NCOs were not present and often compelled less senior soldiers to clean their gear, serve their meals, run errands and do other degrading tasks in the barracks. Seniority, or time in service, became as important if not more so, than rank. The term used to describe their longevity in uniform was *menko* (literally, the wooden tray on which food was served), which was suggestive of the number of meals consumed since being conscripted. *Menko* became more important than rank in this man's army. This made barracks life an endurance test for the average soldier.[3]

Severe punishment was dealt out by NCOs with no attention paid to its prohibition by the Imperial Rescript which read:

> ... Superiors should never treat their inferiors with contempt or arrogance. Except when official duty requires them to be strict and severe, superiors should treat their inferiors with consideration, making kindness their chief aim, so that all grades may unite in their service of the Emperor.[4]

NCOs consistently failed to abide by this principle, which perhaps attracted some NCOs with sadistic tendencies to covet training assignments. Common abuses included punching recruits in the face for no reason, or for poor performance. In extreme cases, NCOs used bamboo rods, swagger sticks, service belts or even rifle butts to issue punishing blows. The soles of slippers (of a sort) made from worn-out marching shoes, which still held the hobnails and heel clip, were used to slap the faces of recruits, often leaving cuts, bruises and permanent scars in their wake.[5]

Taki's training cycle followed a rather precise pattern attuned to the seasons of the year. Since new conscripts were taken in January of each year, until May the programme consisted of squad training, bayonet drills and target practice. In February, a five-day march with a bivouac each night was held to condition troops to cold weather. June and July were spent with more target practice, bayonet, platoon and company training. Hot weather marches of 32 kilometres per day were commonplace to accustom soldiers to the heat. In August, company and battalion-strength exercises were combined with field work, combat firing range practice, swimming and, as always, more bayonet training. The forced marches were increased to 40 kilometres per day in rugged terrain to force the marchers to their fatigue limits. To finish the training cycle, in October and November, battalion and regimental strength operations were taught, plus a return visit to the combat firing range. The highlights of the finale were the autumn manoeuvres involving several divisions in war games.[6]

The offensive mind-set coupled with the organization of a platoon-size basic fire unit (including riflemen, machine guns and mortars) meant that instead of individual marksmanship, volume of fire from the entire small unit was preferable to long range targeting of the enemy. It followed, then, that the training for riflemen emphasized volume of approximate fire rather than pinpoint accuracy. Complicating this training was the fact that pre-1941 liberal use of ammunition was permitted, but from 7 December 1941, for obvious reasons, less was available for training. Most of the marksmanship training was based on a 285-metre range, but it quickly became clear that tropical jungles would render long-range marksmanship training efforts of this sort useless; therefore because of the limited supply of ammunition and in anticipation of jungle combat, the training focus logically shifted from long-range shooting to spend more upon care of the rifle.

His weapon was the standard service rifle, the Arisaka Year 38 bolt-action rifle. Built with a Mauser-type action, it fired a 6.5 x 50 mm (.256 calibre) projectile and was fed by a five-round magazine. Some 1,280 mm long, it weighed 3.95 kg with its 800-mm barrel. It was the longest Japanese rifle due to the emphasis on bayonet fighting, When the 400 mm-long Type 30 bayonet was affixed, from butt plate to tip of bayonet blade, the Type 38 stood at 1,680 mm (5 ft 6 in.) next to the average Japanese soldier who stood just 1,600 mm (5 ft 3 in.).[7]

Taki had excelled on the rifle range and was selected for additional training as scout. The scout/soldier was re-issued a 6.5 x 50 mm Arisaka Type 97 rifle. It had a 2.5-power fixed-focus telescope affixed on the left side of the receiver, and a turned-down bolt handle (to clear the telescope when re-chambering a round). The telescope featured a 10-degree field of vision. It was functional but, with a fixed focus and no graticule (the lines within the scope's optics that enabled aiming points other than the fixed focus point), it required the shooter to adjust his aim manually for ranges beyond the fixed focus point. As a single unit, the rifle and scope weighed in at 4.45 kg.[8] In later stages of the war, the Type 99 rifle firing a heftier 7.7mm x 58 mm (.303 calibre) round was issued and found more effective in smashing through jungle undergrowth en route to its target. The scope supplied with this later rifle was an adjustable one rather than a fixed-focus model. Taki had heard about, but never seen the heavier rifle.

Taki, along with the others in his *han* (group) were taught that their mission was, in order of importance:

- To kill or capture hostile personnel – especially unit leaders and snipers.
- To neutralize or destroy hostile installations which may obstruct the successful completion of a Japanese unit's mission.
- To destroy enemy heavy weapons and the personnel manning them.
- To deal effectively with all targets of opportunity which may come within range.

He learned to estimate ranges with his eyes only. Instructors placed objects at measured distances varying from 200 to 600 metres, which he then had to estimate by sight.[9] He and his classmates spent hours pacing off distances to targets. In order to familiarize themselves with the sight picture differences between 200 metres across flat terrain and 200 metres through jungle foliage, uphill and down, they walked miles. Accurate estimating and shooting were a key part of the training regime.[10]

Once adequately trained on the rifle range for shooting accuracy and in distance estimation, he remembered that the emphasis shifted to concealment and camouflage training. With the primary mission of killing or capturing hostile personnel then reporting back to unit commanders, it was imperative to place scouts on the flanks of automatic weapons installations and to the flanks of any unit. Thus positioned, they would serve as an early warning signal for an imminent attack or spot weaknesses in the enemy defences. They could also fulfill their secondary mission as snipers.

Taki's sniper kit was specially designed to make him effective. It included a gas mask, a combination mosquito net/ camouflage hood (this covered the head and shoulders), a green net to camouflage his torso, a coil of rope, a small sack of rice, a small bag of hard biscuits, 250 grams of boiled sweets, several cans of concentrated food, a small can of coffee, vitamin pills, a can of chlorine tablets to purify water, his mess kit, an antidote for mustard gas, quinine pills, bandages, socks, toothbrush, torch and an assortment of medical items packed in little wicker baskets. These were intended to keep him afield from two weeks up to a month, requiring only a minimum of food and water from the countryside.[11]

Considerable time and effort were expended in teaching the proper identification and use of native plants and their placement in the camouflage net issued to all infantrymen. Foliage had to be coordinated with local plants so the shooter could blend in to his surroundings. He learned that, in some cases, special green uniforms and face paints could be used to deepen cover among the flora between the jungle floor and canopy. Although not specifically trained to use (or *not* use) treetops as hides, some scouts, including Taki, would use trees because the height of trees afforded a better field of vision.

With the benefit of the smokeless projectile propellant, and the low muzzle flash from the long barrel of the Arisaka rifle, a scout could be virtually invisible, locating and eliminating multiple targets from the same hide. Conversely, he knew well that most, if not all, Allied arms featured a bright muzzle flash and accompanying propellant smoke from the barrel with each round fired. It was this small detail that enabled his fellow-scouts to locate and kill commanders and personnel of crew-served weapons effectively. He worked hard to assimilate every aspect of his training, taking it seriously. He knew he would see combat soon. He just didn't know where or when.

In early 1942, with his training completed, Taki was assigned as an infantryman in the 28th Regiment, 7th Division. He was part of a force, embarked at Guam, ordered to occupy Midway Island. As an infantryman, he was trained to close with and destroy the enemy, not simply occupy the post. Garrison life was rife with the mind-numbing boredom of guard duty, coast-watching and endless drills for air raids, drills for sea-borne landing party repelling and the drudgery of close-order drill day after day. But even though the Japanese high command had forecast Midway as perhaps the easternmost point of the Greater East Asia Prosperity Sphere, the Imperial Navy's crushing defeat near there in June dictated a change in plans for the 28th Regiment. The ships carrying the troops were ordered back to Guam then, while en route, detoured once again.

Disappointment reigned supreme among the troops in the berthing compartments of the six destroyers transporting the regiment. They learned that they were being attached to the Seventeenth Army Command, based at Truk in the Caroline Islands, their destination. According to the sailors, who had access to radio traffic, the unthinkable had happened. Japan was being counter-attacked on an island in the Solomon chain.

On 7 August, U.S. forces landed on Guadalcanal, Solomon Islands, just as Imperial Army engineers, supplemented by local labourers, were completing an airstrip. The island was intended as a key location for Japanese aviators when initially conceived. When the enemy landings occurred, the engineers and many of the conscripted labourers escaped into the jungles that surrounded the nearly completed airfield. They had informed the Army of the landings before they escaped and thus caused a great deal of discussion among senior officers. Between the planners on the Army staff and the conflicting information contained in the intelligence reports, two vastly different evaluations emerged:

(1) Enemy forces were on Guadalcanal, but in limited strength, in essence a strong patrol. This school of thought felt certain that those few troops would interrupt construction of the airstrip then leave the island without confronting the Imperial Army.

(2) The enemy were on the island in at least regimental force and intended to capture the entire island in order to use the landing strip as a base for attacks on Japanese shipping and other nearby Japanese-held islands.

All of this was unknown to Taki since it took place at high command levels. In the end, the coterie anticipating minimal enemy troops on Guadalcanal prevailed and the information was communicated through appropriate command levels, finally reaching Colonel Ichiki, commander of the 28th Infantry Regiment. After reviewing the plans for re-taking the island, Ichiki confidently vowed to his superiors that he would recapture the airport on the second day after landing.[12]

Ichiki's men were honoured to be under his command. He had established himself as an aggressive, bold and brave leader. Many believed he had personally started the war with China at the Marco Polo Bridge confrontation at Wanping in 1937. His further experience in Manchuria against the Russians identified him as a young, assertive company commander, a reputation that followed him thus far in his career. It was not lost on his seniors when they were looking for regimental commanders.[13] Taki was proud to be a rifleman of the 4th Company, 2nd Battalion, 28th Regiment – and an expert rifleman at that. The Guadalcanal landing on 19 August was burned within Taki's memory as the day he became a warrior.

Intelligence reports provided to Ichiki indicated only a small enemy force would oppose his men. On 15 August he ordered the regiment's 3,000 soldiers embarked on six destroyers at Truk for a night landing at Guadalcanal's Taivu Point, roughly

35 kilometres east of the enemy encampment around the airstrip. He further reasoned he would not need the entire regiment if the force he faced was indeed small. After arriving offshore of Guadalcanal, he ordered 917 soldiers (about one-third of the regiment) into landing craft to make a silent landing on the beaches. This detached group included the 2nd Battalion, 28th Infantry Regiment, with a few artillery pieces and engineers. Known as the 'Ichiki Detachment', its orders were to remain on the beach until the balance of the regiment landed. The full regiment's mission then, once totally off-loaded, was to recapture the airfield and drive the allied forces from the island. If the enemy could not be driven from the island or annihilated, Ichiki's force would hold at the airfield and execute night attacks to halt construction.

Coupled with the 'Ichiki Detachment' landing was a feint by a small 250-man force of Special Naval Landing Force personnel. They would go ashore at Kokumbona, about 14 kilometres west of the airstrip, to divert enemy attention from the main landing. Taki knew that these were sailors trained in Army tactics and tasked with specific objectives apart from the Army's.

Taki felt it would be a quick victory, because the attacking units were instructed to take only 250 rounds of ammunition, seven days' supply of food and no field packs. He was particularly pleased he would not be laden with the 20-kilo field pack in the heat of this battle. And now, as he stood at the ship's rail in the darkness, only the sound of soldiers quietly working their rifle bolts and the muted squeaks of leather ammunition pouches were audible above the gentle swells of the sea. The air, even at this hour, was moist and hot. He recalled the steam baths of his home town – but only for a moment. Orders to report to debarkation stations broke his reverie.

It was 19 August 1942 at 0100 when Taki stood with his unit at the debarkation station awaiting his turn to go over the rail, down the rope netting and into the small landing craft that would ferry him to shore. After checking and re-checking his equipment, and a last shrug of his shoulder to make sure his rifle was secured by its sling, he clambered over the railing and down the net into the waiting small craft rising and falling gently beneath him. Following his training, he waited until the craft was on the rise of the swell before stepping from the net on to the craft's gunwale and on down to the deck of the boat. The last soldier was off the nets. It was time for his baptism of fire.

As the boat's coxswain steered away from the destroyer, Taki scanned the men aboard. He saw the emotion etched in their faces. He personally was trembling with fear and was somewhere between vomiting and collapse. But knowing the others were feeling the same way somehow made it a little easier for him. As the boat's engine responded to the throttle and its bow turned to port and headed towards the island, he managed to raise his head high enough to get a brief look at the shoreline. He strained his eyes, but saw nothing more than a wide strip of beach and the outline of palm trees in the darkness ahead. Beyond the trees lay the black depth of the jungle. There were no accurate maps of this island so even though, as a trained scout, he was an expert map reader and could find his way using a compass, those skills, he knew, were moot.

The wooden craft skidded up the beach approach, its bow raising slightly as it lurched to a full stop, engine at idle speed, then quiet. Only the waves lapping the beach made any sound now. Upon order from an NCO, the troops stood and clambered up and over the gunwales of the craft to jump down on to the soft, wet sand of the beach. Fearing detection by enemy scouts, the detachment moved quickly across the beach and assembled under the cover offered by the palms and mangroves lining the edge of the jungle.[14]

Expecting token resistance when they alighted from their landing craft, to Taki's surprise and relief, they found the beach deserted. Now, still believing the island to be lightly defended, Colonel Ichiki, who always led from the front, ordered a rearguard of 125 soldiers be left at the landing site at the beach. Taki was glad he would not be left in the rearguard, and looked forward to honouring Japan with his bravery. Unknown to the Ichiki Detachment, however, the command decisions upon which the assault was planned were based on poor intelligence derived from erroneous assessments by Japanese administrators. Those plans would yield horrific results.

Not 2,000, as intelligence reported, but 11,000 U.S. Marines were aware of the landing. Their listening posts had heard the destroyers steam past. They immediately notified their commanders and the Marines quickly formed a full defensive perimeter inland from what they judged as the most logical landing point for Japanese troops; the lagoon that natives called 'Alligator Creek'. The defenders had guessed correctly. Digging in defensive positions became a priority.

Colonel Ichiki's orders were issued for the detachment to march west along the coast under cover of darkness. At 0630, after marching 14 kilometres across the beach, he ordered the troops into the cover of the jungle's edge to rest and avoid detection from the air. During the night march, gunfire had echoed across the water from the direction of Tulagi Island to the north, but it was unclear to Taki who was firing at what target.[15]

Early on 20 August, Ichiki ordered Captain Shibuya to assemble thirty-eight soldiers to take a patrol farther west and establish a communication point at Alligator Creek.[16] In fact, 'Alligator Creek' was not a creek, but rather a tidal stream that held running water only during the rainy season or during high tides. And the reptiles it held were not alligators, but crocodiles, a fine distinction if you were in the water near a large one. This lagoon, approximately 30 metres wide, was contained behind a 3-metre-high sand bar that varied between 10 and 15 metres wide along its length. The side towards the island was higher than the seaward side. It looked like a castle moat, but without a building inside.

Taki was 'volunteered' by his squad leader to go with the Shibuya patrol as a scout. He had not yet met the enemy, but felt honoured that he would be in the lead of this patrol as its point man. Captain Shibuya ordered the men to march through the jungle to avoid detection from the air. As he struggled just 50 metres ahead of the main unit, hacking his way through the dense vegetation with his bayonet, Taki kept his senses on high alert. Fighting through the jungle was a most difficult method of advancing, but he continued to move slowly and cautiously forward. Once he thought he glimpsed an island native scurry away through the bush. Certainly the local population posed no threat to an armed patrol! The thought that the native might report the patrol's movements to the enemy never crossed his mind.

As they marched through the thick, rotting mass of greenery, rifle and automatic weapons fire rang out. The patrol was suddenly engaged from the front. Dropping prone behind a palm trunk, Taki unslung his Arisaka, cycled the bolt to ram the 6.5-mm cartridge into the chamber and carefully slid its muzzle over a protrusion of the palm base. The camouflage he had inserted in the netting of his helmet made it difficult for the enemy to see his position. He wondered, for a second, if he had enough foliage in the net. His heart pounded so loudly in his ears, he was afraid the enemy might hear it. They were trying to kill him!

The patrol was confronted by the enemy in strength. Taki couldn't think or feel anything; it seemed as though his body was moving almost instinctively from the training he had undergone over the past two years. In one sense, the supersonic snap of bullets passing overhead made him want to burrow deeper into the stinking floor of the jungle. In another, detached-from-reality sense, he wanted to fight back. He finally summoned the courage to aim at a helmet just barely visible in the greenery 60 metres ahead.

Not even consciously recalling his rifle training, he formed the proper sight picture, the enemy helmet perched atop his front sight, centred in the rear sight; he slowly inhaled then let part of the air out as he squeezed the trigger steadily with the first joint of his index finger. The play in the trigger was taken up and the firm feel of its resistance led to a loud report from the muzzle. The recoil of the rifle shocked him into an acute awareness of what was going on around him. The helmet in his sight jerked backward as the target toppled over. His first kill.

His senses verified a slowing of fire from the front, but now the rounds were coming from the south, their left flank. The patrol was being outflanked! Unsure of where to direct fire, they were caught in a murderous crossfire of rifle, machine-gun and submachine-gun fire. Captain Shibuya screamed orders to his men, but few heard over the din of the battle at hand. Some turned to fire southward into the flankers; others kept their sights trained on the enemy to the west. It soon became obvious they were trapped.[17] With the enemy in front and to their left, the sea to their right, they had only one route to survival – retreat into the darkness of the jungle. The tables had been turned. They, rather than the enemy, had been surprised. Taki made his way south-eastward, struggling through the undergrowth, evading capture.

Only four others managed to escape the enemy trap into the dark cover of the jungle canopy and its undergrowth. Diving under the exposed roots of the giant trees, Taki burrowed his face into the slimy floor beneath the canopy of palms and mangroves, hoping he had not been seen. His shirt was tattered from several rounds of near-miss rifle fire, and his ears rang from his own gunfire. But he was alive and it was all that mattered to him right now. His rifle and telescope in its leather case were unharmed; his ammunition and rations were still with him. He knew he had seven day's rations, so he felt certain he could survive until the rest of the regiment landed and eliminated the enemy. And he had ammunition with which to 'go hunting' these butchers who killed his friends and fellow soldiers. What he did not know was that the remainder of the regiment would not land this day. The destroyers that delivered the leading part of the detachment into this maelstrom of gunfire were leaving them to fend for themselves on this godforsaken piece of real estate called Guadalcanal.

As the sound of the initial battle faded away to a random rifle shot here and there, Taki began crawling farther into the undergrowth, but now westward towards the enemy positions. He would use the skills he had learned on the rifle range to eliminate as many of them as he could.

After crawling nearly 200 metres, he heard the sound of voices. They were not speaking Japanese, but English! Silently digging a shallow hole with his bare hands, he slowly pulled his rifle by its sling up along his body so he could position his hands in the shooting position. Sliding the sling up on his left bicep, he made the final adjustments in his firing position. Estimating the range at 80 metres, he selected an enemy soldier who appeared to be an NCO or officer. Again his practised trigger squeeze began and the rifle bucked against his shoulder. This time he kept his eyes open as the round slammed home in the neck of his target. The victim dropped straight down, crumpling like a piece of rice paper in an origami contest. The remainder of the enemy soldiers nearby dropped to the ground immediately, all facing outward. He knew the propellant used in his ammunition was nearly smokeless and the muzzle blast of his rifle had hardly moved the underbrush around it. Even knowing all of that, he also knew he could not fire from this position again. To do so would invite accurate return fire.

As he rotated the bolt handle upward and to the rear to eject the spent cartridge, the tree tops to his left were suddenly shredded by gunfire. With his head quickly buried in the soggy slime beneath him, he sensed that the enemy heard the sound of the action of the bolt, but had no idea from where the sound emanated. That information would be useful to him later. He had made mental notes as he watched the way the enemy went through all the pockets of his dead comrades.[18] What were they after? Souvenirs? Information? What information did his patrol carry with them? The questions had no immediate answers for Taki as he lay in his pit of smelly, rotted plant material.

He waited for what seemed hours before the enemy soldiers began to leave the area. Finally, he felt safe enough to move about. Cold, wet and hungry, he still could not be certain of the enemy's locations. He wondered about the fate of his friends. Was he on his own or could he find them? Again, no answers came. When finally the last of the enemy troops left the area, Taki crawled out to the bodies of his dead comrades. Checking what the enemy took from the pockets of the casualties but left behind would give him a good sense of what they took with them. Scattered around the bodies were wallets, photographs, letters from loved ones, cash and even wrist watches. He did *not* see any official documents like orders or maps. Conclusion? They took what they needed from the corpses and left. The damage done to the bodies by enemy bullets sickened him. He vomited and the acidic sourness of an empty stomach would always remind him of his dead comrades.

Ichiki soon learned of Shibuya's rout and elected to respond with the rest of the detachment. His men shouldered their weapons and set a westward course to meet the enemy. They marched through the night, arriving west of the Nalimbu River at 0430. They were just 8 kilometres east of the enemy defensive line. On 20 August at 1200, Ichiki issued the attack plan to his officers. The 1st Company would attack westward on the sandbar, the 2nd Company would attack on the beach and the 3rd Company would attack inland. The intent was to capture the former Special Naval Landing Force camp between the Lunga River and Alligator Creek, fan out to capture the airfield then establish positions east of the Lunga using it as a frontal barrier.

Once all units were in position, the attack began at 0200 with a green signal flare. The 2nd Company's attack across the sand-bar was first decimated by 37-mm canister fire at point-blank range and, as the survivors raced onward, they became entangled in the single strand of barbed wire that fronted the enemy positions. Machine-gun bullets again laced the charging troops but, in spite of the wall of fire, several reached the fighting holes of the defenders. The hand-to-hand combat was ferocious; defenders used their empty rifles as spears or clubs, attackers their bayonets; knives drawn and pistols un-holstered, both attackers and defenders fought for their lives.

The Imperial Japanese Army believed so strongly in the warrior ethic, that in its training, it inculcated the notion that when a Japanese force attacked, the enemy would break and run. This had been their experience in South-east Asia and China. But in their first encounter with U.S. Marines, that did not prove to be the case. Those men fought like devils. In less than an hour, all the Japanese soldiers inside the barbed wire were dead or dying. Ichiki ordered his machine-gun company into action but it was too little, too late. Enemy artillery found the range and quickly put the machine guns out of the fight as they tried to outflank the defenders.

The sound of the battle reached Taki and, duty bound, he turned northward to re-unite with the Detachment. He was tired, hungry, shaken and dripping with the residue of lying on the jungle floor, but after scraping the leeches off his legs and arms with his bayonet, he drove himself onward, hoping to reach his unit in time to fight again. As he neared the area, a cacophony of small-arms, machine-gun and artillery fire coming from enemy weapons pierced his hearing. He could scarcely imagine what was happening to his unit.

As the night of 21 August turned to 22 August, the defenders had launched a counter-attack that compressed Ichiki's force into a triangle near the mouth of Alligator Creek. Trapped, with the sea to their backs, and enemy tanks clanking across the sandbar towards them, some tried to swim to safety but were found with accurate fire. Colonel Ichiki took his own life in atonement for his failure.[19] By 1630, the Ichiki Detachment was non-existent. The wounded prepared themselves as human booby traps, concealing hand grenades beneath their bodies. When a defender approached to inspect the dead, he would be exposed to the blast as the soldier died honourably for his Emperor. Taki was horrified by what happened next.

Quickly coming to realize the Japanese soldier's fight-to-the-death attitude, the enemy coldly went about shooting every body on the battlefield to be sure that they were dead.[20] He watched as the corpses jumped when hit with rifle or pistol shots and it sickened him; and angered him. He vowed they would pay. He was a survivor and managed to escape into the jungle without being detected. How long would it be before reinforcements arrived? What was he to do in the meantime? Where was he? Were there other survivors? Many questions. No answers, yet. Of the 915 men who landed with the Detachment, 777 were dead, 12 wounded (including 1 officer) were captured, 2 unwounded were captured and 1 surrendered voluntarily. Only 123 other soldiers survived.[21]

Finding a glade well inland among the shadowing palms, Taki turned slowly and did a 360-degree survey of the terrain. His training told him to return to the point from which he started, so he headed towards the coast, taking a circuitous route to avoid detection. Other survivors in groups of two or three dutifully followed him back to Taivu Point.[22] With only his bayonet to slash away at the dense undergrowth, it took several hours and multiple rest breaks to move just a short distance. But once free of the jungle, they sped their march back. Ravenously hungry, they raided the produce of local native gardens as they marched. They could not know that they had been 'written off' as casualties by their leadership. Taking to the jungle to avoid being seen from the air during daylight hours, they soon fell into a loose routine of hide, drink, find food, sleep, march then repeat it the next day. Slowly the group began to disintegrate as each soldier, tired, hungry, sick or wounded, began deciding for himself what his duty required.

Each night as he settled down to sleep, Taki was aware of the constant buzz of insects hungry to feed on warm blood. Missing his lost mosquito netting, he slapped and smacked at them for a short time before he dropped into a deep, exhausted slumber, unaware that these little creatures carried diseases that could disable an entire army – malaria and dengue fever. As he slept, they feasted.

As the 23 August morning sun fought its way through the canopy of the jungle, the dreadful feeling of being alone suddenly gripped him, causing him to shudder slightly. Was it from the cold, stinking muck of the jungle floor? Or was it because he was now a target of the enemy's guns? As he stood in the dank air, dim sunlight filtering through the palm leaves, thinking about his situation, his training began to take over. He objectively reviewed his circumstances in the systematic way he was taught: On the positive side of the ledger, he had food, adequate but soaking-wet clothing, ample ammunition, a weapon and, perhaps most importantly, he was unseen and thus had the capability to kill at will. On the negative side, he might well be trapped by enemy forces, unable to contact his commanders for orders. His next steps became crystal clear. He would hide himself in the jungle until Colonel Ichiki brought the rest of the regiment west

Simo Häyhä during his time in action and subsequently with the consequences of his severe wound.

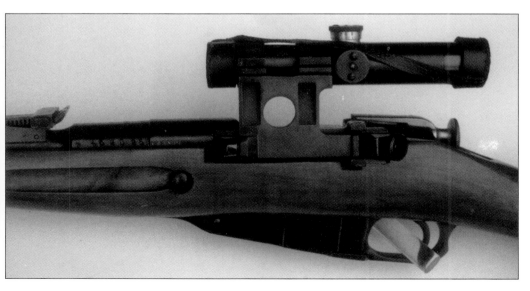

A Soviet Mosin-Nagant 1891/30 rifle with PE scope, the most commonly used rifle and scope combination on the Eastern Front. The Mosin-Nagant rifle was also widely used by Finnish snipers.

British No. 4 Mk 1(T) rifle, with No. 32 scope. The right-side image offers a good view of the cheek pad and scope; note the three sling swivels to allow attachment of a sniping sling. The left-side view shows the two knobs used to tighten the screws which attach the scope. Note that the rifle is cocked and the safety applied for this photo.

Right & below right: Closer views of the No. 32 scope, showing the windage and elevation adjustment dials.

Right : German Kar 98k with Ajak scope on a high turret mount.

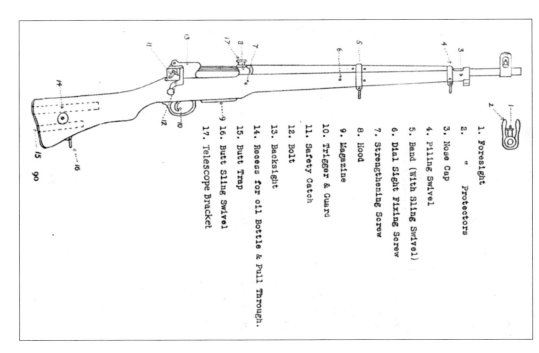

1. Foresight
2. " Protectors
3. Nose Cap
4. Piling Swivel
5. Band (with Sling Swivel)
6. Dial Sight Fixing Screw
7. Strengthening Screw
8. Hood
9. Magazine
10. Trigger & Guard
11. Safety Catch
12. Bolt
13. Backsight
14. Recess for oil Bottle & Pull Through.
15. Butt Trap
16. Butt Sling Swivel
17. Telescope Bracket

Diagram of the preferred British WWII sniper rifle – the P14. Longer and heavier than the SMLE Mk III, the standard British Army rifle in the Second World War, it proved to be more accurate. From Lt Col Nevill Armstrong's *Fieldcraft, Sniping and Intelligence* manual of 1944.

British sniping pioneer of the First World War, H. V. Hesketh-Pritchard.

Sniping trainer and theorist of the Second World War, Captain C. Shore.

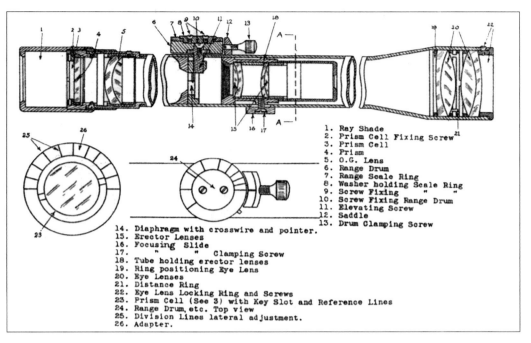

1. Ray Shade
2. Prism Cell Fixing Screw
3. Prism Cell
4. Prism
5. O.G. Lens
6. Range Drum
7. Range Scale Ring
8. Washer holding Scale Ring
9. Screw Fixing   "   "
10. Screw Fixing Range Drum
11. Elevating Screw
12. Saddle
13. Drum Clamping Screw
14. Diaphragm with crosswire and pointer.
15. Erector Lenses
16. Focusing Slide
17.   "   "   Clamping Screw
18. Tube holding erector lenses
19. Ring positioning Eye Lens
20. Eye Lenses
21. Distance Ring
22. Eye Lens Locking Ring and Screws
23. Prism Cell (See 3) with Key Slot and Reference Lines
24. Range Drum, etc. Top view
25. Division Lines lateral adjustment.
26. Adapter.

Diagram of the P18 1940 telescopic sights used with the P14 rifle. To prepare its use, two shots were fired to warm the barrel. The required standard of grouping was five rounds in 3 inches at 100 yards. Any adjustments could then be made. From Lt Col Armstrong's *Fieldcraft, Sniping and Intelligence* manual of 1944.

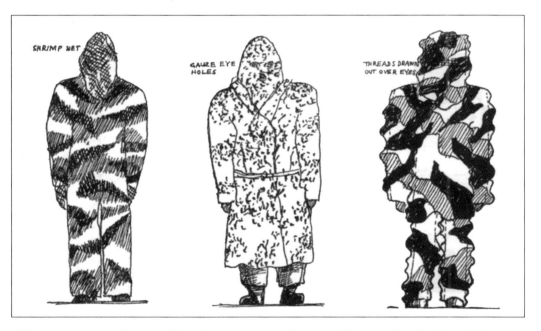

Three versions of camouflaged sniper suits designed for use by the British Home Guard. From Roland Penrose's *Home Guard Manual of Camouflage* of 1941.

Top: Lyudmila Pavlichenko was the most successful Russian female sniper of the Second World War, with over 300 confirmed kills.

Above: Russian sniper Yelizaveta Miranova appeared in a propaganda film, and was reported to have shot 34 Germans.

Left: A student at Kiev University when Germany invaded the Ukraine, within the year Pavlichenko became the most dangerous woman on earth.

Right: Bedecked in medals, sniper Lyudmila Pavlichenko poses following the war. Her awards included Hero of The Soviet Union, the highest distinction offered any Soviet citizen. Of 11,635 HSU recipients during the war, 92 were women and of those only 42 survived the war.

Below: Sniper Lyudmila Pavlichenko at work near Odessa soon after Hitler invaded the Ukraine. When he met her later actor Charlie Chaplin exclaimed, 'It's quite remarkable that these small, delicate hands killed Nazis by the hundreds.'

A U.S. Army sniper seen in a publicity photo with a
Springfield Model 1903-A4 sniper rifle.

Bert Kemp as a little boy, with his sister
Gertie on the horse.

Bert on leave after returning from
Sicily, on the farm with his father.

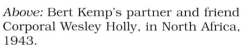

Above: Bert Kemp's partner and friend Corporal Wesley Holly, in North Africa, 1943.

Above right: Bert Kemp at the time of his medical discharge, December 1944.

Right: Bert Kemp in later years.

Left: Masters of camouflage, Japanese snipers often covered their heads with mosquito netting and their shoulders with woven palm fibre to disappear among the palm trees.

Left: Henderson Field, Guadalcanal, seen from a USS *Saratoga*-based aircraft in August 1942. Note the aircraft dispersed at the left end of the runway among bomb and shell craters. The Lunga River is at the top of the photograph. Bloody Ridge is just out of the picture to the left.

Right: To climb palm trees, Japanese snipers tied special climbing spikes to their feet.

Below: Five of the nine destroyed Japanese tanks of the 1st Independent Tank Company at the mouth of the Matanikau River, Guadalcanal, following the fighting on 22 October 1942.

Guadalcanal. Japanese dead on the beach following the battle of Alligator Creek
(or Tenaru River), 20–21 August 1942.

A U.S. Marine sniper on Tarawa poses for the camera.
He is using one of the original Marine match-grade
Springfield M1903 rifles with a pre-WWII Lyman or Stevens scope.

Two Marines with Unertl-equipped Springfields on Okinawa in May 1945.
The Unertl with 8-power magnification excelled at long-range shooting.

A very clean Marine on Russell Island in 1944 with a brand-new Springfield
1903-A4. The lack of iron sights is clearly visible here and was a serious
shortcoming in the close-quarter fighting during many Pacific island battles.

Snipers of the Soviet 104th Rifle Division in March 1943. The man on the left wears a pre-war pattern of winter camouflage, the other a version introduced in 1941.

Soviet snipers on the Karelian Front during the Continuation War against Finland.

A Soviet sniper in action against the Finnish Army. His uniform is well camouflaged, but the failure to camouflage his rifle could be a fatal error.

Generals Chuikov and Gurov examine Vassili Zaitsev's sniper rifle. Zaitsev can be seen on the far right in the white camouflage suit.

Snipers of the Russian 32nd Army after being decorated. They wear summer
overalls as they might in combat, but of course would not sport any conspicuous
decorations in action.

A portrait of Hitler is prepared for service as a target during Soviet
sniper training. The student facing the camera is holding a
Mosin-Nagant 1891/30 rifle with PE sight.

A Soviet illustration (*above right*) of how
to use a camouflage screen during
sniping operations, and (*right*) a screen
of this type being used by a female
sniper–observer pair.

Making good use of natural camouflage to disguise both uniform and helmet, this Soviet sniper prepares to take his shot.

A heavily camouflaged Russian sniper team.

A pair of Russian snipers stalks along a river bank to gain a favourable
position to attack a German unit.

A Red Army soldier takes aim with a M1893/30 Mosin-Nagant rifle, here fitted
with a side-rail mounted PEM telescopic sight.

Sometimes the old methods worked. A squad of American infantry try to locate a German sniper by using a helmet as a target.

A U.S. Army sniper cleans his Model 1903-A4 rifle during the Italian campaign. Its Lyman scope was low-powered but this was not a serious drawback in the street and village fighting of much of the European campaign.

Although more of an aid to aiming than a true sniper scope, the little 1.5-power Zf.41 scope shown here was issued in huge numbers to the German Army.

The German G 43 semi-automatic rifle with Zf.4 scope pictured during trials. Once initial reliability problems were overcome, some 55,000 were issued to snipers.

In the early days of the Eastern Front campaign a German sniper aims a
First World War-vintage Gewehr 98 sniping rifle.

German artist Willy Herman painted
this portrait of a German 73rd Division
sniper, Private Hortnek, watching for
Allied soldiers on the Western Front.

Two British snipers lead a patrol in France, summer 1944. The thick *bocage* terrain is evident here. Neither sniper has a scope fitted to his rifle; these were of little use in such country.

A British sergeant is seen cleaning a Lee-Enfield sniping rifle using a German aluminium pull-through. This is presumably a posed photograph since it will be difficult to carry out this operation with the bolt still in situ!

Above: Patrick Devlin, as seen in a photo preserved with his papers in the Imperial War Museum.

Left: Sgt Harry Furness wearing a two-piece smock over his battledress.

Below left: Sgt Harry Furness at the end of the war.

Below: A Canadian sniper in a Denison smock. His weaponry includes a kukri!

to engage the enemy. In the meantime, he would put his ammunition to good use.

After making his way through the jungle, leaving trail markers in his wake so as to find his way back, he reached an irregular ridge not far from the airstrip. He could hear the take-off and landing roar of the engines as enemy aircraft came and went. He took the body netting from his belt and began to insert the grasses that grew along the ridge. Stuffing some of it in his helmet net, he crept to the top of the ridge to get in position to acquire targets. He crawled to within 200 metres of the field, and chose a rise in the ground that was covered with the same grass as he had stuffed in his camouflage nets. Lying still, he slowly reached behind him and retrieved the telescope from its leather case. He smeared some dirt on the tube to avoid reflection, then attached it to the scope mounts of his rifle.

Peering through the scope, he slowly scanned the enemy perimeter left to right, then back again. There were sentries posted all around the airfield, but they were stationed only about 100 metres distant from the field's edge. He was not interested in them. He wanted bigger game: a senior commander; a pilot perhaps; or at least a senior NCO. He spotted a lone Marine making his way across the end of the runway and began his firing cycle – aim, hold, breathe in, let half out, squeeze the trigger. The round left his rifle but missed its mark as the soldier bent over to pick up a dropped object. The supersonic snap of the round overhead immediately brought the entire section of sentries to high alert. He lay still and waited for another target to appear. He succeeded on his next shot – an officer, he thought. Maybe even a pilot! One more shot and then he would move to another location. That target, too went down when the round hit. It was time to move out. Backing slowly down from the rise, he rose to his feet, and keeping a half-crouch, made his way to the tall grass and the trail markers he would follow back to his hillside hide.

Taki would continue this routine for the next seven days. His food gone, he was reduced to eating betel nuts, coconut, red ants and snails.[23] His water came from a hilltop stream that ran close by his camp. His clothes were nearly in tatters and he was covered with insect bites and leech blisters that nearly drove him insane with the itching that accompanied them. But his rifle was in good order and he had husbanded his ammunition well. On the night of 29 August, from his perch, he saw the approach of ships, darkened for stealth. Some 450 of the 124th Infantry and 300 of Ichiki's Second Echelon were landed at Taivu Point.[24] The next night the balance of the 28th Regiment was landed along with supplies. More would follow. On 31 August, General Kawaguchi, now the senior commander, brought another 1,200 soldiers ashore.[25]

Kawaguchi had ordered Colonel Akinosuku Oka to land 1,000 troops west of the Matanikau River near the site of the former Naval Landing Force camp. In transit, enemy night fighter planes strafed some of the sixty-one barges carrying them, and as a result, Oka's troops became separated, landing at different points along the coast west of the allied perimeter. Finally, only about 600 effectives could be assembled.[26]

By 5 September, Kawaguchi's total force totalled 6,200 versus what he still believed to be 2,000 U.S. Marines defending the airfield and the small perimeter around it. The estimate of enemy strength was low by a factor of six. There were nearly 12,000 U.S. Marines defending what they now called 'Henderson Field'.[27]

After a week of creeping about between his hillside hide and Taivu Point, Taki met more fellow survivors hiding in the jungle. They were elated when Kawaguchi's force landed. The survivors were absorbed into 3rd Battalion, 124th Infantry Regiment (III/124), fed, given clean, dry, uniforms, and de-briefed on what problems the jungle presented. They could relax, even if for a few hours. While Kawaguchi waited on additional forces to land, planning was in motion for the taking of the airstrip – the original objective of the assault.

On 8 September, III/124, now assembled at Koli Point,[28] was ready to head into the jungle, intending to attack the field from the south as their part of the assault on the Marine perimeter. As Taki feared, in spite of his debriefing that warned of the difficulty presented by the jungle, his officers underestimated its resistance to penetration. It became a second enemy to fight. The

III/124 started into the jungle and, soaked by a rain shower and their own sweat, they slipped, tripped and slogged their way towards the airstrip. Mosquitoes feasted on the troops as though they had never had warm human blood before. Slaps and curses were the only sounds apart from the grunts and groans when a soldier fell in the muck beneath his feet. And that was only part of the problem.

Having no accurate maps to guide them, the III/124 got lost and didn't reach their attack position until the early hours of 12 September,[29] the date the attack was to have begun. Kawaguchi was also unaware that part of his force still marching west along the coast had met disaster at Tasimbogo, losing artillery pieces and radio equipment to an enemy seaborne raid. He was also unaware that Oka had not got his troops under way at sundown on 11 September. They did not begin eastward until 0400 on 12 September and by 2200 his troops could hear the gunfire, but were not near enough to assist in the attack. They were hungry, tired, disease-ridden and harried by insects after having marched for eighteen straight hours.[30] Regardless, Kawaguchi's plan continued to unfold because the main force was seemingly undetected.

Native scouts had in fact reported to the defenders that Japanese columns were moving towards the perimeter. The Marines adjusted their defences to meet the new threat. Their artillery and mortars were re-zeroed on the path judged to the one taken by the attackers, a 900-metre-long crooked ridge with a 24-metre high knoll at its south end. There was a second knoll in the centre rising approximately 35 metres above sea level. The ridge resembled an insect with leg-like spurs running off either side. It was covered with grass rather than jungle foliage and its features could allow attacking units to approach unseen. To minimize the chance for a surprise, the defenders had cleared brush to open fields of fire for their machine guns in preparation for the anticipated attack. But even so, the defending forces comprised a thin line of tired, hungry and sleep-deprived fighters.[31]

Taki was sent ahead of the attacking force to scout the defences, but the clearing along the ridge would not allow him to get close enough to make any accurate assessment of the defensive array. Freshening the blended camouflage in his helmet net and on the back and sides of his torso netting, he crept through the heat-holding cogon grass to a rise that allowed him to aim his rifle. Scanning from right to left and back, he observed digging activity, barbed wire being strung, and communication lines being laid all along the ridge before him. An officer appeared to be supervising the work – a perfect target at 150 metres. Taking careful aim, Taki automatically went through his practised sequence of actions – attain the proper sight picture through the scope; inhale; let part of the breath out and hold it; squeeze the trigger slowly and smoothly; let the report of the rifle surprise you. As the rifle slammed back into his shoulder, he watched his target spin to the right and fall to the ground. All work stopped and there were no other targets available. Was it a kill or not? Taki never knew on that particular shot. But it was one officer that would not fight today. He scrambled back to the command area and reported what he had seen to his superiors. It was time to attack, but where was III/124? He was sent towards the Lunga River to find them.

Kawaguchi had set 2000 as the jump-off time of the attack across the ridge, but only I/124 was present. III/124 (except for Taki, the scout) along with II/4 arrived at the jump-off point two hours late. The three battalions, over 2,500 strong, lurched forward only to lose their sense of direction and nearly miss the ridge. They slewed into the swampy lowland area between the edge of the jungle and the ridge.[32] The units broke down into smaller ones, then they scattered and some became intermingled, all this working together to wreak havoc on the command and control effort. It was to be small groups of infantrymen against a thin line of Marines and the jungle.

As Taki caught up with his unit, it met I/124 on the march and the two soon became mixed together. Finally I/124 was ordered to the west side of the Lunga River so the two could be separated. But now it was only an hour before sun-up, much too late for a night attack. III/124, finally separated from I/124, continued forward until it hit the enemy defence line but could not exploit an initial opportunity. Two of its officers were killed, which left the battalion without direction. Some of the men had discovered gaps in the enemy line and raced through them with fixed bayonets, shooting from the hip as they ran. But once within the line, they became confused without leadership and made a careful withdrawal.[33]

The rumour mill had it that Colonel Oka's march eastward had failed to meet orders and, as a result, the enemy perimeter was attacked from one side rather than three, as planned. On 13 September, Oka requested via radio that Kawaguchi delay the jump-off time to enable his men to reach a position to attack from the south-west. An irate General Kawaguchi had suffered all the delays he would tolerate and he ordered the decisive assault to begin at 2200. During the day, bombs rained all along the ridge as the Imperial Army Air Force supported the infantry. But the concentration of bombs served to telegraph to the defenders exactly where the Japanese infantry attack would occur. The defensive positions were re-set 200 metres to the rear to improve the position and confuse the attackers.[34]

In spite of Kawaguchi's orders, I/124 began its attack at 1830 and struck the defence 500 metres east of the Lunga River and south of the ridge. By 2100, enemy artillery, previously ranged, struck the attackers and 'walked' to within 200 metres of the lines. The 1st Battalion commander was killed. Even so, by 2230, the main force had hit the ridge. Mortar fire from the Japanese side began to rain down on the battlefield; in response enemy grenades were rolled down the hill into gathering areas for the attackers. Finally the red flare went up, signalling the general attack. Moving at a crouch, with fixed bayonets, they charged with screams of '*Banzai!*', headlong into the line of rifle and machine-gun fire.

II/4's 5th and 7th Companies struck on the edge of the ridge. 7th Company reached the north-east side of the ridge and commanders committed the remaining fifty or sixty soldiers of the 6th Company to press on even after their commanding officer went down wounded. They arrived at the west edge of the small fighter airstrip at 0530, but were stopped by the defenders there.

Kawaguchi's reserve battalion (III/124) never got into the action, but might have won the day had it been involved. They were lost in the jungle and leaderless until at 1930 they decided to strike out with a junior officer in charge. By the time they reached the battle lines, it was essentially over – it was dawn.[35]

The attack abated with the sunrise, but small groups of both sides exchanged fire frequently as they patrolled their fronts. Taki seized the opportunity to practise his craft, taking numerous shots from between 150 and 300 metres as he moved constantly after each shot. He believed he scored twelve hits – a good day indeed. But the overall verdict on the attack was – in a word – defeat.

On 14 September, Kawaguchi ordered a withdrawal across the Matanikau River. During the days spent on the march westward across the jagged foothills of the mountains, both the jungle and hunger began to pose a threat to his troops. Those who could walk supplemented their meagre diet with betel nuts, snails and other vegetation harvested along the way. The lucky ones found killing fish with hand grenades beneficial.[36] The wounded were carried by four men, a fifth man carrying the gear of the other four. These five were followed by five more who would resume carrying the casualty when the first group needed a rest or could not continue. Some wounded died as the rough handling of the litters opened wounds already infested with maggots. As men marched on, weapons fell by the wayside as the strength to carry them waned. Heavy weapons first, then helmets and rifles. They finally reached Kokumbona at 1400 on 19 August.[37]

Using the next ten days to re-structure, re-supply and receive reinforcements, Kawaguchi made plans for his next attack while organizing his unit for defence. II/124 and III/124 were ordered to hold the high ground along the coast, the expected route of enemy attack. Taki was assigned as a scout for this group and established his post well ahead of the battalions.[38] Orders to seize the east bank of the Matanikau River were finalized, so the now-present artillery pieces could be sighted in there. This did not fit within Kawaguchi's previous plan.[39]

On 27 September, the enemy approached the one-log bridge via the upper Matanikau's east bank and were engaged by the

12th Company, which was supported by mortars from the west bank. Meanwhile, 9th Company attacked across the sandbar at the mouth of the river into the teeth of murderous fire from a battalion of Marines. At 1330, the attack was renewed but again repelled. The enemy reached the rear of the attacking force by barging three companies of Marines to land on a beach west of Point Cruz. They trudged inland 500 metres to the first ridge line. Colonel Oka ordered II/124, which was located west of the Marine landing site, to attack the enemy rear. Oka believed that the enemy were trapped near the beach and issued orders to destroy them.

II/124 moved farther west and left the destruction of the stranded Marines to the 8th Company. A bitter hand-to-hand battle was fought in the attempt, but shelling from enemy ships caused the 8th Company to break off the attack, a move which enabled the trapped Marines to be evacuated via barge.[40]

On 3 October, Lieutenant General Masao Maruyama, commander of the 2nd Division, landed to take command of all forces on the island and began reinforcing and re-supplying the garrison using what the Imperial Navy called the 'Ant Transport', a group of ships dedicated to supporting the troops on the island. Between 1 and 7 October, some 6,000 men, 51 tons of provisions, seven artillery pieces and tons of ammunition were landed at Tassafaronga. Taki could now count on at least one meal a day, meagre though it was.[41]

At 1000 the enemy made contact with III/4, 500 metres east of the Matanikau River, along the coast road (the Government Track), and they managed to wrest control of 500 metres of the east river bank from II/4. The 3rd Company gave ground grudgingly even as they endured point-blank fire from the Marine 75-mm pack howitzers, but they held the west bank. During the night of 7–8 October, the enemy feinted several attacks at the mouth of the Matanikau to draw attention away from two other enemy units making their way north along the river. These enemy units attacked and drove the 3rd Company towards the coast. They were now trapped with their backs to the river.

Rain, torrential rain, provided some relief from the attack. Footing in the jungle, dicey at best, became terrible with men and equipment slipping and sliding off trails and into the underbrush; but it bought time for the force on the Matanikau. About sundown, the 3rd Company attempted to break out of the pocket and cross the sandbar. The smoke from the smoke grenades intended to hide their move was pressed close to the deck by the rain-cooled air and provided little concealment as they struck the enemy line. Barbed wire broke the onrush of the attackers and it became a confused, brutal, fierce, hand-to-hand fight. Precious few of the 3rd Company soldiers made it across the river.[42]

To a soldier of Taki's rank, the days and nights were becoming irrelevant. His training had emphasized night attacks and surprise. Now *his* unit was experiencing night attacks and surprise from the enemy. He continued his assigned role as a scout and added to his kill list at every opportunity. At last estimate, he thought had killed 3 officers, 11 NCOs and at least 15 other enemy soldiers. But he was never sure exactly how many. The Imperial Japanese Army was now in retreat westwards and because of their lack of training in defensive formations, they were building up defensive sites as they thought best.

On 10 October another new commander arrived in the person of General Hyakutake, commander of the Seventeenth Army, who bore orders from Army HQ, orders which he issued on 15 October. The troops had not had sufficient time to recover from illness, wounds and hunger, yet orders were orders. Colonel Ichiki's orders always stressed simplicity, but the new set of orders laid out a complicated advance against the enemy. And in jungle warfare, complex battle plans very often went awry.

The plan was designed to attack the Marines from all directions, making them spread their forces across a wide battlefront. The plan was fashioned as follows:

(1) Major General Tadashi Sumioshi, commanding the artillery of the Seventeenth Army, would take the big guns down the coast as a diversionary move, with five infantry battalions attached.

(2) I/228 and a company of engineers would land at Koli Point at 0200 on X-Day (the attack date to be decided) because air intelligence had informed Hyakutake that the Marines were building a new airstrip near there.

(3) The Sendai (2nd) Division, commanded by Major General Masao Maruyama (to which Hyakutake would attach his staff and headquarters), would march across the foothills of the little mountain (now called Mount Austen) and follow the Maruyama Road.[43] It would then turn northwards towards the airfield. It was hard jungle marching through unmapped territory. The advantage was that neither natives nor enemy scouts would likely detect their advance.

(4) A jungle march commanded by Major General Yumio Nasu would lead to a turn north down the Lunga's east bank to the airstrip. The core element of his force was the balance of 29th Infantry Regiment.

(5) The right wing would be a force under Major General Kiyotaki Kawaguchi. It included the 230th Infantry Regiment with III/124 filling in for III/130.

(6) General Maruyama would control the 16th Regiment as the division reserve.

The first units left the encampment on 16 October with each man carrying ammunition, an artillery round and twelve days' rations, plus his personal weapons and gear. The artillerymen disassembled their guns and had to carry them piecemeal on the march. They marched by compass, in straight lines overland, unable to avoid difficult terrain. It was not until two days later, 18 October, that the tail end of the column finally saddled up and left the encampment. The head of the 30-kilometre-long column had already crossed the Lunga.[44] On 20 October General Maruyama miscalculated his end-of-march position. He thought he was but 7 kilometres from the airfield, but in reality it was twice that distance.

On the coast, Sumioshi divided his force, sending Colonel Oka with the 124th Infantry Regiment (less 3rd Battalion) south along the west bank of the Matanikau to the One Log Bridge. On the signal, he would attack north along the east bank of the Matanikau River, flanking the enemy line. Sumioshi, leading the northern segment of his divided force himself, remained on the coast with III/4, along with Colonel Nakagama, who commanded I/4 and II/4 plus a tank company.

On the opposite flank, based on new aerial photographs, General Kawaguchi requested permission to re-locate the point of his attack farther east. Maruyama refused and Kawaguchi was relieved of his command. He was replaced by the commander of the 230th Infantry Regiment, Colonel Shoji. The western component's orders to strike the enemy from south-east of the Lunga stood even after Shoji objected to Kawaguchi's relief as 'not the way of the samurai'.[45]

Casting objections aside, Maruyama ordered the final advance to begin at 1800 on 22 October. The army cautiously moved forward towards the enemy lines, preceded by Taki and a host of other scouts. Though the approach was difficult, all units proceeded towards their assigned positions and prepared for the attack. In fact, on 22 October, Oka's group, attempting to flank the enemy, could advance only about a kilometre due to the jungle-covered, deep ravines and small, muddy tributary streams that crossed their route. Oka lost track of two of his three rifle battalions, which had unnecessarily marched farther east but he indicated he would be prepared to attack at 1500 the next day.[46]

For his part Taki was sent forward to scout the enemy defences. He reported that there were small enemy patrols out, apparently trying to locate Maruyama's forces.

X-Day was set for 23 October. Soldiers were ordered to drop their packs and move on the enemy perimeter. The scouts sent out on 22 October had reported only heavy jungle in every direction. But after marching in, around, through, and over the jungle trails to the jumping-off point, troops were on the verge of exhaustion and hardly ready for a frontal assault. Because the army was not ready for attack, X-Day was re-set for 24 October.

The jungle created more than marching problems. Command and control of separated forces is difficult under the best of circumstances. Here, the terrain, weather and obstacles combined to disorganize the force approaching the airfield. Many of the scouts sent out failed to return, being lost in the trackless jungle or killed by enemy fire. On the west flank Sumioshi was unable to pass on the order delaying that attack by a day.

However, the uncoordinated approach did allow the nine tanks to move within 200 metres of the enemy positions on the coast. Their noisy advance was unheard by the enemy due to the sporadic artillery fire aimed at the perimeter. But II/4 didn't start forward until 1700 on the 23rd which made the tanks wait. At dusk the first four tanks began to roll forward, but they were stopped by 37-mm anti-tank gunfire. A second wave of five tanks then crawled forward and into the battle zone. Even though one tank broke through the barbed wire and into the enemy lines, it was soon disabled and abandoned. All nine tanks were destroyed and of the 41 tank crew members in the attack, only 17 survived, 10 of them unwounded.[47]

The battle site's coordinates were well-known to the American artillery and, once the battle began, the attackers were pummelled with over 6,000 rounds, ranging up and down the Japanese line. At 2100, it began to rain and, within an hour, the attack faltered. By 0115 on 24 October all was quiet along the Matanikau.[48]

The main attack on Henderson Field from the south was now set for 1900 on 24 October. At 1600 a torrential rainstorm swept across the island making the Japanese advance even more difficult. But, at 2100, the skies cleared and revealed a beautiful star-lit night. Taki and four other scouts were sent out to locate the barbed wire along the enemy lines. This was not a killing mission, so Taki elected to leave his rifle behind. Crawling slowly under the black night sky, he got close enough to hear the talking (and snoring) of the Marines in holes along the ridge. Some 30 metres in front of them lay the strung barbed wire. Empty ration cans, each holding a few pebbles, so as to rattle if touched, hung at intervals along its length. These served as crude early warning signals. Slowly, he slid backward in the cogon grass until the enemy were no longer able to see him. Rising, and moving in a crouch, he made his way back to report what he had seen.

At 0030 on 25 October an uncoordinated attack opened on the American line. At 0115 the 9th Company charged the machine-gun emplacements in their front and within five minutes all were killed. By 0215, enemy artillery were shelling along the attack route, especially on the path of the left wing of the attackers. They were caught in a depression and quickly came to the conclusion that to stay there was to die; and to run was to risk being lost in the jungle. Many chose to die rather than run.[49] Only one small unit made it into the enemy lines and briefly established a salient of 100 by 150 metres. Counter-attacking Marines killed the little group and managed to capture three Nambu machine guns as well as re-capture two U.S. machine guns. Thirty-seven Imperial Japanese soldiers lay dead within that small perimeter.[50]

A further series of desperate attacks the next night proved equally futile and it became clear to the Japanese commanders that the attack had failed. Thus began a fighting retreat west-wards to the north-west coast of the island. The troops suffered from exhaustion, malnutrition, disease and untended wounds, but on they marched. Diary entries reflect the difficulty of the march:

> *October 27* . . . [after three days' march] have only one tiny teaspoon of salt per day and a palmful of rice porridge.

> *October 30* . . . food captures the mind . . . I try to think of other things, but can't.[51]

As they marched west, fighting to their rear, small groups of lost soldiers filtered out of the jungle and joined them. Their condition was equal to, or worse than, their comrades already on the march. They suffered from the effects of leeches, mosquitoes and scorpions plus the never-ending dampness of the jungle floor. Some had managed to eke out their existence eating vegetation or fish, but all were dangerously malnourished.

By 18 December, prospects for a starving soldier were measured in a different, and ghastly way. Life expectancy, according to one diarist, was:

Those who can stand – 30 days.

Those who can sit – 3 weeks.

Those who cannot sit up – 1 week.

Those who urinate lying down – 3 days.

Those who have stopped speaking – 2 days.

Those who have stopped blinking – tomorrow.

As the days wore on, fighting became disorganized and desperate – not really defence. There was a single exception with which Taki allied himself. Units mattered little any longer, so it was his decision to attach himself to the group led by Major Takeyoshi Inagaki.

Inagaki had created the most strongly defendable position on the island in an area he called 'Gifu', after a prefecture on the home island of Honshu. It sat west of the top of Mount Austen between two hills. It held some forty-five crude but effective pillboxes placed in a horseshoe shape, the open end facing west between the two hills. The structures were dug into the ground, lined with logs then reinforced with dirt inside and out. Walls were two logs thick, roofs, three, since coconut wood was easily penetrated by gunfire. Only a direct hit from a 105-mm howitzer could damage these structures.

Each pillbox held one or two Nambu machine guns and two or three riflemen. The placement of the pillboxes enabled them to provide mutually supporting fire. Out in front of the main line, Inagaki placed positions at the bases of the tall banyan and mahogany trees for individual riflemen and light machine gunners. They numbered about 500 in their 'Alamo' fortress. Gifu was also hard to detect. In the jungle, killing ranges rarely exceeded 30 metres, but at the Gifu, an enemy soldier could get within a very few metres of an embrasure without seeing it.[52]

On several occasions, Inagaki sent Taki out behind enemy lines to wreak havoc with his sniping. Working his way beyond the forward company of attackers, he located its headquarters area and methodically began to place one enemy soldier at a time into the cross hairs of his telescope. His kill-shots created fear and confusion among the staff, giving Taki a rare reason to smile.

Stealthily returning to Gifu after dark, he and his fellow scouts traded stories of their 'hunting trips'.

On 25 December, a battalion of enemy forces approached Gifu but was driven back by fire. The mission of these U.S. Army troops (nearly all Marines had left the island by 15 December) was to assault and occupy Mount Austen (a series of hills, not just a single mountain) near Gifu. It took until 1 January for the enemy to take Austen. And on that day, Inagaki distributed the last rations to his troops – two biscuits and a boiled sweet per man.

On 16 January, after receiving permission, preparations to leave the island began immediately. The troops were triaged for departure – first the wounded, then the sick, then the starving, then able-bodied would board the ships when they arrived. They would wait until 2240 on 1 February 1943 before ships finally arrived offshore at Cape Esperance. At 2400, launches were sent shoreward to begin the evacuation.[53]

By 0153 the last soldier boarded at Kamimbo and, by 0158, at Cape Esperance. There remained 1,270 men at Cape Esperance and another 300 at Kamimbo. Admiral Koyanagi, aboard one of the rescue ships, noted:

> [soldiers] wore only the remains of clothes so soiled their physical deterioration was extreme. Probably they were happy but showed no expression. All had dengue or malaria [and] their diarrhoea sent them to the heads [toilets]. Their digestive organs were so completely destroyed [we] couldn't give them good food, only porridge.[54]

Even the inscrutable Admiral Isoroku Yamamoto was horrified by a medical report on the rescue that read:

> [The men] were so undernourished that their beards, nails and hair had all stopped growing, their joints looked pitifully large. Their buttocks were so emaciated that their anuses were completely exposed, and on the destroyers that picked them up they suffered from constant and uncontrolled diarrhoea.[55]

The majority of the pitiful force was safe aboard the Imperial Navy ships, but there were more soldiers to save. The remaining men were organized into a defensive force to protect the evacuation. It was a hotch-potch of men from a variety of units including the last few survivors of Taki's own Ichiki Detachment. The Americans limited their actions to patrols which gave the troops awaiting rescue a break from the continuous tension.

On 4 February, in preparation for final evacuation, Colonel Matsuda, now senior commander on the island, ordered a detachment of 128 men to the east bank of the Segilau River as a rearguard. He also ordered that an additional rearguard of seventy men be posted just west of the Bonegi River and the rest of the command then move to Maravovo to prepare for evacuation. After a heated discussion of how and who should comprise the rearguard, the decision was taken to leave only those who could not walk at the Bonegi River and take the ambulatory wounded to the Segilau at 1500. Those able to fire a weapon were asked to delay the enemy as long as possible, and then kill themselves before being captured. Each soldier in that situation was given two tablets of mercury bichloride, which would bring a sure, but excruciatingly painful death. Other soldiers were ordered to kill those who could not fire their weapons.

This order, Taki could not understand. These men had braved enemy fire, had been seriously wounded, and endured days being carried in litters across the trackless jungle. Now with wounds infested with maggots, and in dire need of medical attention, they were simply shot? And by his own NCOs! It was all too much for him. He turned away in disgust and sorrow. Is this what would happen to him?[56]

A second rescue convoy arrived on the night of 4 February and another 3,921 troops were taken aboard, bound for Bougainville. One skeleton of a man who had cared for and carried his friend aboard now lay beside him on the deck of the ship. His friend was dead, but his insistent companion refused to accept that fact.

Now Colonel Matsuda concerned himself with his rearguard – how to extricate them? Another sea rescue was risky, but ultimately decided upon as the only viable option. With the U.S. Army forces inching westward towards the last perimeter, the remaining soldiers could hear the artillery rounds pounding Maravovo. And there were reports of machine-gun fire at the Segilau to concern the command further. Finally, at sundown, with twenty-six craft still seaworthy, Matsuda re-organized the troops into four groups of 500 each. Between 2130 and 2215 the remaining troops were embarked.[57]

Except for one lone sniper.

At 0030 on 8 February 1943, the word was passed that all the remaining troops were embarked. To fulfill Hashimoto's pledge never to abandon them, the rescue boats sailed up and down the shore, calling out for any they might have missed.[58] Taki heard the calls and for a moment was tempted to answer. But he didn't. Before the others left, he had a friend pull him up into his palm tree hide. It was easy. He now weighed less than 40 kilograms. Wracked with malaria and dysentery, he had not had a meal in weeks. But he was angry and wanted to avenge the deaths of his friends and of those wounded men who were killed by his own NCOs. He wanted to honour his family and the Emperor by dying like a warrior. So he chose to remain ashore to satisfy those yearnings.

*

With his thoughts returning to the present, he is aware of the pain caused by the bench-like seat of his hide. With the seat's pulley-supported rope tied at the bottom of the tree trunk, he waits – patiently, silently, motionless – intent on his mission. The waiting alone is especially difficult when he must remain silent and unmoving for what may be a very long time. Taki's muscles cramp, and nerve endings cry out for relief; yet he remains still and silent. And, as he waits, he is acutely aware of how much his body has endured even when his brain has told him he can do no more. His fatigue seems to sharpen rather than dull his senses of sight and sound. He checks his stock of ammunition and now has but one round left.

He will make it count.

9 February 1943. He has sat in the tree all night, awaiting the arrival of enemy forces. As the lead elements of the 1st Battalion, 161st Infantry Regiment, Americal Division,[59] approach, Taki takes careful aim at the lieutenant with the unit. He squeezes the trigger to fire his last round while keeping the man's face in his scope lens. The Arisaka bucks once again and, through his telescope, Taki watches the officer's head explode in a spray of red and grey.

Even though he has no more ammunition, Taki instinctively pulls the bolt of his rifle to the rear. He can hear the shouts of enemy voices and sees them pointing towards his tree hide.

The world seems to slow down and things can be carefully observed as the American .30-calibre round speeds towards his head. He can almost see it as it enters his skull. He does not feel the fall from the tree. His long walk to a short life is over.

References

Books

Leo J. Daugherty III, *Fighting Techniques of the Japanese Infantryman 1941–45: Training, Techniques and Weapons* (MBI Publishing, 2002)

R. B. Frank, *Guadalcanal, The Definitive Account* (Penguin, 1992)

B. McCoy, *Japanese Army Snipers, World War Two* (e-book available through www.quikmaneuvers.com, 2008)

Gary Nila and Robert A. Rolfe, *Japanese Special Naval Landing Forces: Uniforms and Equipment 1932–45* (Osprey, 2006)

G. L. Rottman, *Japanese Infantryman 1937–45: Sword of the Empire* (Osprey, 2005)

P. R. Senich, *U.S. Marine Corps Scout-Sniper, World War II and Korea* (Paladin Press, 1993)

Internet sources

www.ww2db.com – a database for Second World War battles, units, personnel, ships and photographs

Wikipedia article, 'Battle of Guadalcanal', accessed January 2011

www.lonesentry.com

Notes

1. A fictitious name. The character is used to illustrate the facts of the Second World War in the South Pacific Theater of Operations. According to Japanese sources, few, if any, Japanese snipers survived. This story is based on facts gleaned from indicated references and insofar as possible, describes historical events.
2. Rottman, pp. 30–1.
3. Rottman, p. 26.
4. Rottman, p. 27.
5. Rottman, p. 25 *et seq.*
6. Rottman, p. 1. Daugherty, p. 21
7. Wikipedia article, 'Type 38 rifle', accessed January 2011.
8. Senich, *U.S. Marine Scout Snipers World War Two and Korea.*
9. Senich, pp. 188–9.
10. McCoy, *Japanese Army Snipers World War Two*, chap. 5.
11. *Tactical and Technical Trends, Oct. 1943*, www.lonesentry.com.
12. Frank, pp. 144, 145.
13. Frank, p. 143.
14. Frank, p. 146.
15. Frank, p. 147.
16. Frank, p. 148.
17. Frank, p. 149.
18. Frank, p. 149.
19. Frank, p. 158.
20. Frank, p. 156.
21. Frank, p. 156.
22. Frank, p. 158.
23. Frank, p. 203.
24. Frank, p. 201.
25. Frank, p. 205.
26. Frank, p. 213.
27. Frank, p. 218.
28. Frank, p. 220.
29. Frank, p. 224.
30. Frank, p. 232.

31. Frank, p. 223.
32. Frank, p. 231.
33. Frank, p. 232.
34. Frank, p. 235.
35. Frank, p. 241.
36. Frank, p. 248.
37. Frank, p. 246.
38. Frank, p. 269.
39. Frank, p. 270.
40. Frank, p. 273.
41. Frank, pp. 275–86.
42. Frank, p. 287.
43. Frank, pp. 340–1.
44. Frank, p. 341.
45. Frank, p. 342.
46. Frank, p. 349.
47. Frank, p. 350.
48. Frank, p. 352.
49. Frank, p. 355.
50. Frank, p. 356.
51. Frank, p. 407.
52. Frank, p. 532.
53. Frank, p. 587.
54. Frank, p. 588.
55. Frank, p. 588.
56. Frank, p. 590.
57. Frank, p. 594.
58. Frank, p. 596.
59. Made up of *Ameri-*can Army troops previously stationed on New *Cal-*edonia.

Chapter 6

VASSILI ZAITSEV

The Sailor of Stalingrad

As had been the case for the generation that preceded his, Zaitsev and his contemporaries seemed to have been born with war as their ultimate destiny. Following the October Revolution of 1917, the fledgling Soviet state dedicated itself to a radical overhaul of the armed forces, determined to place Russia on a par militarily with its European neighbours. There is no question that such a reform was long overdue, for the old Russian Army had been woefully under-equipped, poorly trained and indifferently led by an officer elite who regarded the average Russian peasant soldiers as no more than ignorant beasts of burden. During the First World War, the German and Austrian armies had fielded very large numbers of snipers along the Eastern Front and they exacted a terrible toll on the hapless Russians who, despite fielding a huge army, had no snipers or telescopic-sighted rifles and were impotent to respond. Many of the soldiers who survived the terrible fighting on that front were to become the senior NCOs and officers of the new Soviet Army, and they did not forget the hard lessons they had learned in the trenches.

Russia thus set about transforming what was effectively a feudal nineteenth-century army into the largest, most modern and best equipped armed force in Europe. Because of its size (in 1925 the army numbered 560,000 but by 1935 it comprised 1.3 million men) re-arming posed a considerable problem, both logistically and financially. On the thorny question of what to do about re-arming, General Alexei Brusilov (1853–1926), then in overall command of the Red Army, decided that it would retain its old Mosin-Nagant Model 1891/30 rifles (which were adequate if not outstanding] but that a new dedicated sniper rifle would be manufactured.

This was a relatively straightforward process, as from 1926 the Red Army had begun producing good copies of German scopes based on the Zeiss/Kahles and Emil Busch patterns and, with a little modification, the Mosin could be adapted to enable the scope mounts to be fitted to the left side of the receiver. By 1932 the first of these rifles were becoming available to army units.

The new telescope, the 4-power PE, was uniquely fitted with both windage and elevation drums making it easy to use even with gloved hands and between 1932 and 1938 over 54,000 were produced. It proved to be a competent set-up, the rifles being capable of grouping 10 shots into 3.6 cm at 100 metres and 34 cm at 550 metres using ordinary 7.62 x 54mm military ball ammunition and a 13.6-gram spitzer boat-tailed bullet. Later use of a heavier armour-piercing bullet tightened the groups and gave a slightly improved range, with 700 metres being about the maximum for accurate shooting. In 1936 the scope design was simplified and a smaller, lighter scope, the PU, was introduced and this was to become the mainstay of the Soviet sniper through the Second World War and well into the Cold War era.

While it was all very well fabricating the weapons, there was little point unless sufficient men were available to be able to use the rifles so a training scheme was devised by General Voroshilov to produce trained sharpshooters, and by 1939 some 60,000 were believed to have been awarded the Voroshilov Sharpshooters badge. It should be stressed that these were not trained snipers, but marksmen who would later provide much of the raw material for Russia's sniper training schools. To provide practical experience, many hundreds of Soviet snipers were employed during the Spanish Civil War (July 1936–April 1939).

Confident in its new military might, the Red Army launched an attack on Finland late in 1939, little expecting that they would be brought to an unexpected halt by the hundreds of Finnish snipers, who proved murderously effective. They were mostly armed with a near-identical Mosin rifle to that of the Soviet soldiers but few used scopes, finding that they froze and fogged in the bitterly cold conditions. Many were hunters, used to the hostile conditions and terrible cold (-45°C was not uncommon) and they proved superior to the better-equipped Soviet snipers. As a result, the Red Army was forced to retire, having received a terrible battering at the hands of the Finns. This led to a rapid re-evaluation of sniper training and tactics so that when the Germans took the fateful decision to invade Russia in June 1941, they were to be faced by large numbers of Soviet snipers who were arguably the most experienced and best-equipped such force in the world.

Zaitsev's early life

It was into this maelstrom that a young marine named Vassili Zaitsev was thrown.[1] Born on 23 March 1915 into a family of farmers and hunters in Yeleninskoye in the Ural Mountains, he was taught how to handle a firearm from his earliest years, being presented at the age of 12 with a 20-bore shotgun and a belt of cartridges filled with solid slugs. He also received some prophetic advice:

> I became a grown-up . . . an independent hunter. My father, remembering his days fighting under Brusilov, said to me, 'Use every bullet wisely, Vassili. Learn to shoot and never miss. This will help you, and not just when you are hunting four-legged beasts.'

Small in stature (he was about 1.58 metres [5 ft 2 in] tall and one family nickname was 'half-pint') he was nevertheless physically strong and very self-contained, one officer later recalling that he was very modest, with a 'slow grace of movement and an exceptionally calm character'.[2] He was also utterly determined, once spending a night in the open in bitter sub-zero conditions with his cousin Maxim while tracking a wolf, which he caught and killed. He was fascinated by the art of tracking and spent as much time as he possibly could in the forests, stalking and hunting, covering his scent with pungent badger oil, so much so that his sister complained that he 'reeked like an animal'.

I learned to interpret the trails of wild animals like I was reading a book; I tracked down the den of wolves and bears, and built hides that were so well concealed, not even Grandpa could find me until I called out to him.

Using the short-range shotgun meant that he was forced to get very close to his quarry, and the countless hours spent tracking, crawling and patiently waiting were to pay dividends in a way that Zaitsev could never have foreseen.

Military life

In 1937 he was drafted as a sailor into the Soviet Pacific Fleet and for the rest of his career he was proud to have worn the *telnyashka*, the distinctive blue and white striped seaman's shirt. His small stature meant that he was judged unsuitable for front-line service so he was put to work as a clerk in the naval depot at Vladivostok. His duties were undemanding until war began. Then, increasingly angered by reports of German atrocities and moved by the plight of the defenders of Leningrad, he volunteered several times for front-line combat. Eventually, in September 1942, he put on the khaki-green uniform of a private of the 1047th Rifle Regiment, but like all seamen retained his treasured *telnyashka*, which he wore underneath!

His introduction to Stalingrad and fame as a sniper was by means of a training ground on the edge of the shattered city, where, far from honing his shooting ability, he was grounded in the grim skills of close-quarter fighting: the use of submachine guns, bayonets, knives, shovels and hand grenades. 'We sailors were now accustomed to catching grenades in mid-flight, and hurling them back into the trenches.'

Training finished, he and his comrades were taken along the crowded roads to the River Volga, an experience they found profoundly shocking. Scores of old men, women and children dressed in filthy rags passed the army trucks, and streams of wounded soldiers, barely able to walk, staggered past wrapped in bloody bandages.

We wanted to ask them about the battle, but their
appearance spoke for itself. They walked like zombies. The
city looked like a smouldering and sulphurous hell, with
burned-out buildings glowing like red coals, and fires
consuming men and machines.

On the night of 22 September, they crossed the Volga in boats,
and were directed to the Dolgiy Ravine area, which had been the
pre-war metalworking district, where the regiment was at once
launched into the attack. Zaitsev's military career almost ended
before it had begun:

Suddenly a big German was on top of me. He hit me with
the butt of his gun. Fortunately the blow glanced off the
top of my helmet instead of my face. I slipped behind him
and got my arm locked around his neck, then managed to
choke him while he thrashed around.

For a week the regiment withstood full-scale attacks in the
metal factory, and at one point Zaitsev was buried alive in a
bunker full of corpses. It was typical of the fighting in the city,
but was not what he was best suited for.

It was to be a chance meeting that would change the course
of Zaitsev's war. As he and some others from his unit were
crawling forward through the ruins of the blazing fuel depot on
the edge of the industrial district, heavy German machine-gun
fire forced the men to try and find cover and Zaitsev found
himself next to a man even smaller than himself, a 'skinny little
runt of a soldier' as he later described him. He watched in
fascination as the tiny man worked his way forward until he
could see the German machine-gun positions over a pile of old
cobblestones:

He shifted his rifle to his right shoulder. The rifle had some
sort of strange little pipe on top if it. The next second the
short guy was aiming and – WHAM! He shifted his weight
and a few seconds later he fired again, WHAM – and
suddenly both machine guns were silent.

After the capture of the position, Zaitsev enquired about the identity of the soldier and was told he was sniper Sergeant Galifan Abzalov, who had already been credited with over 100 kills. Zaitsev was fascinated and wanted desperately to talk to the sniper, but had little chance as a slight bullet wound to his leg caused him to be withdrawn from the line for a few days.

Zaitsev the sniper

Once he was back in the line, things were relatively quiet and a few men were sitting with Zaitsev in a deep shell crater smoking, when a German machine gun opened up on them. A comrade spotted the position, about 600 metres distant, and handed Zaitsev the periscope:

> I took a quick look, then raised my rifle and practically without aiming, fired a shot. The gunner collapsed. Within seconds, two more gunners appeared and in rapid succession, I plugged each of them with a single bullet.

Bearing in mind this was snap-shooting using a service rifle with no optical sights, it was excellent shooting indeed and under normal circumstances it would have passed unnoticed. However, unbeknown to the young soldier, his work had been witnessed by Brigade Commander Batyuk, who at once ordered Zaitsev be given a scoped rifle. It was a Mosin-Nagant with PE scope, and was the model he favoured through his entire tour of duty. Despite having no official instruction on the care and use of a scoped rifle, Zaitsev at once set to work in his new-found position and he relished killing the hated Nazi invaders:

> I liked being a sniper and having the discretion to pick my prey. With each shot, it seemed as if I could hear the bullet smashing through my enemy's skull, even if my target was six hundred metres away. Sometimes a Nazi would look in my direction, seeming to stare right at me, without having the slightest idea that he was living out his final seconds.

He was forced to learn how to adjust the telescope by trial and error, although fortunately it was not a difficult process, for he was both intelligent and, despite his rural upbringing, mechanically very able. Shooting at longer ranges was, of course, made more difficult by side winds and initially he was unused to having to allow for bullet drift, commenting that he used the smoke from the many fires to determine how strong the wind was:

> I adjusted my sights for 550 metres and looked to see if the wind would throw off my shot. Most of the smoke . . . was wafting straight up, a sign that there was very little wind that day, so I didn't have to compensate for it.

He did his best among the smouldering ruins of the city, but he was more or less working on his own, as no official arrangement had been made to set up a sniper section in the regiment. However, this was all to change on 21 October 1942 when Zaitsev was called to a bunker to meet Commander Yablochkin who was the regimental *zampolit*, or senior political commissar. 'You have new orders,' he was told curtly. 'From now on make eliminating these roving [German] machine gunners your top priority.' Zaitsev protested that it was a task he was unable to accomplish on his own. 'I understand,' the commissar said, 'and that's why I'm giving you this order . . . I want you to look around this room and pick out a couple of sharpshooters, and then I want you to train them.'

It slowly dawned on Zaitsev that he had been told to start the first sniping school by selecting men from a room full of wounded and shell-shocked soldiers. 'How', he wondered, 'did they expect him to pull together a unit of snipers from dregs like this?' Despite his misgivings, he selected a concussed young engineer named Mikhail Ubozhenko, who had refused to be evacuated and handed him his scoped rifle along with five minutes of instruction. Ubozhenko shot two Germans one after another and the furious enemy turned a machine gun on the pair. They slid down quickly from their hide and Zaitsev reflected on his first ever attempt at teaching.

> Thus began our sniper's training school. I, the professor,
> had in reality been the school's first student. Up to now I
> had only learned from my own mistakes.

His selection process was based on the immediate impression
individuals made on him, and his instinct was seldom ever
wrong. He later commented that, 'In general, fate smiled on me
regarding all my snipers.' He soon recruited Nikolai Kulikov ('an
intellectual . . . who chose his words carefully'), Alex Gryazev ('a
giant of a man . . . who would calmly pick up a big lathe, weighing
a couple of hundred pounds and not even break into a sweat')
and another giant of a man, Sasha Reutov, who specialized in
using an PTRD anti-tank rifle for sniping and could carry the
twenty-kilo weapon all day without tiring. He further selected
Riflemen Morozov, Abzalov, Shaikin, Medvedev, Dvoyashkin and
Kostrikov and the little team became known as Zaitsev's *zaichata*
or leverets.

Finding time for instruction during the continual fighting was
almost impossible. Unlike snipers in most other armies, who
were excused normal duties because of the long hours they
worked, Red Army snipers were expected to undertake fighting
patrols and guard duties, to the extent that exhaustion caused
many to fall asleep while under fire. Even the normally inde-
fatigable Vassili reached the limits of his physical strength. Called
in to report to his company commander, Lieutenant Kotov the
sniper recalled that:

> My legs were giving out and I was swaying from side to side.
> When the adjutant informed Kotov that I had arrived, the
> incensed battalion commander looked me up and down,
> saw how far I was gone and snapped . . . 'Take him out of
> here and get him some sleep.'

Sniping in Stalingrad

The fighting in the burning ruins took on an almost surreal
quality, with incessant aerial bombardment from flights of
Heinkels and Stukas and continual pounding from the artillery

of both sides. A pall of smoke hung permanently over the ruins, blotting out the sun and making soldiers wheeze and cough from the acrid fumes. Much of the fighting was by means of underground tunnels and sewers and day and night became as one in the continual half-light. It also became increasingly brutal, with the Germans killing wounded Soviet soldiers by using flame-throwers and the Russians retaliating by cutting the throats of helpless Germans, or lobbing grenades into the packed Red Cross bunkers and finishing off the survivors with submachine guns. The snipers on both sides were particularly loathed and feared and capture by the enemy was an inevitable death sentence, often by methods that harked back to the cruellest medieval forms of torture.

Many snipers carried pistols with them, to use on themselves as a last resort if surrounded. During the defence of Moscow two female snipers, Natalia Koshova and Mariia Polivanova, held out to their last bullet, then reportedly clasped each other in a final embrace and detonated grenades between themselves, each earning posthumous Hero of the Soviet Union awards.

In this chaos of rubble and tunnels, working as a sniper was particularly difficult for the scoped rifle was after all, a long-range weapon and much of the fighting was very close combat indeed. Zaitsev wrote that moving stealthily in the rubble with a sniper's rifle was hard, 'Crawling is difficult when you're a sniper. The long rifle on your back is constantly shifting from side to side, forcing you to stop and adjust its position.' The bolt-action weapons were also slow to use in a fire-fight and awkward in a confined space, so most snipers also carried the PPSh 41 submachine gun, a useful compact weapon with a high 900 rounds per minute rate of fire, and the ubiquitous RGD-33 stick grenades, usually as many as could be crammed into pockets. German MP 40 submachine guns were also popular, but with extra ammunition, grenades and food, it weighed them down and clearly it was not the most efficient method of using their skills.

Both sides had also begun routinely to use explosive bullets – it was against the rules of war of course, but in Stalingrad rules of civilized conduct meant nothing. The Soviet snipers preferred to work close to the German lines and would move into cover between the lines during the night, picking cellars, ruined buildings – anywhere that gave them a clear view and a good field of fire. The constant artillery barrages, far from destroying the city, had effectively turned it into a defender's paradise, for everywhere stood shattered buildings with holes punched through the brickwork by shells or cannon fire, and sitting deep in the shadows of the rooms provided a sniper with excellent cover. He was virtually impossible to spot and only a determined assault by infantry would be able to flush him out:

> We advanced across the rubble, our machine gunners firing at the windows while the grenade-men went in through the big gaps in the wall. They threw their bombs and we ran forward, firing upwards into the stairs and room above. More grenades, flashes and bangs that deafened one, and we burst into the upper room. A dead Ivan lay in a pool of blood, his sniper rifle still in his hand. There was food and water there, and the stink of excrement. He had been living there for days, picking us off one after another. Yet he had made no attempt to escape.[3]

However, the work being done by the leverets in the area they occupied around Mamayev Hill was coming to the notice of the Germans, for it had become a death-trap, as the slightest exposure by a careless soldier resulted in a bullet from one of the Soviet snipers. By November Zaitsev had made about 100 confirmed kills, and in total his men had far exceeded that. The Germans method of sniping was normally to shoot from within their own lines but in an effort to eliminate the small band they began to become more cunning and soon began to pay special attention to the sniper squad. While occupying trenches on the shell-scarred slopes of the hotly contested hill the Russians had spent days repelling counter-attacks with not only their sniping rifles but grenades and submachine guns. The enemy were often so close that Zaitsev commented that at times it wasn't even necessary to aim. But after ten days they were all under-fed, desperately short of water and totally exhausted, and carelessness began to creep in.

> I barely managed to shoulder my rifle before the Fritzes moved up a machine gun . . . and opened fire. But the new gunner of theirs had no cover whatsoever. I took aim and shot and the machine gun fell silent. Then I realized that the enemy were watching me. I knew I had to change my location, I left behind my helmet, using it for a decoy then . . . scurried through the trench in search of another position. Then I started thinking about how the Fritzes had . . . so carelessly allowed us to spot them, and it hit me all in a rush. 'Guys – it's a trap . . .'

But it was too late, Sasha Gryazev, was hit by a single explosive bullet, that tore a huge hole in his chest. Zaitsev and his men buried their comrade and vowed to take more care – and exact their revenge on the German sniper. They settled down to watch and scanned the German line for hours, their eyes sore and red, trying to remain motionless while endlessly looking for a tell-tale sign that would betray a hidden sniper. Through his periscope, Zaitsev idly counted a pile of old German shell-cases, then did a double-take:

> One was missing a bottom! Through a shell case . . . someone could see a long way into the distance. I raised myself up a little. Suddenly there in the casing – it was like a flint striking a spark! An explosive bullet ripped into the embankment behind me.

Shaken but determined, Zaitsev and his fellow sniper Kulikov got some much needed sleep then crept into their position before dawn and eventually spotted the hollow shell-case, now in a new position and well camouflaged.

> Nikolai backed up and used a stick to raise a helmet a few inches above the embankment. The German fired a shot that ripped through the helmet. I was surprised that he went for this bait.

Zaitsev watched patiently as the German reached to pick up the spent cartridge, standard practice for snipers who would leave no tell-tale signs behind. As he did so he moved slightly, raising his head. It was exactly what the Russian needed, a couple of seconds with a clear view:

> It gave me the few inches of scalp I needed to zero on, and at that second my own shot rang out. The bullet struck him in the hairline; his helmet fell forward over his brow and his rifle lay motionless, the barrel still inside the shell-case.

Counter-sniping

The snipers were starting to realize that they no longer had the upper hand, for the Germans were beginning to field some very experienced snipers of their own. As Zaitsev wrote: 'Day by day, they were growing more cautious and more cunning.' But the Russians' dogged defence of the hill continued as they targeted the machine gunners and artillery observers. Not every shot counted though. When a German machine gunner opened fire, both Zaitsev and Kulikov set their sights to 300 metres and fired. To their astonishment, the gun continued to chatter.

> Nikolai and I sat in silence. We were both ashamed because we had missed. Maybe the strain was affecting our vision, or our scopes had gone bad, or perhaps our breathing was unsteady. Then I remembered I had been shooting down[hill] at the target. Under those conditions it is always awkward to measure distance – you always have to add on at least ten per cent of the measured distance. Down in the ravine the Nazi's machine gun opened fire again. 'Listen,' I said, 'I've got him set at three hundred and fifty; you shoot for four hundred.' We aimed again and fired simultaneously. Nikolai had killed the gunner, while my bullet had fallen short.

At the end of autumn, after almost a month in the line, Zaitsev and his men were finally withdrawn from the terrible hill and given a roving commission to try and track down the increasing number of Nazi snipers who were inflicting more and more casualties on the Soviet soldiers. Counter-sniping work was becoming increasingly important and dangerous but occasionally it turned into farce. Near one command post, three men were hit in one day, including Zaitsev's Lieutenant, Arkhip Sukharev. Frustrated by his inability to find the hide of the persistent sniper, Zaitsev began shouting German obscenities through a loud-hailer. First one bullet, then another sang past his ears. The German was under the wheels of a railway carriage, but Zaitsev was unable to get a shot at him, so he ordered a neophyte sniper, Gorozhaev to blind the enemy with the mirror from their periscope. Praying that the ruse would work, Zaitsev crawled to another vantage point, having left a crude dummy behind. Convinced he had made a killing shot, the German committed the cardinal sin of standing upright, slinging his rifle over his shoulder. Gorozhaev took careful aim:

> At that moment I saw that the Nazi must have noticed the reflection from Gorozhaev's scope. His expression changed from gloating to one of alarm and suddenly he was raising his rifle and aiming at us. Gorozhaev's shot rang out. The bullet flattened the Nazi.

By now, the experienced Zaitsev had adopted several methods of dealing with enemy snipers. His modus operandi was to use a lifelike dummy and set up a very well camouflaged post next to it. When a sniper fired at the dummy, apparently to little effect, he often tried a second shot, giving Zaitsev a few seconds in which to snap-shoot. Sometimes he pretended to be a novice. 'I would dull my opponent's vigilance, or simply play around with him a bit.' Then he would substitute himself for the dummy, which by then the German had learned to ignore: 'I'd kick aside the decoy and catch the sniper's head in my crosshairs.'

A legend is born

There was little chance for newly appointed snipers like Gorozhaev to be given any formal sniper training as the need for manpower was all consuming, so most leverets were taught in the front line, one or two being assigned to an experienced sniper. It was often a very brief tour of duty – the average survival time for an infantryman in the line was twenty-four hours, for snipers under a week – but those who lasted beyond that usually became accomplished. Very occasionally men would fail, one sniper, Sidorov, being transferred out of the unit for considering his personal score to be more important than protecting the lives of fellow soldiers. But generally the resolve of those attached to the sniper units was unshakable.

By early winter 1942, Zaitsev had become something of a legend along the front and wherever there was a pressing problem, he and his men would be called on to find a solution, which they always did. Despite being sometimes portrayed as an unschooled peasant, Zaitsev was intelligent and thoughtful, as many snipers were, often preferring silence to speech, but when he had something to say, it was usually worth listening to.

One casual comment made to his officer was picked up on by the Soviet press, desperate to find soldiers to whom they could attach heroic status. Zaitsev had commented that, 'For us, there was no land beyond the Volga,' and this was to become a rallying cry for the desperate defence of Stalingrad.

The work done by the snipers in holding Mamayev Hill had not gone unnoticed by the high command and one afternoon, Zaitsev was called in to an interview with a *politruk*, a political captain, who began questioning the sniper about his work. Zaitsev bridled at what he believed was a question-mark over his dedication and began a tirade which was cut short. 'Vassili, you haven't understood me correctly . . . I'm not knocking your achievements. In fact I've been writing about your exploits in my reports for a month now.'

> Suddenly it hit me, this Captain Grigoriev was a journalist. I told him about the sniper's honour, about my comrades, and about the things I had discovered as I looked into the tactics of the sniper group. Later all this became the object of a discussion in one department of the *Stavka* [General

Staff]; Grigoriev managed to record my ramblings and somehow passed them on to high command in the form of an article.

Unbeknown to Zaitsev, he was about to become a legend.

Tactical change

Dismissing the interview from his mind, Zaitsev hurried back to his men, who had been tasked with finding and eliminating the increasing numbers of German snipers who were picking off Soviet artillery observers. One in particular was a real problem, so, working out the trajectory of the incoming bullets from hits made on the observer's periscope, the snipers calculated that the Nazi marksman was hidden in a huge chimney, so they settled down to wait. After four months of fighting, there had been a gradual shift in emphasis in the tactics of the sniper squad. No longer did they risk exposure by shooting at any German whom they observed. In part this was due to the landscape in which they fought. They now waited specifically for targets of opportunity that were of sufficient importance to warrant being shot. There were too many enemy snipers on the front now to risk giving away their positions without good cause. 'We restricted our shots to enemy snipers and to the most dangerous of their machine-gun posts.'

On one occasion he insisted that neither he nor his fellow snipers fired on an officer, a very tempting target. They waited and also ignored another German who appeared. The snipers grew restive but Zaitsev was adamant. So they waited. Suddenly:

> A heavyset, polished Nazi officer turned the corner . . . he had a colonel's insignia on his jacket. A sniper followed him, carrying a beautiful hunting rifle with a huge scope. Two additional officers emerged . . . one of them was a major wearing a Knight's Cross with oak leaf clusters. Following behind was another colonel. Nikolai and I exchanged a glance. This was what we had been dreaming about . . . we had been willing to wait to catch the sharks. Missing out on

the little fish was the price a sniper had to pay for a moment like this. I nodded a 'yes' to Nikolai and he signalled the others. Our shots rang out . . . we made textbook head shots and all four Nazis dropped to the earth.

So enraged were the Germans that they unleashed not only a terrible artillery bombardment, but also an airstrike on the hapless group, who were lucky to escape with superficial cuts and temporary deafness. No sooner had they crawled back to their lines than an attack erupted across the sector and the snipers were fighting for their lives in the front lines, often working at point-blank ranges. Three were badly wounded, but the attack was eventually repulsed.

Exhausted, the remaining snipers reporting back to their command bunker, where Zaitsev was startled when his colonel burst out laughing. All of the snipers resembled scarecrows, wearing a mix of torn and ragged uniforms, odd headgear, Russian or German greatcoats and sporting assorted bandages and several day's beard growth. Zaitsev was ordered to take his men to the commissar's bunker to obtain new uniforms, As he entered an officer regarded him thoughtfully. 'I've been waiting for you scarecrow. Come in.' To his astonishment he was given a beautiful uniform that had belonged to Brigade Commissar Zubkov.

As soon as he and the rest of his men were re-equipped, they were ushered into the command bunker, resplendent in their new uniforms, but with sticking plasters all over their cut and bruised faces. To their astonishment Lieutenant General Chuikov, commander of the 62nd Army, walked in. He confirmed that the days of using highly skilled snipers as infantry were over:

> You fellows are fighting brilliantly. I'm aware that three of your comrades lie wounded . . . but that happened for a simple reason. You forgot your assignment. You turned into submachine gunners, into normal infantrymen. I'm not going to waste any more of your time . . . remember; you have to pick your targets carefully. We pay for every mistake in blood. Try to see this struggle from a broader

perspective. Then it will be clear to you how you must act.

I wish you success.

He left and the silent snipers filed out, save for Zaitsev, who sat and pondered. 'The fighting at Stalingrad had taught me a great deal. I had matured and become stronger. I knew I was a different soldier than the one I had been just a month before.'

The game was still being played, but the rules were changing fast.

The duel

The meeting with Chuikov had incurred the displeasure of Zaitsev's jealous captain, who relieved him of command of the sniper group and ordered him back to Mamayev Hill, effectively a death sentence by now. Working with one other sniper, Pytor Tyurin, Zaitsev was determined to dominate the area once again but found himself over-run by a sudden German assault. Using captured enemy weapons, he and Tyurin ignored their new orders and launched a furious counter-attack from behind the German lines, forcing the enemy into a confused retreat.

By now, he had been fighting constantly for four months and Zaitsev was suffering from battle fatigue:

> I was worn down and tired to the bone, and fatigue is the sniper's worst enemy. Also I was calculating my odds, and the probability of my continued survival. Every day on average I was killing four of five Germans – this had continued since my arrival in Stalingrad. As day after day passed without my being hit, I kept thinking it was like having a run of luck at cards; I knew it couldn't last forever.

He was also aware that the press coverage about him and his snipers would be closely monitored by the Germans, and this was borne out when a prisoner was interrogated who said that the head of the Berlin sniper school, Major König,[4] was being brought to the front to eliminate Zaitsev, who in typical fashion was proud that his group's achievements had resulted in such an event. But he also admitted, for the first time, to having some doubts.

Although outwardly confident he was well aware that if the story was true he was going to face the most experienced sniper he had ever come up against. One factor in his favour was that he was used to determining the operating characteristics of enemy snipers: 'I was able to pick out the more experienced . . . from the beginners; and the cowards from the patient and determined.'

Zaitsev usually set about locating a new sniper's position by working in two stages. He would interview soldiers about where and how men had been sniped and work out the likely position of the sniper's post from bullet trajectory. He would then begin to search the lines with a periscope, which he believed was better than a rifle scope or binoculars and far less noticeable. He was also acutely aware of changes in the level of activity along the front. 'Experience told me that locations that had once been bristling with activity, but which later became dead silent, probably hid a cunning sniper.' However, he conceded that 'the characteristics of this new-super sniper remained difficult for me to identify'.

There was no doubt that there was an excellent sniper facing the Russians, for in one day he shattered the scope on Morozov's rifle and wounded Sahikin, both very experienced snipers. Zaitsev and Kulikov took over the wounded pair's position and began patiently scanning the enemy lines. They ignored a helmet raised opposite them, clearly a ruse, but it was a clue that someone wanted them to betray their positions. So they sat, and watched and waited. One morning they were joined by their political officer, Danilov, who was sure he had spotted the sniper, rising up in his excitement and getting a bullet across his scalp in response. It was the proof Zaitsev needed. 'Only a top sniper could have made that shot, could have fired with such quickness and precision. I peered into my scope for hour upon hour, but couldn't locate him.'

Somehow the sniper needed to be lured out, so Zaitsev put a glove on a piece of wood and slowly raised it. The shot that hit it was fired from directly in front, where a sheet of steel and a pile of bricks lay. They had always been there, and Zaitsev had ignored them . . . until now. Kicking himself, he and Kulikov conferred. Kulikov began raising his helmet very slowly, as only an experienced observer would do. A shot rang out and Kulikov threw himself up with a loud cry and fall. Convinced that he had finally found his target, the German raised his head from behind the sheet of iron. It was a brief glimpse but all Zaitsev needed. 'I pulled the trigger and the Nazi's head sunk. The scope of his rifle lay unmoving, still flashing in the light of the sun.' After dark, the two snipers dragged the dead German from his lair, took his rifle and documents and sent them to their divisional commander.

The final battle

There was to be no rest for the sniper group, now comprising thirteen men, seven having been killed or wounded, for in early January 1943 they were ordered to a new front. Although he did not know it, it was to prove Zaitsev's final battle, ironically resulting in injuries that doubtless saved his life, for no one could survive in Stalingrad for ever. A new German assault was forthcoming and they were to target all of the officers they could. In Zaitsev's words they were to 'behead' the German infantry by removing their leaders. This they did, with huge success, using concentrated sniper fire. It was an unusual tactic, but in this instance undeniably effective for three of the snipers made over fifty hits between them.

Forgetting his own rules, Zaitsev ran towards a group of Germans who were surrendering – right into the path of a rocket barrage. 'I could see how it [the rocket] turned end over end through the air. The round landed about thirty metres from me, bounced once and – boom!' The blast scorched his head and drove tiny steel splinters into his face and eyes. He awoke in hospital, swathed in bandages. For a month he lived in darkness, learning to identify various sounds from around the ward and suffering from post-traumatic stress, his moods swinging between wild laughter and tears. In a way, the enforced rest was the therapy he needed and, in typically stubborn style, he refused to accept his blindness as anything other than temporary.

After five weeks, the bandages were carefully unwound, and he could see the pale outlines of the staff around him. He still needed intensive treatment and was to be sent to the eye hospital in Moscow, but en route he was ordered to meet Chuikov, who promoted him to lieutenant. Stalingrad had finally been retaken by the Red Army, and the frozen, starving Germans had surrendered in colossal numbers.[5] Zaitsev continued to receive treatment for his blurred vision from the pioneering surgeon Professor Filatov, eventually recovering full sight.

He was interviewed on several occasions by members of the Politburo and Red Army leaders about his experiences and thoughts on the value of sniping, details that were later fundamentally to influence Soviet Russia's sniper training. After one such interview with Mikhail Kalinin[6] to Zaitsev's amazement, he was handed the gold badge of the Order of Lenin, the state's highest award:

> For the next few minutes I was afraid even to breathe. My ears were buzzing from all the excitement. The sound was like an echo of the battle of Stalingrad . . . where for a time we had to forget that beyond the Volga there was still land.

After the war Zaitsev left the army with the rank of captain, having assisted with sniper training and toured widely, lecturing on his experiences. Although probably the most famous of Russia's snipers, his official score of 242 enemy was nowhere near the highest.[7] He went to university and studied engineering, receiving a degree in 1952. He continued with his career, becoming a professor of engineering. He died in 1991 at the age of 76, just ten days before the fall of the old Soviet Union.

It was Zaitsev's dying wish to be buried at the monument to the defenders of Stalingrad in the Mamayev Hill war cemetery where so many of his comrades gave their lives in Russia's defence. In accordance with his request, on 31 January 2006, he was reburied with full military honours. His coffin was interred near the monument that carries his famous quote: 'For us there was no land beyond the Volga.'

Notes

All quotes included in this chapter come from Zaitsev's autobiography: Vassili Zaitsev, *Notes of a Russian Sniper*, Frontline Books, 2010.

1. The root of the surname came from the Russian word for rabbit, *zayit*.
2. General V. Chuikov, later Marshal of the Soviet Union.
3. Otto Bildmann, *Memoirs of the Eastern Front*. Private publication, 1996.
4. There has been much discussion about the actual events of this counter-sniping duel. There is no doubt that Zaitsev did fight an experienced German sniper, but so did most long-term snipers at some time. *König* (meaning 'king') may simply have been a nickname for a sniper who was known to be the king of his particular front. The name Thorvald has also been used in connection with this fight, but no such person exists in German records, nor was the head of the Berlin Sniper School so named.
5. In all 91,000 were captured. When finally released in 1955 only 6,000 survived to return to Germany.
6. Mikhail Kalinin 1875–1946, Chairman of the Supreme Soviet and titular head of the U.S.S.R. 1919–46.
7. His actual score was over 400, but only observed kills were officially recorded. The highest scoring Soviet sniper is believed to have been Ivan Sidorenko of the 1112th Rifle Regiment, with over 500 kills officially recorded.

Chapter 7

CLIFFORD SHORE

British Sniper, Trainer, Theorist and Historian

Captain Clifford Shore played an important role in the development of Britain's Second World War sniping capability by establishing an effective sniper training programme. His book *With British Snipers to the Reich* is also regarded as one of the classic works on sniping and is still considered an essential source today, both for its historical perspective and its insights on the deployment and use of snipers.

In early 1943, Shore attempted to establish a sniping school in England, but at the time there was little interest in his suggestion. However, Shore mentioned that there were at least some sniping schools in existence prior to that time. The first he discussed was a small one in Scotland designed primarily to teach ghillies, who were already good shots and expert stalkers, the use of telescopic sights and techniques for passing on their stalking and shooting skills. At least some sniping was taught at the Commando Training Depot in Scotland as well. Although Shore later discussed why he did not feel that the typical Bisley shooter made a good sniper, he commented that a sniping school established at Bisley early in the war did turn out some useful personnel. Another school in North Wales gave sniper training, but Shore felt that the most useful aspect of this school was a two-day course for battalion commanders which taught them to appreciate the use of snipers. He considered this, in some ways, more valuable than sniper training as it helped ranking officers to understand how to employ snipers. Although he mentioned that little sniping was done by the British Expeditionary Force in 1940, at least one source claims that one of the early impetuses for establishing the first British Second World War sniping schools was the success British 'snipers' had in delaying German infantry advances during the evacuation at Dunkirk. This discrepancy may result from semantics as some members of the BEF may have performed well at 'potting' Germans even though they were not trained snipers.

Later, in the months before the D-Day landings, Shore attempted to acquire sniping rifles to equip the best marksmen in his unit, but was unsuccessful. Even his attempts to acquire a scoped rifle, military or commercial, to take into combat were not successful. As his troops embarked for landings at Normandy, he had to be content with a Lee-Enfield P14 rifle with iron sights.

Upon landing on the beachhead, Shore immediately noticed the effectiveness of German 'snipers', who for the most part were actually infantry marksmen rather than trained specialists. Nevertheless, their aimed fire kept units pinned down on the beach, afraid to move inland. He immediately realized what a force multiplier trained snipers could be in slowing an enemy advance. He concluded that, if these regular troops acting as marksmen could create so much fear, a 'one shot, one kill' trained sniper could wreak havoc. Shore astutely realized that the psychological effect of trained snipers could be even greater than their actual killing effect.

After the Second World War, but before his book was published in 1948, Shore talked with combat veterans and found that overwhelmingly they feared accurate sniper fire more than mortars, artillery, bombs, or machine guns. In simple terms, troops feared the bullet that had their name on it more than those marked 'To whom it may concern'.

As a marksman himself and with a basic understanding of sniping, Shore covered his own officer's insignia and ordered his NCOs to cover their chevrons since snipers normally shoot for officers, radiomen, NCOs, and others whose death can disrupt a unit. However, his commanding officer countermanded his orders, thus putting the troops in greater danger. Though Shore may have understood snipers and sniping, obviously his superiors did not. This attitude did change as the war progressed and German snipers took their toll on officers and NCOs wearing soft caps, carrying binoculars or map cases, and lacking rifles or carbines. Eventually, standard procedure dictated covering rank insignia and avoiding other clothing or equipment that identified the user as an officer or NCO.

As his troops advanced out of the beachhead, Shore made it a point to examine any sniper hides which were discovered and showed special interest in how they were sited for best fields of fire. During the advance through Belgium and Holland, Shore's unit still encountered occasional fire from German shooters, but he doubted they were true snipers. In Belgium, at least, the local Resistance generally eliminated the snipers but, though Shore was willing to purchase one had the Resistance captured it, they never acquired a true sniping rifle.

Shore also tried to follow up the myths he encountered about German sharpshooters including that there were trained women snipers, possibly French women married to Germans, or that there were German snipers operating from treetops. There were occasional Germans encountered in the treetops, but Shore felt most were observers rather than shooters. As a marksman himself, Shore found it difficult to believe that a German marksman could get a solid shooting position while trying to remain in a tree. Additionally, shooting from the tree would make escape after a few shots almost impossible. Nevertheless he did note that he later saw German training manuals which illustrated the use of treetops as shooting positions.

In October 1944, Shore spotted a sign for a 'Sniper School' near Eindhoven, Holland, and convinced his commanding officer to allow him to attend. Once this was approved and he was at the school, Shore was in his element. He found that the instructors from the Lovat Scouts regiment, many of them Highland ghillies before the war, were excellent, and threw himself into the training in stalking, observation and shooting. Shore, the oldest officer on the course, was surprised to find that some of the other officers attending were surprisingly poor shots, even with excellent coaching. He also noted that some of the sniping rifles were quite inaccurate.

The wartime shooting standard for snipers coming out of training was the ability to hit a man's head regularly at 200 yards and a man's torso at 400 yards. These were minimum standards and most snipers could achieve these hits at longer distances.

The Sniper School curriculum covered various subjects:

General: Organization, Equipment, and Tactical Handling of Snipers;

Observation: General, Telescope, Binoculars, Location of Fire;

Fieldcraft: Concealment, Camouflage, Movement, Stalking;

Shooting: General, Sources of Error, Zeroing, the Sniper Rifle, Dusk Firing, Holding, Elevation Table, Aiming Off – Wind and Movement, Recognition of Targets, Judging Distance, Field Firing Exercises.

Major Underhill, who commanded the school, believed that a wartime sniping school should be located as close to the front lines as possible to allow trainees to get real sniping experience. However, by the time Shore's class was ready to graduate, the front lines were moving rapidly due to the advance into Germany. In an attempt to give the trainees some actual sniping experience they were attached to the Highland Division after the Rhine Crossings. Another advantage Shore noted of the sniping school moving along with the advancing troops was that sniper instructors could spend a day or two at a time working with front-line 'snipers', some of whom had actually had little training. Although Shore notes that a German bullet came close to him at one point, it was not from a real German sniper, and he had little chance to use his newly acquired sniping skills before the end of the war.

British Sniper Equipment
As recommended by the Sniper School
No. 4 Rifle (T), Denison smock, face veil, Scout Regiment Telescope, binoculars, compass, 50 rounds .303 ball,

2 No. 36 grenades, 5 rounds tracer ammunition,
5 rounds armour-piercing ammunition, water bottle,
1 emergency ration.
Shore noted that although the above equipment was
recommended snipers often adjusted what they carried to
the mission.

The No. 4 Rifle (T) was the standard sniping rifle worked over
by Holland & Holland. In his section on British sniping rifles,
Shore spoke highly of the No. 4 Mk 1 (T) and pointed out that
each rifle was selected for accuracy, then fitted with two metal
plates to take the telescopic sight (No. 32 TS), a cheek rest, and
a special shooting sling. The No. 32 TS scope was only 3-power
and incorporated a drum for elevation adjustments between 100
and 1,000 yards. The Mk 1 version of the scope allowed elevation
adjustments in 50-yard increments and the Mks II and III in 100-
yard increments. A windage drum ('deflection drum' as Shore
terms it) was located on the left side of the No. 32 scope. This
scope was renowned for its durability, no doubt because it had
originally been developed for use on the fully automatic Bren
gun. Shore made a point of noting that an important part of
training the sniper was inculcating the methods of caring for the
sniper rifle properly as many weapons came into the sniping
school that were virtually useless after time in the field.

The Denison smock had been designed for airborne troops. It
was waterproof, windproof and camouflaged and had an array of
pockets and proved very popular with snipers. Face veils
camouflaged in brown and green broke up the outline and colour
of the sniper's face when in a hide.

A Scout Regiment Telescope was issued to each sniper team,
with the spotter normally carrying it. This was a 20-power three-
draw telescope with three sets of lenses. Some snipers, including
many of the Lovat Scouts, considered the Scout Regiment
Telescope too bulky, but Shore felt it performed well, as the Ross
telescope which was also available was only a 15-power even
though it was lighter. As with rifles, Shore emphasized that
snipers had to learn to maintain and take care of their telescopes,

especially learning not to scratch the lens when cleaning it. In discussing the advantages of the Scout Telescope, he pointed out that it was capable of picking up troop movements at over 16 kilometres. Among other hints offered by Shore was the importance of sniper and observer alternating on the telescope every twenty minutes or so to avoid losing concentration.

Binoculars were also normally issued. The types of binoculars varied but they were normally carried by the sniper to scan for targets using their wider field of view. Binoculars were most commonly of 7-power, but Shore notes that his were of 10-power. If he spotted a potential target he would normally alert the spotter to check it with the telescope. One excellent point made by Shore is that the binoculars were especially valuable at dusk or in moonlight because of their light-gathering ability.

The final item of 'observation' equipment was a prismatic compass, carried by the sniper and used for reporting observed artillery or mortar targets or other information.

The main ammunition supply consisted of fifty rounds .303 ball. This standard rifle ammunition was carried in a bandolier and used for zeroing the rifle or normal shooting. Generally, snipers were issued with the standard 174-grain Mk VII load; however, some snipers tried to obtain the 175-grain Mk VIIIz boat-tail load which was intended for use in the Vickers machine gun and gave more range. The 'z' indicates the use of nitro-cellulose powder. This round had the reputation of being more accurate at ranges past 300 metres. Additionally, as the front one-third of the bullet's interior was filled with aluminium, tenite (plastic), or even compressed paper, upon impact with flesh, the back-heavy bullet would tumble causing a larger wound cavity. This bullet remained stable in flight but would have retained more killing potential at longer ranges. Whatever ammunition the sniper chose, and for which he zeroed his rifle, he tried to have a good supply so he did not have to re-zero the rifle to a new load.

Snipers were also recommended to carry two No. 36 grenades. Also known as the Mills Bomb, the No. 36 grenade was a pineapple-type fragmentation grenade, carried by snipers in case they unexpectedly stumbled upon a German position during a stalk. Many snipers did not like crawling around with No. 36 grenades in their pockets!

Snipers were also instructed to carry both tracer and armour-piercing ammunition. Five rounds of tracer were to be carried in the right trouser pocket and were intended for use in indicating a target. Shore states that he never knew of a British sniper using his tracer ammo. The left trouser pocket was used for five rounds of armour-piercing ammunition. AP ammunition was used to shoot at German machine-gun positions as it would often put the machine-gun out of action with a hit.

A standard water bottle was slung over the shoulder and carried for refreshment. However, some experienced snipers would use water to dampen ground in front of their muzzle to keep dust from being kicked up. Or, to keep their water supply, they would urinate on the area to dampen it. An emergency ration was also recommended, useful if a sniper remained in position all day.

Shore also noted that tubes of camouflage cream were available at the sniping school but that most snipers used improvised materials such as blacking from cooking pots to break up the white of their faces and often made up burlap gloves to camouflage their hands.

Almost immediately upon graduation, Shore applied for a posting as instructor at the Sniping School. By the time his assignment came through, however, the war in Europe was over, and the school, which would be part of what came to be known as the British Army of the Rhine Training Centre, was now located in Germany. Prior to assignment to the Sniping School staff, Shore found his firearms knowledge often called upon to examine and repair 'liberated' firearms for other soldiers.

Once he reported to the Sniping School, Shore lectured on 'History of the British Service Rifle', 'Small Arms Ammunition', and 'Comparison of British Small Arms with Other Countries' Small Arms'. Though his time was spent in lecturing, Shore kept his stalking skills sharp by hunting with his friends among the Lovat Scouts NCOs assigned as instructors. Later, when he ran sniping courses, he often used some of the Lovat Scouts to demonstrate the ability to move long distances on stalks without being detected.

In *With British Snipers to the Reich*, Shore discusses how trainees soon learned that techniques of concealment and stalking were not rocket science:

> The man of average intelligence quickly saw that fieldcraft was mainly the exercise of common sense, hunter's sense: the avoidance of breaking skylines, looking around cover, not over it; keeping in shadow, mindful that the position of shadow can change; the merging into one's background; the avoidance of isolated or conspicuous cover and all unnecessary movement. He realized the value of camouflage, the necessity of having some contrast in colour and tone so that a disruptive effect was obtained. He was shown what practical camouflage methods he could take towards personal concealment including the head and face covered with a camouflage veil; the hands smeared with camouflage cream, mud or dirt, or gloves; the body by wearing the Denison smock which could be improved for some purposes of concealment by tufts of hessian garnish stitched onto it; some protection for the rifle could be obtained by painting it or wrapping garnish around it; the body of his telescope could be covered by a face veil or an old khaki sock with the foot cut out; the binoculars obscured by a strip of camouflage hessian tied around the front of the bracket.
>
> Emphasis was laid on the fact he should train himself to be able to 'pierce' enemy attempts at concealment; this had a double purpose – he became more careful with his own forms of camouflage . . .

Throughout his time in Europe prior to attending and instructing at the Sniping School and while affiliated with the school, Shore had observed and developed his own ideas about what should be included in a sniping course. Upon return to his regiment prior to discharge, he got a chance to put his theories into practice when he was assigned to give sniper training to members of his unit.

In retrospect, Shore decided that the 10–14 day sniping courses run during the war were probably too short to give really effective training. However, they certainly proved better than no training and produced some highly effective snipers. He noted, too, that the school which moved along with the British Army in northern Europe was better organized and more effective than some others. As examples, he cited one school for troops in the Mediterranean which did not even have scoped sniping rifles. He did note, however, that the Mountain Warfare School in Lebanon incorporated sniping and stalking into its curriculum.

One of the most important conclusions Shore drew in relation to sniper training was that those acting as instructors should have combat-sniping experience. Not only did this make them more credible, especially when they were training combat veterans, but it allowed them to offer authoritative practical advice. In cases where instructors were chosen because of their ability as teachers, Shore felt they should spend at least some time on the front lines to add experience to their instructional ability. This was one reason why locating the sniper school near the front lines was highly advisable.

One aspect of the sniper to which Shore had given substantial thought was temperament and background. In *With British Snipers to the Reich* he commented:

But it is a fact that a sniper will kill with less conscience-pricking than a man in close combat. Personal feelings of remorse or questioning of motives will slow down a man's critical killing instinct and the sniper who allows himself to fall into such a train of thought will not last long. It is imperative to look upon the killing of an enemy as swatting a fly, an unthinking, automatic action. Two things only should really interest the sniper – getting the job done and getting away unscathed. To become accustomed to 'sniper killing' is not so difficult or hard as close quarter killing. A man dies more slowly than the average person thinks; he often grins foolishly when he's hit, the whites of his eyes roll upwards, death sweat gleams on his forehead and he sags to the ground with a retching gurgle in his throat –

and it is difficult to hear that gurgle without emotion. The sniper is usually spared all this unless he's quick enough to get his binoculars on his victim, or the 'sniped' is at such close range that the telescope sight will give him all the motion pictures he needs.

Sniping is not the vague, haphazard shooting of the unknown in a sort of detached combat. It is the personal individual killing of a man in cold blood, and is an art which must be studied, practised, and perfected. I often heard it said that a sniper should be a man filled with a deadly hatred of the Hun, or enemy. But I found the men that had seething hatred in their hearts for all things German, such as those who had lost their wives and children and homes in the blitzed cities, were not the type to make good rifle killers. The type I wanted was the man of cold precision, the peace-time hunter who had no hatred for his enemy but just a great interest in the stalk and the kill.

When one was in position for a shot there came an 'inner freezing'; the breathing was not quite normal; the hearing sense was magnified and there came too that sense of excitement which all hunters know and which results in an unconscious nerve-hardening, and once the Hun was in the sight and the pointer steady at the killing spot there was no qualm of conscience about hitting him or taking life. The true hunter is never a butcher; he does not desire to kill for killing's sake, but there is something elemental in the stalk and slaying which swamps every other feeling and makes the heart and brain exultant, and filled with action-elation.

Although British snipers were mostly involved in mobile warfare during the Second World War, Shore still emphasized the ability to build a hide or hides for situations where a sniper would be in position for any amount of time. A well-built hide would offer protection from the weather as well as concealment and should also offer the possibility of a limited amount of movement without detection. The size and structure of a hide would vary by terrain and material available. Shore emphasized that care must be taken that light would not shine from loopholes in a poorly constructed hide.

Shore emphasized three warnings when shooting from a hide:

- the danger of firing from a hide at dusk or dawn when muzzle flash could give the sniper away;
- the danger of smoke showing when firing on frosty mornings and damp days;
- the need to dampen the ground outside the hide if danger of dust being thrown up existed.

A common problem noted by Shore was the tendency to build hides without enough headroom. Among possible locations he mentioned were beneath hedgerows, in rubbish heaps, in destroyed buildings, or in slit trenches with camouflage overhead cover. When ruined buildings were used, it was recommended to build a rest well back from windows or loopholes so the sniper remained in shadow. Wherever the hide was built, Shore emphasized having good fields of fire and alternative hides which the sniper would use on a variable schedule.

After the war, Shore made it a point to talk with as many snipers as he could to assemble as much useful data as possible. He was particularly interested in determining the missions which snipers could perform most effectively. Among those he cited as best suited to the sniper sections assigned to British battalions were: control of no-man's land between the British and enemy positions, elimination of enemy machine-gun crews, assumption of hidden positions in no-man's land to snipe at enemy positions (he cited many cases of eliminating German sentries as they were entering or leaving positions), elimination of enemy artillery or other observers, elimination of officers and NCOs (British snipers were trained to recognize German and other enemy rank insignia), and making use of their spotting scopes to function as observers to gather intelligence for their own unit. Battalion officers seemed especially to appreciate the sniper's value in dominating no-man's land since it allowed troops to be pulled back from the front line during the daytime for rest or hot food.

Shore pointed out as well some instances where he felt snipers could be invaluable but for which they were not used very often during the war. Snipers are invaluable in the counter-sniper role to neutralize enemy snipers left behind to slow an advance. He also pointed out that use of snipers to infiltrate through enemy lines ahead of an advance, so that they could engage enemy weapons crews from the rear and eliminate them, could speed an advance and break-through dramatically.

In discussing the counter-sniper role, Shore made some interesting comments about the 'dummy heads' which had been widely used in the trenches during the First World War to draw enemy sniper fire so that the snipers could be located and eliminated. Although British sniper schools usually had a few of these heads, which were of high quality, in the Second World War the mobile nature of warfare rendered them of little use. Still, at times when a particularly annoying German sniper was at work, one of the dummy heads might be deployed.

The more he analysed successful deployment of snipers, the more Shore felt that a hunting background was a huge advantage. For example, he found that many skilled hunters acting as snipers could identify enemy movement by watching the reaction of animals in the area. He also noted that a good precept for British snipers was to attempt to emulate a successful poacher! When discussing snipers from various countries, he emphasized the success of those with a hunting background. For example, he noted how successful Norwegian mountain hunters were at sniping from the mountains at Germans in villages during the invasion and occupation of Norway. Likewise, Shore praised the skills of Finnish snipers who were skilled hunters and woodsmen.

In fact, Shore concluded that a successful background as hunter was a much better indicator of success as a sniper than marksmanship skill of the type attained on the ranges at Bisley. He felt that, in addition to learning to take a shot at a partially hidden target, hunters had developed the ability to estimate range and windage quickly and practically. His own experience was that teaching trainees about minute of angle for making elevation and windage adjustments was generally not successful for most. Additionally, hunters had a better feel for terrain and choosing shooting positions where sun would not glint on telescope lenses or muzzle blast would not throw up debris. In his discussion of how a sniper training programme should be run, Shore even suggested that hunting of game should be part of the curriculum.

Shore used some Australian snipers who were former kangaroo hunters as an example of his thesis. Many of these men killed substantial numbers of Japanese using the same skills which allowed them to place a shot carefully enough not to damage a kangaroo pelt and lower its value. He also noted that many Australian snipers were trained to shoot at longer ranges than typical British snipers. This is not to say there were not British snipers who could shoot at long range. He also mentioned a technique used at longer ranges when multiple snipers were working together. If they could not agree on the range to the target, each sniper would set his sights for the range he believed correct and all would shoot simultaneously at the enemy. Normally, at least one shot would be true. This same technique of using multiple snipers was sometimes used for very long range shots as well and often proved successful.

Shore made an interesting observation about British snipers operating against the Japanese in the tropics. Their success was noticeably less than in Europe, and Shore speculated that this was at least partially due to the fact the heat caused them to carry out their mission wearing just shirt sleeves which did not allow cushioning for the elbows or shoulder when in the shooting position. He suggested that lighter clothing of the bush-jacket type with padded elbows and shoulders would have improved performance substantially.

Shore felt that many of the tales of Soviet snipers were propaganda and that they were not as good as portrayed. He did feel there were some very effective snipers who had grown up in the Urals or Siberia and were skilled stalkers or hunters, but suggested that they were the exception. At least some of the rationale for Shores's conclusions came from debriefing Germans after the war who had fought on the Eastern Front, many of whom claimed that they had faced few if any skilled snipers. It may be argued, however, that many of the most successful Soviet snipers fought at Stalingrad, and the Germans who had faced them were still in POW camps in the Soviet Union for many years after the war and could not be interviewed by Shore.

Always interested in sniper tactics, Shore made note of the use of Soviet snipers who would move into forward positions prior to a Soviet offensive. Once the artillery preparation of the German lines had taken place, the snipers would fire at troops preparing to meet the Soviet advance. He also noted the use of armoured shields by Soviet snipers so they could occupy forward positions. These forward Soviet snipers often sniped at machine-gun positions or used tracer ammunition to pinpoint a tank or artillery position for Soviet artillery. Shore expressed some scepticism about the effectiveness of this technique, though he did make an interesting point about use of tracer when he noted the Soviets were using white tracer which got lost against the snow, while the Germans used red tracer which showed up well against the snow.

From D-Day onward, Shore had attempted to gather information about German snipers and came to the conclusion that there were really few trained snipers deployed. Once again, this may have been because most German snipers were deployed on the Eastern Front. He did note, however, that in Italy British troops encountered some very skilled German *Fallschirmjäger* snipers. In discussing the tactical use of snipers, Shore commented that the Germans missed a real chance to disrupt Allied air support by not deploying a few snipers in the wooded areas surrounding the hastily built airfields from which aircraft flew in support of Allied advances. The occasional sniper kill would have made airmen and support personnel maintaining the aircraft much less free to move around the airfields and would have tied down infantry in the sniper suppression role.

On at least one occasion an instructor from the sniping school was in Italy and made at least two kills at 650 metres, a distance at which the Germans felt safe. This same instructor related to

Shore a good example of the strategy that is often involved in sniping/counter-sniping encounters:

> Jerry was very keen to find out where we were; we knew that he could not see us. One day he put up a dummy target over his trench to draw our fire whilst he watched through a periscope situated nearby. Both the dummy and the periscope I picked up through my telescope, and so I am quite sure he was most disappointed at the failure of his ruse.
>
> Next day we expected the obvious – that he would try a little bout of counter-sniping. So at dawn we watched the only piece of cover he could get to during the hours of darkness where he could snipe back at us under 300 yards range. Like a Good Little German he had done the obvious and he was there all right. One burst from a Bren which had been lined up in readiness for him finished him off before he had time to become a nuisance.

Of course, it is important to bear in mind that the Lovat Scouts, the best snipers and stalkers in the British Army, had been deployed to Italy in 1944 where their mountaineering, stalking, and sniping skills were put to good use.

Shore was a great believer in the British system of using a sniper/observer team as it enabled the observer to use his more powerful spotting scope to help the sniper find targets as well as offering psychological support to avoid some of the loneliness of sniping. Shore felt the perfect weapon for the observer was the M1 Carbine, which could be carried easily, but gave substantial firepower if needed. Debriefing Germans after the war, he found that many of them believed that the British system of using a sniper and observer team gave a definite advantage compared to German snipers. He allowed for individual preference, however, and noted that some snipers preferred to operate entirely alone.

A practical use of multiple snipers occurred along the Lamone River, where a patrol had crossed, then come under fire. Although the patrol escaped back across the river, one wounded soldier was left behind. By British use of multiple snipers, the Germans were kept from approaching the wounded soldier until a boat, under cover of the snipers, could be sent across to rescue him.

As he developed his own sniper programmes, Shore drew on his wartime experience and the experiences of others. It has already been pointed out that Shore did not feel standard bulls-eye shooting was good training for snipers other than to evaluate their marksmanship initially. He concluded that the perfect sniper training range would offer a variety of terrain which would allow training in observation, stalking and camouflage, and practical shooting at three-dimensional dummy targets. This training area should be available twenty-four hours a day so day and night training could be carried out. Also counter to standard wisdom among competition shooters, Shore believed that snipers should be taught the value of shooting from a rest as often they would have to use a rest of some type to take their shot.

In sniper courses and during demonstrations of sniper employment for battalion or higher command officers, Shore noted that an extremely useful demonstration of the 'economy of force' value of the sniper was having a sniper fire at targets versus a Bren gun firing at the targets at a like distance. Each was to engage six targets and, invariably, the sniper prevailed.

Shore hoped that his book would help avoid the common problem of developing a sniper training programme during wartime, then losing the skills during peacetime, to the extent that sniper rifles deteriorated in storage from lack of use and maintenance. He also hoped to argue for snipers to be included in the unit organization of an infantry battalion. Shore pointed out that in some of the units where snipers were employed most usefully, they were assigned to the support company and were under direct orders from the battalion commander through the support company commander. Placing snipers under an officer with sniper training was also deemed most effective rather than having the sniper unit commanded by an NCO who would have less ability to influence decisions on their employment. This was rarely the case, however. Standard organization of a battalion sniping section consisted of one sergeant, one corporal, two lance corporals, and four privates.

As part of sniper employment Shore was also emphatic that snipers should have clear-cut missions rather than just be sent to wander the front lines. But, at one point, he admitted that there were some very effective 'lone wolf' snipers who could be employed very effectively by just sending them where the action was.

Combining his own background in shooting and hunting, his sniper training, and his experiences with snipers and their rifles, Shore drew some conclusions about the characteristics of the ideal sniper rifle. Shore began his discussion by pointing out that the traditional military sniping rifle in the British forces had been a service rifle chambered for the standard service round and chosen for above average accuracy, then fitted with a telescopic sight with windage and elevation adjustments.

Shore, however, argued that a smaller calibre than .303-inch firing a lighter bullet at higher velocity, would be preferable for the sniper as it would shoot flatter and hence require less adjustment for range. He offered .276 as a likely calibre. Shore also felt that a 4-power or 5-power scope would be desirable. In discussing his ideas with experienced snipers, Shore found most agreed, though he did receive comments that they would like to see better lens covers for the scope, that they would like to see it lighter in weight, though of 4- or 5-power, and they would prefer it to be mounted by sliding on rather than the screw-on method used on the No. 4 Mk 1 (T). As an alternative to the higher-velocity .276 round, Shore also mentioned the possibility of using a high-velocity, accurate .303 round designed for snipers. Should snipers not be able to receive a supply of the special ammunition, they could still use standard service .303 ammunition.

Shore's contribution to sniping was not in the number of kills he registered. Instead, it was in his observation and analysis of sniper training and tactics and his reportage of his conclusions in *With British Snipers to the Reich*. As Shore's book did not initially appear until 1948, its influence was primarily felt in sniper training for Korea and later conflicts. However, as a sniper trainer during the Second World War, Shore did impart some of his knowledge to various snipers whom he instructed. In fact, he felt the necessity of sound instruction so important that he put off his own return to Great Britain and discharge for some weeks single-handedly to run sniper courses for NCOs in his unit.

In 1946, 'By Command of the Army Council' a manual titled *Small Arms Training: Sniping* was published to gather the information learned regarding training and use of snipers during the war. Much of the information about sniper training is obviously based on the sniper schools established during the war and which Shore had attended. Whether Shore made any contribution is unknown as no authorship is attributed. However, this manual, taken in conjunction to *With British Snipers to the Reich*, would undoubtedly offer a wealth of information to future trainers of snipers.

Certainly, Shore would not disagree with the section on 'Characteristics and Training of Snipers' early in the manual:

7. A fully trained sniper can be defined as a soldier, who is trained to locate an enemy, however well hidden, who can stalk or lie in wait for him unseen, and who is an expert shot with the rifle. His object is to kill with one round. He is the big game hunter of the battlefield, and must combine the art of the hunter, the wiles of a poacher and the skill of a target shot, with the determination to seek out his enemy.

8. He must be trained not only in rifle marksmanship, but also to a high degree in observation and in fieldcraft. Without great skill as an observer, he will seldom be able to find suitable targets; and without a comprehensive knowledge of fieldcraft, he will rarely get to a fire position within shot of his quarry; thus observation and fieldcraft must be thoroughly understood by him.

Certainly, the comments about the sniper as big game hunter or poacher could have been made by Shore but also by some of his cohorts from the Lovat Scouts. As in *With British Snipers to the Reich*, the publication of *Small Arms Training: Sniping* shows a clear intent to avoid the mistake of letting sniping knowledge and training stagnate as after the First World War.

References

As well as Clifford Shore's own book, *With British Snipers to the Reich* (Greenhill Books, 1997), the following are recommended.

British Army Instructions on Snipers and Sniping (The War Office, 1946)

John Plaster, *The History of Sniping and Sharpshooting* (Paladin Press, 2008)

Ian Skennerton, *The British Sniper: British and Commonwealth Sniping and Equipment, 1915–1983* (Privately published, 1984)

Chapter 8

SEPP ALLERBERGER

Wehrmacht Scharfschützen

Newly assigned to sniper duties in his German Army mountain regiment, Private Josef 'Sepp' Allerberger had been ordered to eliminate a Soviet sharpshooter who had killed several of his comrades. During August 1943, operations in the southern part of the Eastern Front had coalesced into the type of temporary trench warfare that brought sniper activities to the fore. Allerberger's unit – the Austrian-recruited, 2nd Battalion, 144th Gebirgsjäger (Mountain Troops) Regiment – had established a reputation for sniping, but this was to be his first mission.

Fortunately for Allerberger, the Soviet marksman was poorly trained and over-confident. Allerberger instructed a soldier to wave a cap above the trench. The inexperienced Soviet rifleman blasted away at the cap, the muzzle-flash of his rifle giving away his position to Allerberger, who had been carefully scanning the enemy line with his binoculars. The Soviet sniper committed a further cardinal error in remaining in his firing position – Allerberger could even see the light glinting on his telescopic sight.

The young Austrian sniper prepared to take his shot, adopting a firing position behind some logs in the German entrenchments. There was a small gap between the logs, just wide enough for the muzzle of his rifle, but too small to permit the use of a telescopic sight. But as the range was short – just about 100 metres – the rifle's conventional iron sights were sufficient for the task. As he looked along his sights at the enemy soldier, Allerberger – like so many snipers before him – was seized by a spasm of conscience, but his training soon took over and, bringing his breathing under control, he gently pulled the trigger.

The shot rang out across no-man's land. The blast of dust raised by the bullet leaving the muzzle obscured his view, but an infantryman shouted out: 'Perfect shot! You've got the swine!' Allerberger's comrades gathered around him, congratulating his shooting prowess. As a young soldier only recently arrived at the front, he was a little overwhelmed by the praise from these hardened veterans but was privately delighted that he had found his vocation as a sharpshooter in the German Wehrmacht.

Allerberger did not fit the traditional mould for a sniper. Many had experienced an extended background as game hunters in their youth: the Red Army sniper Vassili Zaitsev had developed his skills shooting game in the great northern forest, as had Simo Häyhä in his native Finland; while a youthful Bert Kemp had been sent out to down squirrels for the family pot in the wooded hills of Tennessee. By contrast, Allerberger was an apprentice carpenter who had followed his father into the trade. But during his two years fighting on the Eastern Front he would amass 257 certified kills, making him the second most successful sniper in the German Army during the Second World War.

Born on 24 December 1924 in a village close to the Austrian city of Salzburg, Sepp Allerberger was brought up in a strict, authoritarian environment where military service was not only the norm but also a source of pride. He had few reservations when declared medically fit for service in the Wehrmacht during the autumn of 1942. According to the all-persuasive propaganda machine of Reich Minister Josef Goebbels, the war in the East was all but won, and only a last push was needed to secure final victory.

In February 1943 Allerberger was inducted into the *Gebirgs-jäger* – whose Austrian headquarters was in the Tyrolean town of Kufstein – before being despatched to Mittenwald to begin his basic training, which in the German Army was hard and thorough. While at Mittenwald he was assigned as a machine gunner, and it was with this speciality that he was sent with other reinforcements to the join his regiment on the Eastern Front in the summer of 1943.

The 144th Mountain Regiment was part of the 3rd Mountain Division, deployed in the southern Ukraine on the west bank of the River Donets near Voroshilovgrad. Almost immediately on arrival at the front, Allerberger found himself in the thick of a Soviet offensive, launched in July 1943 and designed to force the Germans back to the River Dnieper. It was a fearsome introduction to the war on the Eastern Front, where the outnumbered German forces were subjected to massive artillery bombardments from the Red Army, followed by wave after wave of infantry assaults that almost inevitably forced the Germans to retreat.

During the Soviet offensive it soon became obvious to Allerberger that machine gunners were a focus for Soviet fire, especially from the many Red Army sharpshooters who helped ensure that casualties among German machine-gun teams were disproportionately high. After five days of fighting, Allerberger was hit – not, in fact, by a sniper's rifle bullet but by a shell splinter that cut into his left hand. Although this was a minor wound, he was sent to the regimental headquarters to convalesce while performing light duties.

One of his tasks was to repair damaged German weapons and to sort the piles of captured Soviet small arms. While sifting through some Soviet weapons he came across a sniper rifle, a Mosin-Nagant 91/30 with a 3.5-power PU telescopic sight. This rugged, reliable and accurate bolt-action rifle, fitted with a five-round box magazine, intrigued Allerberger; he sought and was given permission to try it out, using the copious supplies of captured Soviet ammunition for target practice. This was essentially the same weapon that proved so deadly in the hands of both Vassili Zaitsev and Simo Häyhä. Allerberger also proved a natural with the rifle, and was encouraged by the Weapons NCO to develop his shooting prowess. Soon he was capable of hitting a matchbox out to a range of 100 metres.

Allerberger's regiment took sniping seriously, and it was no coincidence that among its ranks was Matthias Hetzenauer from the Tyrol, who was to achieve an incredible score of 345 certified kills, making him Nazi Germany's top sniper. When news of

Allerberger's skill with a rifle reached his company commander, he was released from his duties as a machine gunner and reassigned as the sniper for his company. Although a daunting prospect, this change of role provided the independently minded Allerberger with new challenges.

During the remainder of 1943 the Germans were relentlessly pushed backwards by the Red Army, in a series of cataclysmic attacks that could not be held for long. Between the offensives, the Germans withdrew to new defensive lines, which they would hold until the next Soviet assault. These withdrawal and defensive phases gave great scope for German snipers to deliver telling blows against Soviet targets.

By mid-September the Germans had fallen back to a new defensive line in front of the Dnieper. It was clear to the Germans that the Soviets were planning to resume their offensive, if only from the number of reconnaissance patrols that were being sent out to probe German positions. Allerberger was given wide latitude by his superiors to wage his sniper war in the way he thought best. During this period he would often slip out into no-man's land during darkness, establish a good firing position and await events. On one clear morning he observed a Soviet patrol pushing forward out of a small stand of trees, entering his field of fire only 150 metres away.

Officers were a priority target for snipers, and on this morning Allerberger was in luck: leading the patrol was an extremely well-dressed officer, the smartness of his uniform giving him away. Looking through his telescopic sight, Allerberger could see the fine detail of the man's polished leather boots as he paused to look around. It was an easy shot, aimed at the torso. As the muzzle-blast smoke disappeared, Allerberger saw the officer sink to his knees and then fall to the ground. The other Soviet soldiers initially scattered in panic, unaware of the source of the shot. Normally, Allerberger would have slipped away unobserved, but on this occasion he could see that his position was un-compromised and he quickly despatched two more enemy soldiers who were bravely but foolishly attempting to recover the body of their now dead officer.

After the war, Allerberger, Hetzenauer and another sniper from the 3rd Mountain Division, Helmut Wirnsberger, were interviewed about their sniping techniques and tactics, and all three made the point that eliminating officers could stall an enemy attack, and one even laconically noted: 'Shot the respective leaders of enemy's attack eight times in one day!'

Although the Red Army smashed its way across the Dnieper in October, the Germans maintained a bridgehead on the eastern bank of the river at Nikopol, and the mountain troops were assigned to help defend the bridgehead.

As the weather worsened and snow began to fall, they received a new batch of winter camouflage uniforms: reversible cotton suits (padded with cotton wool) with white on one side and a regular camouflage pattern on the other. The sniper version had loops fitted so that natural camouflage could be easily attached to the clothing. Snipers had their reservations about these uniforms, however, as they found it difficult to conceal all of the white when the temperate side was being worn, especially with the hoods that left the sniper with a potentially fatal white ring around his face. Unsurprisingly, Allerberger went his own way, and after conducting various experiments he persuaded the regimental tailor to make him a bespoke sniper suit in temperate camouflage, as well as a light-cotton white oversuit that was worn in winter conditions but was easy to fold away when the snows melted.

Although Allerberger had opened his sharpshooting career as a 'lone wolf' he began to follow standard sniping practice by using an observer to help locate targets, spot the fall of shot and provide vital moral support. He had struck up a friendship with a soldier called Balduin Moser and they worked effectively with each other – although their relationship was to end in tragedy.

Allerberger had begun to use a Soviet tank knocked out in no-man's land as both an observational and firing platform. The protection the tank provided had made the normally careful German marksman dangerously over-confident, and he and Moser repeatedly used the position. This had come to the attention of a Soviet sniper who patiently waited for the two

Germans to return to the tank. As Moser was scouting targets for Allerberger, the Red Army sniper struck. A bullet hit Moser in the lower face, smashing his jaw and ripping away his lips and much of his tongue. It was a desperate wound, requiring immediate medical attention, but if they attempted to move from the safety of the tank they would be hit again by the Soviet marksman. Allerberger looked on in helpless desperation as what remained of Moser's tongue began to swell, blocking the airway to his lungs. During what seemed an eternity, Moser slowly asphyxiated. Only when night fell was Allerberger able to drag his dead companion back to German lines. It had been a salutary lesson in not taking anything for granted.

The regular breakdowns in the food supply chain to front-line troops forced them to forage from the land, and after more than two years of war in the East there was pitifully little to eat, with the troops often reliant on a diet of apples and pickled cucumbers. Worn out by the strain of combat, poor weather conditions and a poor diet, Allerberger succumbed to a severe bout of gastro-enteritis as he and his comrades withdrew from the Nikopol bridgehead in January 1944. He was withdrawn from the front, but after a vital period of rest and good medical treatment he was strong enough to return to active service. While at the front he had come to the attention of the new CO of 2nd Battalion, Captain Max Kloss, and from then on he operated at battalion level, often under the immediate direction of Kloss.

The death of Moser had profoundly affected Allerberger. For a while he went back to operating on his own, but eventually returned to using a partner for particular missions, drawing from a pool of men with sharpshooting or reconnaissance experience. He also enlisted the help of his infantry comrades for specific operations, one of which involved using machine guns to fire in the general direction of the enemy to mask his own more accurate aimed fire, which netted an extraordinary figure of eighteen kills against Soviet infantry in one operation.

But, despite their best efforts, the Germans could not hold the Soviet juggernaut, and as they retreated from the River Dneiper back to the Bug and then the Dniester they were pressed so hard that, at the end of March 1944, they were cut off by the advancing Red Army. Charging Cossack cavalry nearly overran Allerberger's position, and he was forced to exchange his sniper rifle for the 9-mm MP 40 machine-pistol that he always carried for close protection. After the Cossacks were repulsed, the 144th Mountain Regiment's commander, Colonel Anton Lorch, made the painful decision to order an immediate break-out, which meant leaving behind the seriously wounded. Knowing their likely fate, they were left with weapons to end their suffering swiftly before capture. The break-out succeeded and by 10 April the remains of the regiment had crossed over the Dniester to relative safety.

Once on the far bank of the Dniester the mountain troops had an opportunity for recuperation and reinforcement during the following weeks. To Allerberger's and his comrades' relief this was a quiet sector, although Soviet troops held positions on the other side of the river, which at this point was as much as 400 metres wide – too far for ordinary shooting but perfect for sniping. Allerberger patrolled his section of the river, taking shots at Soviet soldiers lulled into the false sense of security provided by their distance from German lines.

On one occasion, during May, he came across a group of Soviet soldiers bathing noisily in the river some 600 metres from his position. It was a difficult long-range shot for Allerberger and his Mosin-Nagant rifle, but there was minimal wind and the light was good. Resting his rifle on a stack of turf squares he had just cut, he prepared to take the shot. His target was sunbathing naked on the river bank, and was accordingly easy to pick out. Quickly looking through his sight after firing the shot, he knew he had been successful: the enemy soldier lay immobile on the bank, while his comrades ran for cover. Allerberger had long since surrendered any scruples about shooting unarmed men; war on the Eastern Front was a simple case of 'kill or be killed', and he took a quiet satisfaction from having hit the mark at such long range.

While the units of the 3rd Mountain Division rebuilt their strength, Captain Kloss engineered things so that Allerberger was sent back to Austria to attend a sniper-school course. By this time, Allerberger had pretty much learned all there was to know about sniping in the field, but Kloss decided to give his young protégé a well-earned break from front-line fighting and a chance to see his family.

On 30 May, Allerberger handed over his trusty Mosin-Nagant rifle and boarded a waiting truck, the first stage in a five-day trek back to Austria. The four-week course was held at Seetaleralpe, and Allerberger was surprised – and relieved – to find the instructors friendly and the atmosphere relaxed – in marked contrast to the unremitting harshness of basic training. Allerberger was also pleased to discover that his instructors knew their job, most of them ex-snipers whose wounds had removed them from front-line service.

The German Army had neglected sniping in the early phases of the war, but the heavy casualties inflicted by Soviet snipers on the Eastern Front forced a rethink, and from 1943 onwards sniper schools began to produce highly trained marksmen. The course followed the basic elements of sniper technique: marksmanship, fieldcraft, reconnaissance and tactical awareness. The German and Soviet attitude to sniping as an important military discipline contrasted favourably with the haphazard approaches adopted by the Western Allies. The British sniper trainer Captain Clifford Shore despaired at the British Army's cavalier approach to the subject, a state of affairs that also bedevilled the U.S. Army.

At the German sniper school, special attention was paid to camouflage, the instructors emphasizing the point with the motto: 'Camouflage ten times, shoot once!' The camouflage techniques developed at the sniper schools were often highly elaborate, the recommended hides taking a sniper several hours to construct properly. Allerberger had his reservations about some of these more elaborate schemes, believing a sniper needed to maintain flexibility and freedom of movement. He did, however, find the camouflage umbrella highly effective. This was, in effect, half an ordinary umbrella, its 'circumference' spanning only 180 degrees. It was painted to match the terrain and was covered in natural camouflage, with the sniper crawling along the ground, pushing the umbrella ahead of him as a form of concealment.

When operating in static positions, Allerberger did use some elaborate dummies to draw out enemy marksmen. Some were kitted out in full German Army uniform, with masks for faces, and were fitted with cigarettes that were smoked by the sniper's assistant using a long rubber tube. At other times, the dummy would be 'armed' with a rifle that could be fired using a wire pulley.

Allerberger had been happy with his old Soviet sniper rifle but at Seetaleralpe he had the chance to try out other weapons, including the 7.92-mm Mauser Karabiner 98k, which equipped the ordinary infantryman but was popular with snipers because it was highly reliable and its forward-lug locking system made it more accurate than other bolt-action rifles. Snipers received superior quality rifles from the manufacturer and unit armourers were able to make minor improvements. They also received top quality, match-grade ammunition. A variety of telescopic sights were issued for the 98k, including the official Zeiss 1.5-power and 4-power sights and the commercially acquired 6-power Hensoldt sight. Allerberger was issued with a rifle fitted with a Hensoldt sight, which he found highly satisfactory and used for the remainder of the war.

Another rifle offered to snipers was the 7.92-mm Walther Gewehr 43, a self-loading rifle that had been designed with an integral telescopic-sight mount, enabling its easy use as a sniper rifle. Despite the advantage of an increased rate of fire – allowing a follow-up shot by simply pulling the trigger – it was not popular with snipers: it was heavier than the 98k, lacked long-range accuracy and had a tendency to jam at critical moments. Allerberger favoured the 98k for sniper operations, as did Matthias Hetzenauer, who believed the G 43 went against the sniper philosophy of 'one shot, one kill'.

Allerberger passed out of the sniper course in the top three and, instead of returning directly to the front, he was given a few days' leave with his family. After nearly a year of combat, Allerberger was no longer the callow youth who had optimistically departed his Austrian village. He was now a hardened veteran, who had witnessed terrible scenes and personally killed scores of Soviet soldiers. Like so many other front-line soldiers he found it impossible to talk truthfully of his experiences – even to his father, a veteran of the First World War. It was a strangely unsettling interlude, and it was with a sense of relief that he bade his parents and sisters farewell and climbed aboard the train taking him to the front.

He arrived back with the 144th Mountain Regiment in mid-August. They were occupying a quiet sector alongside units from their Romanian ally, although it was common knowledge that a Soviet attack was imminent. Complicating matters were a succession of rumours that placed doubt on the reliability of the Romanians. When the Soviet offensive was launched on 20 August, the rumours turned into fact, and three days later the Romanian government was overthrown in a coup with the new leaders taking their country over to the Soviet side. This caused enormous problems for the German mountain troops who were fighting Soviet forces to their front, and now had to contend with hostile Romanians on their flanks and to their rear.

Cut off on several occasions, the Germans were nevertheless able to conduct a fighting retreat into the Carpathian mountains that helped stabilize the line. Allerberger and other snipers were repeatedly employed to act as rearguards. German field commanders often preferred them to machine guns – the standard rearguard weapon – because the flexible sniper teams could disengage more easily. Allerberger found that a few well aimed sniper shots could bring a Soviet attack to a complete halt, without the enemy being aware of his position. A machine gun, by comparison, would immediately give its position away, inviting retaliatory counter-fire.

The new rifle/scope combination now being used by Aller-berger was an aid to improved accuracy, and the superior 6-power magnification not only increased the size of the target, but, through a larger objective lens, it provided a better image in low-light conditions.

Rather than having to rely on captured Soviet ammunition, he now had access to regular supplies of high-quality German cartridges. These included the B or *Beobachtung* (observation) round that was fitted with a small explosive charge that ignited on impact and provided a puff of smoke to indicate the fall of shot. These were used by Allerberger and his sniper comrades to mark out enemy positions for machine-gun and mortar crews, and in dry weather they could set alight straw-thatched wooden buildings. Expensive, and lacking the long-range accuracy of conventional ball rounds, they were seldom employed against enemy personnel – despite the many lurid accounts of their use against human targets (a standard high-velocity bullet hitting the body is sufficiently explosive in itself).

As they fell back to the Carpathians, a group of soldiers that included Allerberger witnessed the destruction of a German patrol caught by heavy Soviet fire in open ground ahead of them. Only one German survived, and he was severely wounded, his screams ringing out across what was effectively no-man's land. The wounded man lay in highly exposed ground, and any attempt at rescue would have been suicidal folly. Allerberger's comrades gathered around him, and pleaded with him to end the man's agony. He hesitated but then reluctantly agreed to take the shot. By careful manoeuvring he was able to get an image of the man's head in his sights, and with a sick feeling in his stomach he pulled the trigger. After the shot there was silence, and Allerberger's unit continued the retreat.

Later that day, as night fell, they spotted a Red Army position some 150 metres away, which they carefully skirted. Looking through the semi-darkness Allerberger could see a pale patch close to the position, which, through telescopic sights, proved to be a Soviet soldier bending down to defecate, his trousers by his ankles. A swift, well-aimed shot hit the man in the stomach; his cries alerted his comrades who loosed off a fusillade of wild shots in the general direction of Allerberger's patrol, which slipped away into the darkness. It was a revenge of sorts.

As the Germans were slowly forced back towards Hungary, Allerberger now worked closely with his battalion commander, the newly promoted Major Kloss, often acting as his bodyguard. Allerberger liked working for Kloss – both men having a natural affinity for the other – and by operating from battalion head-quarters he had more freedom of action, and, not least, access to better food. It was during this period that Allerberger tried out one of three scoped G 43 rifles that had been sent to the 144th Mountain Regiment. Never regarding it as a sniper weapon, he found the semi-automatic rifle, with its ten-round magazine, a useful tool for rapid, medium-range shooting, and used it to good effect on a number of occasions.

While defending the Hungarian city of Miskolc, Allerberger was grazed by a fragment from a mortar round. This was the third time he had been hit, but they had all been minor wounds, and given the amount of combat he had endured, he led something of a charmed life. Less fortunate was Major Kloss, who was killed during a Red Army artillery bombardment on 10 November – a profound loss for Allerberger, who, now more than ever, had to inure himself to the consequences of death all around him.

Allerberger was welcomed back to his company, which with the rest of the regiment began the process of withdrawal into the Tatra mountains of the German rump state of Slovakia. As the Red Army pressed inexorably forward, so Slovakia's loyalty waned, and groups of Slovakian partisans emerged to ambush the Germans in the region's steep-sided valleys. During their retreat, the mountain troops passed briefly through southern Poland, and there had time to adopt a defensive position on the edge of a village, with Soviet forces approximately 500 metres away – a good distance for long-range sniping.

Allerberger developed several sniping platforms in the attic roofs of the village, following the cardinal rule of not firing more than a couple of shots from any one position. And, in accordance with his sniper training, he would knock out several slates or shingles from a roof to disguise the origin of the shot further. He had little difficulty in taking out careless Soviet infantrymen who erroneously believed themselves safe from the German lines opposite them.

Eventually, the exasperated Red Army commander of the section opposite Allerberger ordered up a light anti-tank gun to blast away the enemy sniper's position – wherever it was. The gun's three-man crew had not been properly briefed on the dangers facing them, and they pushed the artillery piece forward in direct view of Allerberger. His first two shots each downed an artilleryman; the third crew member, instead of fleeing to safety, attempted to rescue one of his comrades. As he carried him away, Allerberger's third shot hit home. The anti-tank gun remained in the open for the rest of the day, unfired. Only with the onset of darkness was it towed away.

A special badge for *Scharfschützen* (sharpshooters) had been issued on 20 August 1944 to encourage high scores among Germany's snipers. Oval in shape, and to be worn on the cuff, the badge consisted of an eagle's head surrounded by oak leaves and was awarded in three classes: the first for 20 confirmed kills, the second for 40 confirmed kills, the third for 60 confirmed kills. Only a few were awarded, however, and Allerberger had to wait until early March 1945 before receiving all three classes simultaneously. Although gratified to receive the award, Allerberger did not sew any of the badges onto his sleeve, fully aware that to be captured with such a badge would mean a particularly brutal end. He simply put the badges into an envelope and posted them to his parents back in Austria.

In early April 1945 he was awarded the Iron Cross First Class, which, given his contribution to his battalion's performance on the Eastern Front, was long overdue. According to his biographer, Albrecht Wacker, he also received the Knight's Cross of the Iron Cross later in that month, but no mention of this award can be found in official records (a grainy photograph of Allerberger shows him with the Knight's Cross at his throat, but this part of the image does not fully convince).

By now the war was, at last, drawing to a close. The 3rd Mountain Division had been forced back towards the Czech city of Olmütz early in May, while rumours circulated through the ranks that the Red Army had captured Berlin and that the Führer was dead. On 9 May the Wehrmacht High Command confirmed the inevitable and ordered its forces to end hostilities and lay down their arms. Lieutenant General Paul Klatt, commander of the 3rd Mountain Division, decided not to surrender his men to the Red Army, but instead released them from their soldiers' oath and told them to make their way west to U.S. Army lines as best they could.

While the majority of the mountain troops marched westward, Allerberger teamed up with a soldier called Peter Gollup and decided to head due south to Austria. But the two men faced the problem of reaching the Austrian border, which was about 200 kilometres away, all the while avoiding the Red Army and armed gangs of local Czechs, out for vengeance. Before they set out, Allerberger destroyed his sniper rifle; it was a painful moment, but he would have no need for it now, and to be captured with it would be to invite almost certain death. Instead, he relied on his MP 40 machine-pistol to get them out of trouble.

They decided to walk by night and hide during the day to escape being sighted by the civilian population or encountering any roving enemy patrols. On the second night of their journey, a desperate need for food forced them to approach an isolated farmhouse. In this region there were a number of Sudeten Germans, and this building had a generally German look to it. When a man opened a bedroom window and shouted down to them in very broken German, it was obvious to Allerberger that he was a Czech and so he hung back. But Gollup was more desperate for food and advanced further, only to be hit by a hail of machine-pistol fire. Allerberger helped him back into some nearby bushes, but his wound was mortal and he died a few minutes later.

Once more on his own, Allerberger was even more guarded about revealing himself to others, relying on his excellent field-craft skills to see him through. While in hiding, however, he heard German voices and recognized the advancing troops as men from his own division. He teamed up with them and continued southwards towards the border. Having survived an attack by Czech partisans, Allerberger and three other companions came across a farmhouse and discovered that they were more than 15 kilometres over the border. They were back in their homeland.

They were subsequently captured by troops from the occupying U.S. Army near the city of Linz, and then taken to a temporary POW camp at Mauerkirchen where they were processed by their captors. The sheer volume of prisoners began to overwhelm the American authorities, who decided to release the walking wounded. Allerberger was able to persuade the American guards to release him to look after one of his wounded comrades. As a free man, Allerberger returned to his village and a tearful reunion with his parents and sisters.

Allerberger was inevitably scarred by his two years of murderous fighting on the Eastern Front. But, like so many men of his generation, he suppressed these horrifying experiences, speaking little of his time at the front. He was simply relieved to have survived the war. Any interest he may have had for travel and adventure had been sated by his wartime service, and with the peace he returned to the family carpentry business, eventually taking over from his father. Other leading snipers – such as Zaitsev and Häyhä – followed a similar pattern of avoiding the limelight in favour of a quiet life.

Among the many people Allerberger did business with in the postwar years, few could have realized that this modest man had been one of the Wehrmacht's top snipers, with 257 official kills, with many more going unrecorded – an extraordinary achievement. When asked what were the chief qualities required of a sniper beyond marksmanship, he replied: 'calmness, good judgement, courage'. These, of course, were the qualities displayed by Allerberger himself. Another quality would have been caution, which ensured that the Austrian sniper survived the war and died at the ripe old age of 85 on 2 March 2010.

References

Erich Kern, *Dance of Death* (Collins, 1951)

James Lucas, *Hitler's Mountain Troops* (Weidenfeld, 1992)

Peter R. Senich, *The German Sniper 1914–45* (Paladin Press, 1982)

Snipers in Action: The Unseen Weapon (Wehrmacht, 1944; International Historic Films [DVD], 1988)

Sniper: The Invisible Enemy (Wehrmacht, 1944; International Historic Films [DVD], 1988)

William H. Tantum, *Sniper Rifles of the Two World Wars* (Ottawa
  Museum Restoration Service, 1967)

Albrecht Wacker, *Sniper on the Eastern Front: The Memoirs of Sepp
  Allerberger* (Pen & Sword Military, 2005)

Charles Winchester, *Ostfront: Hitler's War on Russia 1941–45*
  (Osprey, 1998)

Chapter 9

PATRICK DEVLIN

Fighting Irishman

During the night of 31 August 1939, Nazi forces posing as Polish saboteurs seized the Gleiwitz Radio Station in Silesia, Poland, and sent an anti-German broadcast across the radio waves. It was the eve of the planned Nazi invasion of Poland and a ruse to the world, a false provocation, and justification for Germany to attack. Operation Himmler had started, comprising twenty-one incidents in all along the border between the neighbouring countries. and was intended to give the appearance of Polish aggression against Germany. In supposed retaliation the German Army invaded Poland on 1 September, attacking from three directions, north, south and west. Striking almost at dawn, German tanks, infantry and cavalry penetrated Polish territory on three fronts with five armies, a total of 1.5 million troops. The Poles were no match for the Germans and retreated to pre-prepared defensive positions. However, all defiance became futile after the Soviets then attacked from the east on 17 September, effectively surrounding the Poles. Small pockets of resistance remained but it was all over by 6 October. Britain and France had mobilized and declared war on Germany on 3 September and for the second time that century set about preparations for battle.

Almost two years from the capitulation of Poland, with the Second World War now in its third calendar year, a 17-year-old left Galway in neutral Eire in great haste. Straight after leaving school he crossed the border into the Northern counties, and on 1 July 1941 promptly volunteered to enlist and fight against the Germans after signing on at the Army recruiting office in Clifton Street, Belfast. Patrick Devlin, not wanting to miss out on the big adventure, worried that it would pass him by, had lied about his age, stating that he was twenty. Freshly enlisted, 6410458 Private P. Devlin was sent to England.

This indeed was the start of a big adventure that would take the young man from basic training in England to the Normandy bridgehead during Operation Overlord, the break-out and push through France leading ultimately to his being wounded in action after the Rhine crossing.

England

Paddy Devlin was not alone. So many of his Irish peers found their way to England and uniformed service that some line regiments ended up Irish-heavy. This led to fights breaking out so often that a disgruntled Monty split the Irish up, sending them in much smaller numbers throughout the infantry as a punishment. Devlin's first regiment, the 8th Battalion, Royal Sussex Regiment, was based in Colchester, and after a massive fight against Canadians in the town Monty disbanded the battalion. Devlin was sent to the 11th Battalion, Queen's Royal Regiment (West Surrey) .

During the build-up training for D-Day Devlin volunteered for a brand-new airborne unit being formed from Irish volunteers; this was to be an Irish parachute battalion and was to be part of a brigade set to play a major part in the coming invasion campaign. However, after gathering many volunteers together, the 'top brass' had a re-think. Not wanting to put all the Irish back in the same basket and go through similar discipline problems, they decided they should be scattered throughout the airborne brigades. Rifleman Devlin therefore found himself in 18 Platoon, C Company, 1st Battalion, Royal Ulster Rifles, part of 6th Air Landing Brigade in the 6th Airborne Division, destined for the Normandy landings and led by Major General Richard Gale.

By this time Devlin had become a battalion scout-sniper. After the end of the Great War, sniper training and a sniper establishment had disappeared from the order of battle of most

British infantry units. No progress in developing sniping had been made in the years between the two world wars, and when war came again in 1939 it was considered a low priority. Even sniper rifles were in short supply, leading to any old First World War rifles that had not been sold off or committed to service elsewhere, being reissued. In the early days urgent requests were made for snipers, leading to the establishment of a small training school in France, and later one at Hythe. Even after the debacle leading to Dunkirk a negative attitude was taken towards this much-needed skill. By the time of the Normandy landings, however, things had changed. The British Army sniper was well equipped, trained and classed as a specialist.

The typical kit and equipment carried by such on the eve of Overlord was in Devlin's own words:

> The .303-inch British Enfield Rifle, Telescope No 32, GS Watch, Denison Smock, Face Veil, Binoculars, Compass Prismatic Mk3, x2 No 36 (Mills) Grenades, Bandolier of 50 rounds, Water bottle, x5 rounds Tracer, x5 rounds AP and Emergency Rations.

The war establishment for infantry battalions set during 1942 included 8 snipers: 1 sergeant, 1 corporal, 2 lance corporals and 4 privates. The specialist units were allocated even larger establishments, 32 snipers for a parachute battalion and 38 snipers for an air landing battalion. After Normandy a sniper school was again set up in France and this school also held courses to train instructors. These newly qualified trainers then went back to their respective units to run basic level and continuation courses for the snipers of each battalion.

After 1942 the First World War SMLE (Short Magazine Lee Enfield) and its back-up the P14, were officially replaced for sniper use by the Lee-Enfield Rifle No. 4, Mk 1 (T). Like its predecessors this was a bolt-action weapon, this time fitted with a 10-round magazine and a 3-power telescopic sight (No. 32), plus iron sights. The sniper rifles were selected from the standard factory production line, picked as superior from the batch. They were then stripped down and rebuilt with a new stock and a wooden cheek piece fitted. At this stage standard issue ammunition was still supplied.

Operation Tonga

Operation Tonga was the code-name given to the British airborne element of D-Day, the parachute and glider-borne force which was to land and secure vital objectives hours before the seaborne invasion, thus protecting the eastern flank of operations inland from Sword Beach. Objectives were the seizure and capture of two vital bridges over the Caen Canal and River Orne, later to become known as Pegasus and Horsa bridges, and the destruction of various German positions, including the Merville battery, which could make life uncomfortable for those on Sword Beach. All of this would help prevent the 21st Panzer Division from racing towards the allied bridgehead to sweep the attackers back into the sea.

Like many others during the build-up, Rifleman Devlin found himself in one of the little barbed-wire transit camps popping up all over England. These camps were all part of the operational security; the barbed wire was not only there to keep out the unwanted, but to keep the operationally briefed troops in.

Here the battalion was fully informed of its mission and tasks for D-Day, and what was expected from each and every man. After the brief a 'special' pay parade was held, with the officer commanding sat behind a table. Each man was given 200 francs along with the offer of three condoms. Devlin: 'I thought we were going to fight the Germans, sir? Not to breed.' After his initial refusal Patrick was persuaded by the CQMS to take them anyway, if only to give them away.

On the eve of 6 June 24,000 airborne soldiers at 22 airfields across England, boarded 1,200 transport planes and 700 gliders. 1st Royal Ulster Rifles (1 RUR) boarded their Horsa gliders; every platoon had been earmarked one each and in a unit of 750 men that makes for many airframes. The men of 2nd Oxfordshire and Buckinghamshire Light Infantry (2 OBLI), also of 6th Air Landing Brigade, were doing the same, and would be the first to leave.

Unfortunately. though. this could not be said for the third and final battalion of the brigade, 12th Devonshire Regiment (12 Devons). The RAF had run out of Halifax and Stirling tugs so apart from one company, the Devons had to travel by sea, and catch up via the beaches!

Devlin, with his Enfield .303 cradled in his arms, by now with his face blackened, climbed aboard and picked a seat portside by a window. This way he could keep his eye on the exit door – he liked it that way. During take-off, however, the towing aircraft belly dived and released the tow rope, 18 Platoon came to a standstill on the runway, before being towed away, this time by a tractor! Thus it was that Patrick Devlin was in the very last Horsa glider to take off for the air landing operation.

Normandy

During the night flight the wind was strong and gusting, blowing the gliders, hanging on at the end of their tow ropes, in all directions. Now and then, by the light of the moon, Devlin could see through gaps in the clouds down to the massive armada of ships heading into position.

Over Normandy tow ropes were released and hundreds of gliders steered their way to their respective landing zones. In the first wave behind the Pathfinders, the Ox and Bucks had already swooped down onto their target bridges. 1st Royal Ulster Rifles landed near Ranville. The men were then assembled by whistle, and companies were formed up and marched off to complete missions as tasked. C Company was formed up on the road and sent on its way, heading through Le Bas de Ranville and on up to a feature known as the 'Ring Contour', so called simply because that was how it appeared on the map. Whilst marching Paddy realized that this was for real this time when he saw his first dead German soldier, a *Fallschirmjäger* (German Para-trooper) crumpled up by the side of the road, most probably from 1st Battalion, Fallschirmjäger Regiment 6, elite troops who were known to be operating in the area and who would fight a very tough rearguard action.

On arrival at the Ring Contour Devlin and the remainder of his section were tasked to dig in under the cover of darkness to cover the approach routes to Ste-Honorine la Chardonnerette, in preparation to provide covering fire for the remainder of the battalion during an attack on the village via the Longueval flank early the following morning, 7 June.

Overall the situation at this time was considered to be largely successful, though many of the units were under-strength. Strong winds blowing at the time of the drop had driven many gliders and paratroops way off course; as the sun fell on D-Day many men were still making their way towards their units' objectives. Those already in place had to repel counter-attacks as a much smaller force than anticipated. This said, all tasks had been accomplished and all units were sited to defend the bridgehead.

Errors were made, however, At dawn the following day it was found that Two Section's position faced in the wrong direction – they could not even see the village let alone provide covering fire. This was quite a common siting mistake during the war. Lazy marking out in the dark by tired troops, and poor supervision by NCOs, often led to this error being made.

The first shots were then fired overhead when, to the delight of those manning the hilltop, two Spitfires chased a fleeing Junkers 88 escaping from an attack on the beaches and shot it down right in front of the position, to a tumultuous cheer from the trenches. On seeing this, the German defenders of Ste-Honorine opened up, shelling the RUR positions. Immediately work began to build up the hastily dug trenches to provide better protection, another lesson learnt the hard way. Some time during this barrage the attack from 1 RUR started. After what seemed a long pounding, followed by silence, it became apparent that Devlin and Two Section were on their own; the remainder had moved off without sending word to the small group. On top of this shock discovery, the Ulsters' attack was faltering, then as if nothing could get worse, the cry of 'Tanks!' went up. Tanks were spotted leaving the village, heading directly towards Two Section to clear them off the feature. Devlin hurriedly prepared for withdrawal, quickly packing away his range card and panoramic sketch of his firing position's given arcs. Under the section commander they legged it back towards Ranville, which had been the first French village to be liberated.

On their arrival a paratrooper sentry informed them that the Ulsters' attack had failed, and that, after retreating, the battalion had headed for Longueval. Getting a grip on his sniper rifle once more, Devlin headed off with Two Section and found the remainder of the company digging in at a holding position on the 'Top Road'. 18 Platoon lined the bank of a sunken road interlocked with the other platoons. Two Section joined them and hurriedly dug in again, awaiting the expected German counter-attack. Devlin was pushed forward of the emerging position, just out of earshot of the hasty digging, to be used as a forward early warning to the remainder of the company, a routine task for any sniper.

After such a counter-attack failed to materialize the company was ordered to push to the southern end of Longueval village where they were told to dig in for the third time that day, Devlin dug his new shell scrape by the former German headquarters, now being used as the regimental aid post (RAP). On completing his new scrape and before settling down, he made out a new range card and sketched a new panorama detailing known distances, and identifying, marking and listing reference points. These were to help in target indication and fire control. Finally Paddy was able to put something on to eat and boil a brew, not forgetting also to clean his sniper rifle. The remainder of 7 June was uneventful. However, after a night of routine, the position was attacked, this time by two Spitfires mistaking them for Germans! The division suffered 800 casualties between 5 and 7 June.

Night patrol

The young platoon commander of 18 Platoon, Lieutenant Mike Gann, who had left Two Section behind on the Ring Contour, was tasked to carry out a reconnaissance of his old position, for the night of 9 June. To help carry out his task he picked his scout-sniper, Devlin, to lead the way, navigate into the target area and, he hoped, back out again. Patrick relished the chance to show what he could do. The mission was to recce Two Section's old position to see if it was now occupied by enemy forces. For Devlin, this was a typical sniper skill and one in which he was well rehearsed. To keep noise to a minimum it was to be a very small, three-man, patrol. The final member was one who always looking for some action; Lance Corporal Geordie Gibbs would bring up the rear.

This patrol was useful for Devlin as it enabled him to shake out his scouting skills and get some experience under his belt. En route the patrol passed by the lone para sentry and, after exchanging passwords, gained the information that to his knowledge the contour feature was definitely now occupied by the Germans, 'Yes, they are on the hill.' After leaving the relative safety of the defensive position, Devlin signalled a patrol stop, spending several minutes in all-round defence to ensure eyes and ears were adjusted to the conditions.

Now moving on, Paddy and his companions crept ever nearer, and with the certain knowledge of its occupation ever more cautious, until within earshot of the trenches where they lay low and listened to German voices talking. Mission accomplished, the lead scout then led the satisfied patrol back to headquarters where Lieutenant Gann made his report.

Several days later another sniper task came in. C Company commander wanted Devlin to flush out a German sniper from a building that overlooked the defensive positions from 100 metres or so outside the village. Paddy quickly gathered up his sniping equipment and set off in the direction of the barn on task.

To ensure he kept out of line of sight he went up the street using the walls, alleyways, windows, doorways and gardens for concealment. He well knew the superiority of the German machine guns and feared a burst along the street or indeed a shot from the sniper he hunted. He worked his way up the street, house by house, garden by garden, until the last house but one. The final house was a large two-storey stone barn-type dwelling.

This he reckoned would provide him with a decent position from which to search out the enemy hide in the wooden barn not far distant.

All but the second-last house had been deserted, and in it he discovered a lone Frenchwoman cowering from view and peeping out at him and then indicating the direction from which the fire had come. Paddy made his way through her house and into the last one. Here he took in what he could see of the stone barn. He would have liked to remove roof tiles from several places and use one of the holes to shoot from, but decided not to. He had to assume that the building was under observation so no change to the appearance could happen. Instead he crept inside, keeping in the shadow and avoiding any doors and windows in plain view of the enemy arc of fire as he searched up and down the house for a fire position but found none suitable.

Instead of lying in a observation position waiting for any sign of movement from his enemy, and to the dismay of the company commander who had been following his progress, a frustrated Devlin simply jumped into the street, adopted the kneeling position and fired off two rounds rapid into the barn in the hope of enticing his opponent into giving away his position, whilst using the covering fire to get himself a better look! The OC grabbed him by the shoulder of his Denison smock and pulled him back into cover as several shots rang out from the German.

This method of 'locating the enemy' is normally used as a last resort in order to entice an enemy observer to open fire, and it comes with risk. The least important member of a sub-unit would usually be tasked to provide the movement not a sniper, a most valuable asset! In this case the move led to a tit-for-tat counter-snipe match between the two snipers with neither side hitting the other. This duel went on for some while until it became apparent the German sniper was not alone. After the German fire intensified Patrick Devlin was recalled.

Whilst Devlin was battling it out at the barn, the remainder of his company had taken their first casualties during repeated counter-attacks by the German forces. He was then ordered to pack up his kit and get back to his company. Several days of relative inactivity in the trenches followed, until 1 RUR was relieved by 5th Cameron Highlanders of 51st Highland Division. As the Camerons took over each position from the Ulsters the Scotsmen bragged that they would show the Irish how to attack! The Highlanders' attack went in but the bragging Scots never lasted long – within minutes they were defeated and came running back through the Ulsters! The Ulsters then had to quickly re-man the trenches that had been far too easily abandoned.

The bombardment that followed that incident seemed similar to Devlin to one he suffered on an occasion when he was caught out in the open whilst out sniping one day. With only a skinny lone tree for cover, he lay in the open ground for thirty minutes under incoming fire. This is one of the reasons that snipers were often disliked by their own side during the Second World War. Any sign of sniper activity along the lines or in no-man's land could easily result in the area concerned being pounded by artillery – a once peaceful scene would turn violent due to the presence of a sniper. Indirect fire was one of the only effective ways to catch a sniper out and kill him.

Through the second half of June and into July 1944 the fighting in Normandy developed into a virtual stalemate; the Germans' quick reaction to the Allied landings had prevented a rapid break-out from the bridgehead. Instead, every metre was going to have to be cleared and fought for. Allied losses to German snipers at night were particularly noticed, as was the Germans' clever concealment and use of cleared passageways through the Normandy hedgerows, providing cover from view and from fire. This pretty little area, known as La Suisse Normande ('Swiss Normandy'), with its rolling hills, thick hedgerows, streams, rivers, orchards, patchwork fields and dense woods, stone-built towns and picturesque villages, favoured defence not attack, and therefore assisted the Germans. The Germans, too, showed their superior combat skills and experience, retaining the determination and the ability to fight even after suffering heavy casualties, often reforming broken units to continue the battle. The stubborn and resourceful character of German troops involved in a rearguard action was well known amongst the advancing Allied units.

Scout-snipers were trained to a high level of fieldcraft and were considered among the best in those skills within a battalion. Good ones were hard to come by. Because of their specialist skills they were trusted to lead patrols of the highest level, advising company command and battalion headquarters. Unfortunately young officers often struggled to accept the word of the sniper and would doubt or disregard him, instead favouring their own opinions. This could lead to disastrous results, as Devlin found out towards the end of June 1944.

During a scouting task for B Company, Paddy was ordered to infiltrate the forward enemy positions and help B Company troops to capture a prisoner. Snipers get to know the ground they operate in like their back garden and this ground knowledge soon came in handy. Devlin led a platoon out through their own lines into no-man's land towards the enemy. Before they had even passed through the sentry position of their own defences, and were still in relative safety, one of the platoon feigned illness and refused to be budged, not wanting to risk his life. After this was finally sorted out, Paddy shook his head then continued on; he could see that discipline was poor and was expecting a long night of it. His idea was to lead them to a forward sentry machine-gun position he had noted on an earlier patrol. As far as he was concerned that part was routine.

After stopping short of the intended objective Devlin called forward the platoon commander. Paddy briefed him on the exact location of the German position but from there it all turned into a shambles. The young officer scolded Devlin for his actions and refused to accept his directions, stating that there was no way the enemy were anywhere near the said location. At this he promptly walked along the hedge to the position Devlin had shown him, only to be challenged in German! On being challenged, the foolish but brave officer jumped into the hedge firing a burst from his Sten gun to which machine-gun fire was returned. He was never seen again. The rest of the platoon all ran off back to their own lines, chased by bullets spraying the area from the German machine gunner. They left the officer to his fate; not one man from the patrol stepped forward to help. The dejected sniper, not wanting to leave the officer like this but unable to do much about it on his own, patrolled back to friendly lines. When he got there, the sentry stated that 'the shambles' had returned a good twenty minutes beforehand. In the aftermath Devlin made a detailed and frank report of what had happened and handed it in to headquarters.

Later on in the war, whilst wounded and in hospital, Devlin was shown a long list of the 'missing in action'. The only name he recalled was of this tragic officer, whom Devlin had to assume was dead.

Allied casualties during the first phase of Operation Overlord, including killed, wounded, missing and captured, were later estimated to be approximately 10,000 for the invaders against 4,000–9,000 German defenders. For 1st Royal Ulster Rifles the figures were killed 85, wounded 235 and missing 35. One of the wounded was Devlin's company commander, though he would later return to lead C Company to the Seine after the breakout.

After numerous weeks on the defensive east of the River Orne, many of the airborne troops were chomping at the bit, wanting to get on, out of the bridgehead and away from the normal infantry defensive role. In the middle of August the order to advance came and 6th Airborne eyes turned towards the open countryside between the Rivers Orne and Seine. Rifleman Devlin, C Company, 1st Royal Ulster Rifles, and the rest of 6th Airborne Division advanced, continually harrying the Germans as they retreated to the Seine near the port at Le Havre, fighting through and capturing Deauville, Trouville and Honfleur en route.

The high command decided that the better to control and coordinate all the different airborne units during the push into Germany that a unified, single headquarters and structure was required for the airborne forces. Therefore, during August 1944, the Allied First Airborne Army was formed. It gathered into its structure several American and all of the British airborne units. The first mission for the new army was only weeks away, Operation Market Garden. Preparations for this were already under way, but because the men of 6th Airborne had fought long and hard in Normandy, they were to miss it. Instead, having left their weapons in France, they went home on leave! As Devlin put it after the event, 'By luck I've missed the Arnhem shambles.'

Leave and new battles

Early in September 1944 the whole 6th Airborne Division was sent back to England to rest and reorganize. The men left via the Mulberry harbour built at Arromanches on the invasion beaches. There were two of these temporary harbours built for the Normandy invasion, designed and developed to off-load men and equipment. Various pier and breakwater structures were made in Britain, then floated very slowly, piece by piece, across the English Channel to be assembled and positioned off the landing beaches and then anchored to the seabed by chains – an amazing feat of military engineering. Mulberry A for the American forces was built off the coast at St-Laurent-sur-Mer by Omaha Beach, and Mulberry B was the harbour assembled for Gold Beach at Arromanches, for use by the British and Canadian invasion forces.

After some reorganization back in England, Devlin and his mates were rushed back into action in late December, arriving in Belgium on Boxing Day. They found themselves fighting off a major German counter-attack in the forests of the Ardennes for a month in absolutely freezing conditions. The Battle of the Bulge, as it became known, was Hitler's attempt to retake the initiative earlier lost at Normandy. Towards the end of February 1945, after tough fighting all the way to the banks of the Maas River, capturing the villages of Bures and Wavreille en route, the division was again sent back to England, this time to Salisbury Plain where they practised for the next and possibly their last operation of the war, the crossing of the Rhine.

The Rhine crossing

HQ XVIII Corps (of First Allied Airborne Army) now planned Operation Varsity. This was executed and led by Major General

Matthew Ridgway. Lieutenant-General Gale had moved up to Deputy Corps Commander and Major-General Eric Bols had taken over 6th Airborne. Operation Varsity was to be the biggest airborne assault of the Second World War. The plan was to land gliders and parachutists slap bang in the middle of the German forces, thus preventing them from counter-attacking against ground forces making the river crossing. What was more, like Arnhem, it was to be achieved in broad daylight.

After a spot of home leave, Rifleman Patrick Devlin found himself once again preparing for a major operation. He travelled from Bulford to another wire-enclosed transit camp, this time in Essex, where after the briefing about the forthcoming event, he and the rest of the participants were routinely barred from leaving camp. During this confinement Devlin questioned himself about his voluntary return to the war.

At home in Galway, his mother had brought much pressure onto Patrick to decline to return to England and the certainty of further combat, even going so far as inviting a priest to the house in the hope of dissuading him. 'After all,' they said to Paddy, 'it's not our war. You've done your bit lad, and no one could speak ill of you for not wanting to go back. Eire is neutral.'

Paddy turned to his father for advice, 'The decision is yours, son' said Patrick's father. Young Devlin was adamant. Not pausing for one moment, he chose to return to the front. But here, in confinement once again, once more on the eve of battle, he had time and second thoughts about his romantic fool-hardiness to have returned so eagerly .

24 March 1945

Up early at 0245 hours, breakfast, followed by a chilly truck ride to RAF Rivenhall near Colchester to emplane. On arrival at the airfield after the journey, the troops were taken straight to their gliders; hundreds of them littered the field. Lift-off was not for a few hours so to keep warm the soldiers played football in the dark. The weather status was good, ideal conditions for the morning's flight.

As before, each platoon had been allocated its own glider. On boarding Devlin sat in the same seat as he had done before for D-Day, by the window, with the exit door in view. He had learnt from experience that on landing gliders quickly became shot up. He wanted to be first out the forward port door on landing and not be left queuing to exit. Varsity was to become the largest single airborne operation in history – 1,348 gliders and 1,696 aircraft took 21,680 airborne soldiers, in one lift, towards Germany.

After a smooth, uneventful take-off Devlin dozed for the 3½-hour flight, and perhaps 'with the carefree attitude of the young', thinking 'it won't happen to me', was much more relaxed this time. Devlin mentioned after the war that, despite the danger, travelling by glider was less nerve-wracking than advancing across ground, because you cannot hear much because of the slipstream.

On their arrival over the landing zones things were different. Devlin could now hear the sounds of battle. To add to the confusion, there was fog, dust and smoke all over the field. Around 1030 hours the tug cast away the tow rope and the pilots guided the glider down to its final destination, LZ U3. The glider landed on the correct LZ but on the wrong side, far away from the objective. This, however, turned out to be a stroke of luck. One of the five gliders involved in this part of the operation was badly shot up. By landing at the wrong end of the LZ Devlin's glider had managed to miss most of the incoming fire. And thus it was that Paddy Devlin made his second operational air landing.

The 6th Air Landing Brigade had been given the hardest task of all, capturing the town of Hamminklen and the bridges over the River Issel. The initial task for 18 Platoon was to take a t-junction on the road to the south of Hamminklen, with the river, being a couple of kilometres away (though this distance was now greater as they had landed nowhere near the intended location). The glider carrying 18 Platoon put down in a ploughed field. On landing, whilst others over-cautiously stowed the door into the ceiling, Paddy sprinted through the doorway, leapt to the ground and then ran down the length of the glider to take up a fire position at the rear. As he did so he realized he was being shot at by two Germans, about fifty metres away in the front doorway of a two-storey farmhouse. One Jerry was firing an MP 40 at the glider as the troops debussed. Devlin returned the fire, chasing the pair of them into the farmhouse. Who knows what damage they would have caused against the glider troops but for Devlin's quick response?

At that moment two enemy armoured personnel carriers sped into view heading down the road from behind the farmhouse. It was not clear whether they were trying to reinforce the enemy position or run away. In any case Devlin hit several soldiers in both vehicles as they sped past – this raised his morale a bit. Once the platoon commander had got his bearings and the men were reorganized, they were ready to move off to the objective.

Two Section took point, spread out and headed off across the ploughed field in the direction of the road junction. Paddy Devlin felt exposed as he walked across the open field so he decided to move closer to a ditch running along the edge of a wood. As he moved nearer, though, he noticed a German MG 34 gun team, who seemed to be clearing a stoppage from their gun. Paddy knew he had to reach the ditch before they had cleared the stoppage and gunned him down; he was right in their view. When Devlin was less than 100 metres from the gun team they opened fire. The burst hit Paddy in the arm and the small of his back down the right side. Dropping his weapon, he fell face first to the ground and froze still. The Germans, thinking they had killed him, did not shoot at him again. His right arm was broken from the impact of the rounds, and he felt blood running down his right thigh as he lay there unable to move.

Devlin had to stay there for some while until, the Germans having moved off, the pilots from the glider crawled past keeping low. Devlin called for help, which startled them – they stated afterwards that they had thought he was a goner. Paddy pleaded for help to get into the ditch but they continued on their way, much to his anger. Lucky for Patrick he had friends and soon after Rifleman Bertie Birchall came back looking for him. After an unsuccessful attempt on his own to lift his wounded friend

Bertie left, coming back with Rifleman McCrea. At this point they discovered that the 'blood' Devlin had pouring onto his legs was in fact leaking from tins of condensed milk intended for their tea break! Devlin was dragged off towards the regimental aid post.

Outside the aid post was a smashed glider lying partially in the road, and partially in the ditch; scenes of battle were all around. Before reaching the RAP Devlin and his helpers came under fire from two more enemy vehicles, this time eight-wheeled APCs that came into view shooting everywhere. Both sides were letting loose at each other so Birchall and McCrea dropped Devlin and legged it for cover. Patrick fell into the ditch just as a PIAT took out a German vehicle. This then crashed into the ditch next to Paddy and the broken glider, with the soldiers in it trying to jump out and take cover from the overwhelming British fire. Germans were shot all around Paddy as he lay there in the middle of it all! After this battle had finished Devlin finally reached the medical officer, who tended his wounds.

Casualties

Allied casualties in the airborne attack were lighter than expected when planning the operation. They were significant all the same, mainly because of the decision to go in daylight rather than risk scattering the troops in the darkness. Of the 7,220 men who had landed as part of 6th Airborne Division, by the end of the first day of Varsity about 1,400 were killed, wounded or missing in action. This figure, sadly for Devlin, included Lieutenant Mike Gann, his platoon commander, who was killed in action.

For Rifleman Patrick Devlin the war was over and he was sent back to England along the casualty evacuation chain. From the aid post he went back to the Rhine bridgehead, going over the newly built Bailey bridge back over the river to the field hospital. From hospital he moved on to Goch, then Venrey where he had plaster put on his arm, and then to Bruges in Belgium. Finally he flew to RAF Lyneham in Wiltshire by Dakota and on landing he was sent to Basingstoke hospital for further treatment.

Devlin's kitbag caught up with him eventually, so on VE-Day, 8 May 1945, he sneaked out of bed, donned his best uniform and went absent without leave for three days. He went to London where, by his own admission, he 'whooped it up!' When he returned he was unceremoniously told off and sent to Shaftesbury military hospital, which was much stricter and harder to abscond from. After a while Paddy was discharged from Shaftesbury, downgraded and sent to Villach in south Austria, from where he was finally demobbed in September 1946.

Author's note

'Kill one man, terrify a thousand' – Ancient Chinese Proverb. From the outset I was very interested in writing this chapter and in particular I wanted to write it about a British Army sniper. Not only because I was one but for several other reasons. Firstly, this is the first piece of sniper writing I have done since my book *Sniper One: The Blistering True Story of a British Battle group Under Siege* was published. Secondly, and more importantly, because so little is written or known about British snipers, I hope my choice helps in some small way to redress the balance.

Snipers were not popular soldiers back then and were thought of as 'unsporting'. Of course another reason is that so few actually survived the war at all. There are now many 'famous' snipers – Zaitsev, Allerberger and others – but very few British ones. It proved very difficult to find a subject to write my chapter about. Rifleman Patrick Devlin came to me after much reading and researching of websites, ending up with a written request to the Imperial War Museum for assistance. The help I received was enormous and immediately the private papers of Patrick Devlin were offered to me amongst others and it was then I decided to write about him. All quotes in the chapter are taken from the private papers, though I have filled in some detail using a bit of artistic license.

References

Patrick R. Devlin, Private Papers: Unpublished

Gregor Ferguson, *The Paras: British Airborne Forces 1940–1984* (Osprey, 1984)

Adrian Gilbert, *Sniper One On One: The World of Combat Sniping* (Sidgwick and Jackson, 1994)

John Man, *The Penguin Atlas of D-Day and the Normandy Campaign* (Penguin, 1994)

Chapter 10

HARRY M. FURNESS

Fieldcraft Expert

In the British Army of the Second World War the art of sniping was not the respected skill that it is today and so for a young soldier to be selected and accept the challenge of this very dangerous and much misunderstood profession is indeed a testament to his commitment to the defence of his country and to the character held within.

One such was a sixteen-year-old Manchester lad, who, like many across the country, decided he wanted to do his bit and took himself off to sign up for the infantry in 1941. Little were his recruiters to know that the young Harry Furness was to become one of the most successful snipers in British Army history.

Harry's desire to fight should come as no surprise since his dad was a famous boxing champion and promoter. Harry was the son of Harry ('Kid') Furness, a flyweight champion who then went into boxing promoting, and of whom it is said that his work as a showman would have put Don King in the shade.

Harry almost immediately showed a skill for soldiering that caught his instructors' attention, in particular excelling in shooting and fieldcraft activities, both skills needed in the demanding world of the sniper. He was duly selected to attend a sniper course, which he passed with flying colours, and earned a posting to HQ Company, 6th Battalion, The Green Howards. Being posted to HQ Company was not the rear-line non-combat destination that it might first appear, as a battalion's snipers were viewed as a battalion asset in much the same way as the mortars or heavy machine-gun crews were. It was therefore normal practice for snipers to be attached to battalion HQ. This gave the battalion intelligence officer (IO), who also acted as the deployment and controlling officer for the snipers, close access to them on a day-to-day basis.

Battalion snipers were seen not only as a direct-action asset, but also as an extension of the commanding officer's eyes and ears, and as such were often deployed in a reconnaissance role to gather information and intelligence to allow the battalion IO to formulate a broader picture of the battlefield ahead to aid in the CO's plans, an action not truly appreciated by the normal infantry soldiers, who viewed snipers with a certain mistrust and disdain, often labelling them 'Murder Incorporated' or complaining about the backlash from the German mortars or artillery that often followed after a successful sniper mission. None of this fazed the young and determined Harry Furness, who very quickly established himself as a dedicated and ruthless professional, who by the time of his deployment on D-Day, was a seasoned sniper corporal at the tender age of nineteen.

The 50th (Northumbrian) Infantry Division was to establish a beachhead between Arromanches and Ver-sur-Mer on Juno Beach and then head south towards Route Nationale 13, linking Caen with Bayeux. The first wave was to be made of the 231st and 69th Infantry Brigades. Once the initial assault was over and the beachhead established, the follow-up brigades, the 56th and 151st, were to push inland to the south-west towards RN13 supported by the tanks of the 8th Armoured Brigade.

In the landings the Nottinghamshire Yeomanry (Sherwood Rangers), the 1st Battalion, Hampshire Regiment, and the 1st Battalion, Dorset Regiment, fought their way ashore on the western side, while the 5th Battalion, East Yorkshire Regiment, and the 6th Battalion, Green Howards, with Harry Furness and his sniper section, assaulted the eastern side of their objective area.

As a side note to Harry's D-Day deployment, Company Sergeant-Major Stanley Hollis of the Green Howards single-handedly captured a pillbox which had been bypassed by the first waves of troops. For his action he was awarded the Victoria Cross. He was the only soldier to earn that medal on D-Day. Later that day he led an assault to destroy German gun positions, and must have served as a great role model for young soldiers like Harry.

Harry came ashore to a wall of withering fire, as did all the brave men of the assault waves who would land on those beaches that day, and remembers using condoms and tape to seal his Lee-Enfield No. 4T, the standard-issue sniper rifle of the British Army, from the seawater and harsh conditions, unwrapping it only when safely ashore, and very happy to be away from the rolling ships and sea sickness of the D-Day armada. Harry was wounded during a mortar attack in the early stages of the Normandy campaign, but recovered and was posted to the Hallamshire Battalion of the York & Lancaster Regiment, part of the 49th 'Polar Bear' Division, as a battlefield replacement after it took heavy casualties. Harry served with distinction for the remainder of the campaign, through to the end in May 1945.

A great part of the sniper's role was observation and Harry generally operated in front of the battalion position, often alone, usually deploying at last light, to the abuse and cat calls of his fellow soldiers. He would locate a position of advantage over-looking the coming terrain and build a carefully camouflaged position before dawn, and have to remain in it, effectively motionless, until dusk allowed him to move again. In at least one incident Harry and his snipers were concealed for several days while observing a German unit. During this time, they were able to build up a very detailed record of the German strengths, weapons, morale, positions and routines and were so close to the German unit that they could not withdraw to pass on this vital information to their own unit until the Germans actually retreated a little. Upon returning to their own lines and reporting to the Hallamshires' IO, Harry found out that they had all been posted missing in action due to the time they had been gone. A sniper's dedication and patience are unmatched on the battlefield.

The selection of any position had to be very carefully thought out, as a sniper's worst-case scenario is that of an enemy sniper looking for him, or operating in the same area. This becomes a problem as both men are highly trained soldiers who think and act alike, and so a position that was workable for Harry would have been a position identified as a potential sniper hide by a German sniper and hence targeted. The skill is to select the position that is not obvious, and this tends to mean that it is generally more uncomfortable. German snipers were very well respected and feared opponents and Harry was to meet and kill several of them in the coming months, although in his humility, he argues that one of them could not have been a trained sniper, as even though he had a sniper's rifle and equipment, his lack of skill and general mistakes made it too easy for Harry to win. However, there are those who would suggest that in fact it was Harry's own level of skill that made it seem that way.

A little-known fact is that German snipers deployed throughout Normandy with subsonic ammunition and clip-on suppressors for their Kar 98 rifles, as the Germans had recognized the psychological effects of sniping with a silenced rifle and the increased life expectancy of their snipers when equipped this way. Harry had suspected this early on in the campaign when he was searching through a German Army supply vehicle, abandoned in the retreat, and found box after box of subsonic ammunition. Proof was to come many years later from documentation and discovery of the previously unknown suppressors that had indeed been issued to German snipers.

All German soldiers were aware of the threat posed by snipers and therefore set out their defences to cover likely British observation positions and sniper firing points. During a moment of weakness in such circumstances, Harry almost lost his life.

After a night of stalking Germans Harry was aware of the impending arrival of daylight but was too far away from his own unit to return and needed to locate a safe place to hole up for the day. After much searching, he came across an old isolated barn, and even though he admits his sixth sense was 'screaming' at him not to use it, his tiredness, the lack of time left before daylight and fear of being caught over-ruled his common sense and he cautiously advanced towards the barn. Having climbed onto the stack of hay, Harry started to pull some out so that he could slide in feet first and then conceal himself. Within minutes of starting work he felt bullets tearing into the hay around him and then heard a sound he knew too well. A German machine gun was sending its fire ploughing into the hay. Harry threw himself to the floor as the bullets continued to impact above him and took off running back the way he came for all he was worth, stealth no longer an option. The noise of a German MG 42 being cocked and rounds entering the chamber commonly brought fear to Allied soldiers who heard it. Harry knew the noise well, and hearing it now he was aware that at any moment 'Hitler's buzz saw' would try to cut him down. Harry remembers the sound of bees buzzing past him as he ran as fast as he could towards the hedge line and sunken track that would provide him with sanctuary. He saw the hedge 'dance' ahead of him, but did not know what was causing it at the time as his racing mind was concerned with his own survival. He was later to realize that the 'dancing bush' was in fact the hedge being destroyed by the impact of bullets from the MG 42 that had just missed him.

As Harry approached the hedge, he summoned up all his strength and launched himself headlong over the foliage and down into the safety of dead ground, hardly feeling the impact on the floor, before being up on his feet again and running away from the area as fast as he could. He became aware of the fact that his left leg was not functioning properly as his stride was awkward and ungainly, but at this stage he had no time to check his wounds. After a run of over a kilometre, Harry fell into a patch of dense foliage to catch his breath, prepare a fighting position in case of pursuit and to check his leg injury, and it was now that he found out how close to death he had come. Looking down at his leg he found no signs of any injury, but when he touched his boot, he found that it had in fact been all but shot off by rounds from the German machine gun – it was the flapping heel and not a wound that had caused his ungainly run. Relieved, Harry swore never again to discount his sixth sense, and returned to his unit lines safely.

As the Allied advance continued, the inevitable move into urban areas increased the risk to Allied soldiers, especially the snipers. When a platoon had to advance down a new street, it was Harry's job, with the rest of his sniper section, to move on a flank and identify and eliminate the German machine-gun positions and any other weapon that posed a major threat to the advancing troops. The hazards were obvious; the snipers were few in number and vulnerable to getting caught in a large fire-fight with overwhelming odds, but since they were a battalion asset and therefore a support weapon system, it was their role – they were trained to much higher standards for a very good reason.

In one incident, a sniper from Harry's section was quietly moving to the upper floor of a abandoned building when, without warning, the door at the top of the stairs opened, and a very frightened German soldier bulldozed over the sniper, down the stairs and out of sight. Assuming the German would bring additional troops, the sniper was left with no choice but to relocate as quickly as he could.

It was during one such advance that Harry got momentarily left behind, as he identified a German soldier with a *Panzerfaust* anti-armour weapon concealed and awaiting an Allied tank. Harry rapidly worked his way to the optimum shooting position and removed the threat. During this time the platoon had advanced and Harry had lost his link with them and realized he had to catch up fast both to cover their movement and also to avoid possible fratricide. He did not want to be engaged by friendly fire when he appeared in a position in which they were not expecting to see movement. Looking down the street, Harry saw a burnt-out German tank and decided to sprint from his present covered position to the tank and then use it as cover to plan his next rapid movement. As his heart raced, he fully expected to hear weapons fire the second he broke cover. Harry sprinted straight towards the disabled German tank. After what must have seemed an age, he found himself sliding under the protective armour of the tank beside its tracks, and looking further down the street to a corner, his next objective.

With the next bound decided, Harry was poised to break cover again and sprint for the corner, when he became aware of

German voices coming from inside the tank, and to his horror he realized that it was not disabled at all and was indeed manned and fully functional, no doubt waiting to ambush the Allied Sherman tanks. With no choice, as to stay there would invite certain death sooner or later, Harry ran for his life, expecting to be cut down by the tank's machine guns as he went. Harry's luck was to hold and, gasping for breath, he rounded the corner and got out of line of sight of the tank's gunners. Still trying to regain his breath, he risked a look back round the corner, as the soldier in him took over and he looked for vulnerabilities he could exploit on the tank. Open hatches, exposed fuel cans, even track linkage can be targets for a sniper with armour-piercing ammunition, a type all Allied snipers carried. Harry's professionalism led him to overcome the fear he had just faced and resume his role of destroying the enemy, so he scanned for potential targets. It would appear that the tank crew had no idea a British sniper had just used them as cover to advance down the street. They never fired and instead started up and moved away while Harry was looking for targets. With no shots available, Harry resumed his role protecting the platoon as it advanced on its mission, its members unaware of the life-threatening situation one of their snipers had just faced.

As the campaign moved into Holland, Harry was called forward to assist the men of a company who were taking a large number of casualties from a German sniper concealed somewhere ahead of them. After receiving his brief, Harry set out with one of the company's officers to locate an observation position from which to carry out his counter-sniper task. After a detailed reconnaissance, Harry settled on a large multi-storey building that gave a commanding view of the area and secluded himself and the accompanying officer among the broken roof rafters. There then began the long and laborious task of searching and scanning the ground ahead of them for likely enemy sniper positions, and both Harry and the officer spent much time using their binoculars to try and locate the German sniper.

After a period of several hours' searching, the officer had to return to his unit and this left Harry alone to continue the task.

As the German sniper had not fired for almost a day now, Harry wondered if he had withdrawn to a new location, waiting to ambush the advancing Allied troops again, thereby delaying the advance a second time, a common sniper tactic. At this time a building almost opposite Harry and some 400 metres away caught his eye. The building had been hit in the fighting and now had broken windows and damage to the wooden walls, that had left several planks swaying around every time a gust of wind blew. As Harry watched through his Scout Regiment scope, he spotted what he believed to be a slight movement in the shadows of one of the damaged planks and quickly swapped his spotting scope for his rifle and waited.

As Harry continued to watch he saw what he considered to be a hand moving to lift the damaged plank slightly and he aimed and fired at the area he assessed would hold the body belonging to the arm he could now make out in the shadows. After watching the area for another hour and seeing no further movement, Harry withdrew to the company location and briefed the company commander on what had happened and his belief that the German sniper now lay dead in the building he indicated.

That night the company sent out a fighting patrol to snatch a prisoner for HQ to question. During this foray, a corporal and two men from the patrol entered the building Harry believed the German sniper was in. On their return to the British lines, the corporal sought Harry out and handed him a German 4-power telescopic-sighted G 43 sniper rifle that they had found in the building on top of a table set back in the shadows, and that in front of it next to the house's wooden walls, was the dead body of the German sniper, hit in the head by Harry's bullet. Harry kept the telescopic scope but not the rifle, as he did with all sniper against sniper incidents – the rifles were too heavy to keep and using them, with their different sound to Allied weapons, would invite friendly fire. Harry ended the war with several enemy telescopic sights in his possession and kept them for many years before finally parting with them, reluctantly, for financial reasons.

*

Due to the high levels of stress and the physical effort required during a sniper mission, snipers are trained to operate as individuals, to allow them to continue the fight even if one is killed, but even so are generally deployed in pairs to reduce the workload and stress. Harry Furness preferred to work alone and it makes his achievements even more impressive. Deploying alone and in advance of your own unit had many disadvantages as, with the loneliness of being isolated, often far from immediate friendly supporting fire or back-up, it was not uncommon for units to forget or even discount their deployed snipers if a major opportunity presented itself. Many a sniper found himself left behind with only his skills as a soldier to aid him in surviving and finding his parent unit again. On more than one occasion, Harry was to find himself hungry and without supplies, as the resupply and feeding had taken place while he was deployed, and nobody thought or cared about the 'murdering snipers' out ahead of the unit, completely unaware of the mortar crews, machine gunners and enemy raiding patrols that had fallen foul of these lone hunters during the night, and how this had in fact increased the line infantryman's life expectancy. It was to be another sixty years or more before the sniper would receive the accolades he deserved from his fellow soldiers and the world's media.

Harry's time was largely spent searching and scanning the ground ahead of his unit, looking for signs of German positions, equipment and, of course, German snipers. To do this he would have followed the taught methods of searching and scanning using the issued 7-magnification binoculars (binoculars of the type that I was myself issued with, still stamped 1944 on the side, some fifty years later thanks to lack of investment in sniper equipment!). The system calls for a sniper to break down the ground into sections of left–centre–right, and near–middle–distant and follow a logical scan, near–to–far looking for threats and enemy positions. Harry would have been taught to check the ground nearest to him first as this was the biggest threat to his safety.

For longer distances and for target identification, Harry would use the Scout Regiment telescope. The Scout Regiment telescope was a relic of the nineteenth century in design and would not have looked out of place in the hands of Admiral Nelson at the battle of Trafalgar. It was, however, a very good optical instrument and telescoped into itself for ease of carrying in its purpose-designed leather case and could be stripped down into its component parts for ease of cleaning the lenses. However, it was far from an easy design to master and many a sniper put the lenses in backwards or in the wrong place and struggled over several hours trying to work out why his scope no longer worked! (I was also issued with a Scout Regiment spotting scope when I became a sniper fifty-plus years later, again highlighting the lack of understanding and commitment to the skills of the sniper.)

Harry did not always have the security of darkness to hide him from German eyes. Movement in daylight towards or around an enemy formation was a day-to-day occurrence for Harry and all British snipers. When it was essential to move during daylight, this was done with extreme care, and generally by crawling, unless the sniper was concealed by cover. A sniper's role is that of gathering intelligence and engaging targets of opportunity to reduce the enemy's ability to fight, and so Harry would be on the look-out for officers, or for specialists such as engineers, machine-gun and mortar crews, exposed tank crews, and personnel manning the dreaded 88-mm guns. Once he identified a target, Harry would have to consider very carefully what effects his possible actions would create. If his unit was advancing covertly, or the Germans did not know they were moving towards them, then a single shot would provide an indication of a British presence in the area and place the Germans on high alert. He also had to consider the retaliatory actions of the Germans against his own lines and weigh this up in comparison to the value of his target, as the life he took might well cost several lives among those behind him in defensive positions.

So firing a shot was best considered rather carefully, even though the lowly sniper did not always have the tactical knowledge and understanding of the big picture – firing a shot could bring massive retribution in the form of a mortar or artillery barrage. The sniper might well find himself between a rock and a hard place. On one occasion, ahead of his own lines and alone, Harry identified an orders group involving several German officers, clearly discussing their next plan of action, huddled around a set of maps spread over a vehicle body. After several minutes of close observation, watching for signs of deference to rank – no unit wore rank in the field because of snipers – Harry settled on the one he believed to be the senior officer and began to make the calculations needed to adjust his No. 32 sniper scope to maintain point of aim and achieve point of impact on his selected target. Harry's opinion on what happened next is based on the reaction of the German troops in the surrounding area. Harry believes he killed either a very high-ranking or a very popular officer, as within a matter of minutes his world became a vibrating, deafening hell on earth, as everything from small arms fire through mortar and artillery and even tank rounds poured into his general vicinity, as the Germans vented their anger and tried to avenge the loss of one of their own. For a very long eight minutes, Harry was thrown around like a rag doll as the very ground on which he lay, bounced and shook from the impact of the German assault, and a very lucky and partially deaf Harry Furness crawled back into his own lines some time later to such encouragement as 'Serves you right' from his own troops.

Harry would have several encounters like this throughout his advance through Europe and into Germany and his luck would hold out, where others failed, and he soon became one of only a few snipers left from his original section. When I asked Harry what had made him better than anyone else and helped his survival during the campaign, he told me attention to detail and luck.

*

Harry's world was often one of split-second decisions. His ability to remain unseen in any terrain was the key to his survival, along with learning to trust his 'sixth sense', something I have instilled in all the snipers I have trained in my career. And a good sniper always has one up the spout, just in case. After firing, Harry would remain completely motionless for about half an hour, since the enemy would be searching intently to identify his location, kill him and remove the threat. Being a sniper has never carried the option of surrender; history has shown that few soldiers are willing to take snipers prisoner, and so remaining undiscovered and unseen is the best defence a sniper has. Even reloading a rifle has to be done very slowly and where possible in dead ground. It is a proven fact that movement catches the eye, and so any sudden or quick motion will draw attention, even if it is only caught in an enemy's peripheral vision. Once a sniper's general area is known, artillery or mortars will usually find him. Harry was to suffer several minor wounds from mortar and artillery fragments during the war.

Harry would adopt the shooting position best suited to his environment but more often than not chose the Hawkins position, a very low-profile firing position, in which the rifle is effectively on the ground, with the butt in a little scrape, and the shoulder over rather than behind it. The barrel is supported by the left fist and the sling wrapped around the left arm, with the sniper's cheek flat on the butt-stock and at the correct eye position for the No. 32 scope. A little trick in dry weather was to pour water or lay a dampened cloth in front of the barrel to prevent dust being kicked up by the muzzle blast and presenting any German observer with an indication as to where the sniper was concealed; this would invariably bring retaliatory fire and increase the chances of death or injury .

Harry was never a smoker but learnt very quickly that the daily cigarette issue could be used as hard currency to secure items he needed or desired to make his life easier. One such trade involved frequent visits to the machine-gun crews who, in exchange for cigarettes, would allow Harry to search through their ammunition supplies to locate batches of ammunition with the same production run numbers on them. Harry, and indeed all snipers, knew that ammunition from the same production batch had a higher level of consistency of manufacture, which translated to better accuracy over longer ranges. This was clearly of importance to snipers, who have to engage targets of opportunity and also fire at longer ranges, and so this was a great trade in Harry's eyes. For a machine-gun crew, whose weapon is an area weapon with a 'beaten zone' of impact to hit as many men in a given area as possible, consistency was irrelevant, and even detrimental to their task, and so Harry's cigarettes were of much higher value to them.

Harry was also very careful not to use German equipment left behind or found, as in his worst-case scenario, that of being captured, any chance of survival, assuming he had managed to conceal his sniper's role, would quickly disappear if the Germans were to find some of their own side's equipment on him. They would assume that Harry had looted dead German soldiers, as did happen, which would anger his captors and probably lead to his death. Harry also rarely approached any of his targeted quarry, as he was never sure who else had witnessed his actions and might well be lying in wait, bent on revenge. Confirmation of a sniper kill was far less important than staying alive in Harry's eyes.

One exception to this rule was when, deployed ahead of the main Allied thrust and prowling around for targets, Harry was preparing to cross a rural road when he heard the increasing noise of an engine approaching his location. Aware that the approaching vehicle could only be German, Harry concealed himself overlooking a place where the road emerged from a tree line, from where the engine noise was coming. With little delay a German dispatch rider came into view riding a military motor-cycle and carrying a message satchel. Harry was faced with a decision: the satchel could contain vital intelligence but he had not watched the area long enough to be sure there were no German units concealed in the tree line opposite and so firing could expose his own position. In the end, well used to split-second decisions, Harry fired and the dispatch rider was knocked clean off his motorcycle by the impact of Harry's .303 round. The easy part was done; the enemy rider had been cleanly killed and lay on the road some 300 metres from Harry's concealed position, so now the wait began. Harry knew that to approach the body quickly to secure the satchel and its possible intelligence could be a death sentence for him should there be any enemy witnesses to his actions, but to wait raised the likelihood of another German vehicle arriving and the satchel being lost. Harry had to weigh the value of his life against the satchel's possible contents – after all it might just contain the week's weather reports. He began very slowly to stalk his way around by a covered route towards the downed rider, always being careful to remain in sight of the motionless figure.

After a painful and time-consuming stalk, Harry was at the road's edge, almost within arm's reach of the body, but still he had to resist the temptation to cut corners and make a sudden movement, and so he lay motionless and concealed for a further thirty minutes until he was as certain as he could be that the body was not under enemy observation. With heart racing and sure he would hear the sound of gunfire as soon as he rose, Harry broke cover and moved to the body, retrieved the satchel and a Luger handgun from the rider's holster, ever aware of the trade value of such an item, which over-ruled his fear of being caught with it. He was later to sell it to an American soldier. The satchel now slung around his body, Harry started the long stalk back to his own lines where he would hand in the bag to the IO, never caring to ask about its contents, merely intent on doing his job.

Harry's war would come to an end on the outskirts of a small German village where, having received the order to halt all movement, and be prepared for a ceasefire, Harry's commander deployed him, alone as usual, to scout ahead and around the village for German forces, just in case they were told to resume the advance. After circumnavigating the village he found himself concealed a short distance from a German girl in her late teens, hanging laundry on a washing line to the rear of her home. Having been very active over the last few days and having missed all meals, Harry was very hungry and so made a calculated risk to expose his position and approach the girl and ask for food. His hunch that the girl would not run or panic was a sound one, and in true German hospitality she led him into the house, introduced him to her elderly parents who then prepared him a meal from the meagre rations they had, a sign of the respect the

German people had for soldiers, be they their own or others. Being touched by the generosity and hospitality of the family, not to mention the obvious beauty of the young girl, Harry went back to his commander, reported that the village was indeed devoid of any and all military units, and proceeded to trade all his booty for tea, coffee, sugar and other foodstuffs. He then stalked into the woods and shot a deer, and with this and all his traded food, returned to the house and repaid the kindness shown to him the day before.

Harry's unit did then indeed receive the order to cease all hostilities and the war in Europe came to an end. For Harry, the end of the war had started a new chapter in his life, and his relationship with the young German girl would develop into a love that lasts to this day. The very successful British sniper would spend the rest of his life with a German girl he met at war's end.

*

By that time Harry was a sniper sergeant, and being a lover of military history, was well versed in the story of Major Hesketh-Pritchard, an officer considered to be the founding father of British sniping after his ideas led to the first dedicated sniper school during the First World War. In a famous portrait photo of Hesketh-Pritchard, he is seen to wear a tie pin through his uniform tie, a non-regulation practice considered the sniper equivalent of RAF fighter pilots leaving their top button unclasped. In a postwar publicity shot of Harry he is seen to wear just such a pin in his uniform tie, no doubt a tribute to Major Hesketh-Pritchard, the great sniping instructor, and an indication of the immense pride Harry and all snipers have in their trade.

The Sniper's Uniform and Equipment

When Harry deployed from the landing craft onto Juno Beach, he and all of his snipers were dressed as per any other infantry-man, and the order of the day was the issued battledress uniform, standard for the British and Commonwealth army. Most snipers had found ways to add to or modify their uniforms the better to suit the specialist task they performed, and while this went against the traditional uniform and turn-out standards of the British system, it was overlooked to a certain extent as sniping was recognized as a skill that suits the individual and so what worked for one might not work for another. As the war progressed camouflage uniforms started to come online and the famous Denison smock, as worn by British paratroopers, was also issued to snipers, with many sewing socks to the cuffs to add insulation to the jacket and stave off the cold European winters. Many also had unit tailors add a wide zip pocket on the lower rear of the jacket to allow for carriage of the Scout Regiment telescope, to avoid having to sling it over the shoulder in its leather case, which proved to be cumbersome and noisy.

To ensure a greater degree of camouflage snipers dyed their web gear with a dark green form of blanco, the dye normally used to colour webbing white for ceremonial peacetime duty, and used vehicle paint to cover the brass of the metal fittings. Snipers carried an entrenching tool to dig a shallow scrape or hide a position, rucksack, water bottles and food. As with today's snipers they were issued a sidearm for close-quarter combat and this would have been the standard British-issue .38 pistol, holster and ammunition pouch, although many swapped these for Colt .45 automatic pistols once they came into contact with American forces for that weapon's greater magazine capacity and the knock-down effect of the .45 round.

Snipers also carried the Fairbairn–Sykes fighting knife that was issued to commando and paratrooper units and this was normally carried in the knife pocket incorporated into the battle-dress trousers or secured in the issue scabbard and tied to the lower leg. Whilst designed for fighting and sentry removal, the knife was mainly used by snipers for probing for mines. Snipers were also issued with a prismatic compass to allow the precise navigation they needed and this was generally kept on the web waist belt in the issued compass pouch, and secured to the sniper by a lanyard to avoid its accidental loss. The issued binoculars were often painted in a camouflage paint and covered with strips of hessian to conceal their shape (as was the Lee-Enfield rifle), and were hung around the neck, but secured inside the top of the smock to stop them bouncing around or impairing movement.

After a severe mortaring incident in Normandy, where his helmet deflected a large piece of shrapnel, Harry always wore a helmet, somewhat unusually for a sniper. Many a picture from the time will show snipers in makeshift headgear, normally including a face veil and cap comforter, but this best explains how individual snipers were, and how the system allowed them to remain flexible in their individual dress. Harry did, however, secure a face veil to the front of his helmet and attached to the hessian camouflage cover, to allow for it to be drawn forward and over his rifle while in a firing position the better to break up his outline and aid in his concealment.

Face camouflage was very important, and also improvised as much of the snipers' gear was. Harry used soot from cooking fires and burnt cork to stripe his face and hands as camouflage. Max Factor make-up was used in training but was hard to get hold of in theatre and so snipers improvised. This improvisation also saw many snipers carrying additional hessian sandbags, which they used to cover their boots, and the boots' tread pattern, to avoid leaving ground sign for the Germans to discover and realize that snipers had been moving around their areas.

As the war progressed, more and more specific-to-task equipment was designed and issued to specialist troops, with snipers always at the forefront of kit issue. The suppressed Sten gun was one such addition. A sniper and observer team might be issued a suppressed Sten as the observer's weapon, to allow for the silent removal of sentries or enemy troops in an accidental discovery situation, allowing the sniper pair to withdraw quickly and avoid a fire-fight with superior numbers. Another upgrade was the issue of the first camouflage windproof smock and trousers, made famous by being issued to members of commando and airborne units, and the SAS, who continued to use it for many years, some still preferring its random camouflage pattern today. Harry was issued the windproofs and believed them to be an experimental pattern at the time, not knowing of their widespread issue to specialist units and also the entire infantry of the 52nd Lowland Division.

The European winter of 1944–5 was as severe as any recorded and it saw large falls of snow across much of Europe. The German Army with its Eastern Front experience and the Alps on its back doorstep, was well in advance of the Allies in winter camouflage and this proved to be a major advantage during the Battle of the Bulge, where U.S. troops had such a hard time locating German soldiers moving through the wood lines. The British Army saw a need to improve its troops' camouflage and so took the basic windproof clothing and produced it in a flat white colour for issue to snipers and limited numbers of specialists and infantry troops. Harry was one of the snipers who received a set of the snow whites, and used his knowledge of camouflage and his operational area to make the decision to 'modify' his own snow whites. Harry scrounged some green vehicle paint and proceeded to add a few green stripes and shapes to his suit the better to match the snow-draped trees and high foliage he had to deploy into. He also modified his rifle and helmet camouflage with strips of white cloth and bandages bartered for with his cigarette ration.

*

Overall, British snipers during the Second World War begged stole or improvised the equipment needed to achieve their goals, and this was never helped by the general misconception of their role in the eyes of their fellow soldiers. The ingenuity and resourcefulness of those men was captured in the subsequent manuals and teachings given to the snipers who followed them, and it is a tradition carried on by today's snipers. The experiences and skill of such men as Harry Furness have made the British sniper of today a force to be reckoned with.